The Best That I Can Be

Rafer Johnson

with Philip Goldberg

Introduction by Tom Brokaw

DOUBLEDAY
New York
London
Toronto
Sydney
Auckland

THE BEST THAT I CAN BE

An Autobiography

PUBLISHED BY DOUBLEDAY
a division of Bantam Doubleday Dell Publishing Group, Inc.
1540 Broadway, New York, New York 10036

DOUBLEDAY and the portrayal of an anchor with a dolphin are trademarks of Doubleday, a division of Bantam Doubleday Dell Publishing Group, Inc.

Library of Congress Cataloging-in-Publication Data

Johnson, Rafer, 1935–
The best that I can be: an autobiography / by Rafer Johnson with Philip Goldberg; introduction by Tom Brokaw. — 1st ed.
p. cm.
Includes index.
1. Johnson, Rafer, 1935– . 2. Decathletes—United States—Biography. 3. Track and field athletes—United States—Biography.
I. Goldberg, Philip, 1944– . II. Title.
GV697.J67A3 1998
796.42'092—dc21
[B] 98-3174
CIP

ISBN 0-385-48760-6

Printed in the United States of America
September 1998
First Edition

10 9 8 7 6 5 4 3 2 1

To my family

My parents, Lewis and Alma Johnson, who worked hard to give their children a better life than they had.

My brothers and sisters, Ed, Jim, Erma, and Dolores.

My wife Betsy and our children, Jennifer and Joshua.

CONTENTS

PREFACE

IN 1960 I won the gold medal in the decathlon at the Rome Olympics. In 1968 I was standing close to my friend Robert Kennedy when he was shot, and I helped to subdue the assassin. In 1984 I was given the honor of lighting the Olympic torch at the Los Angeles Games. After each of these milestones in my public life, numerous people suggested that I write my memoirs. Some came forward with propositions to collaborate on such a book, or to sell it or publish it.

For me, the time never seemed right. At the end of the Olympic games in Rome, I was eager to get on with life after sports; and besides, I felt I was too young to write an autobiography. It was enough that an hour-long television documentary was being made about me. Eight years later, the parties that approached me about a book wanted to focus on the assassination and my relationship with the Kennedys. I did not want to sensationalize such a grievous loss; and even if it could be handled with dignity, I could not bear the thought of reliving the traumatic event. Sixteen years later, when the opening ceremonies of the 1984 Olympics sparked new interest in my life story, I was still reluctant to dredge up those dark memories. In addition, exciting new opportunities had opened up to me; I wanted to turn my attention to the future, and not so much to the past.

By 1995 the thought of writing an autobiography began to come from inside me instead of from other people. At the age of sixty, with my children in college and my parents gone, I found myself reflecting on the past. I could now see my life with greater clarity and detachment. The turning point came at a reception for Archbishop Desmond Tutu of South Africa, after a Mass he led in Los Angeles. I told another guest, a minister, that I had been thinking of writing my autobiography. He offered to introduce me to Lynn Franklin, the agent who had represented the archbishop's book. Lynn and I hit it off immediately.

At her suggestion I met with Phil Goldberg about collaborating on the book. I felt that he and I were a good match. At one point, we reviewed my life to see if it could be divided into ten segments—one chapter for each event in the decathlon. I had always thought that the course of an individual's life was like the decathlon. It moves in a series of phases, each one representing a different set of challenges and calling on different skills. And, like the decathlon, life appears to be orderly but is in fact unpredictable, demanding constant adjustments. When we saw that the phases of my life matched well with the sequence of decathlon events, Phil and I knew we were on the right track. The final piece of the puzzle fell into place when I met Eric Major of Doubleday and learned that not only was he enthusiastic about the book but he had actually been present when I won the decathlon in Rome.

I have been blessed with an exceptional life. My reasons

for telling my story are several: First, I want to pay homage to all those who made it possible—my family, coaches, religious advisers, friends, and teammates as well as the members of every community that shaped me; second, I want to leave a legacy to my children and grandchildren so they will have an accurate record of my life and understand the forces that made me who I am; third, I hope that my story will inspire young people to aim high and work hard to be the best that they can be; and fourth, I want to encourage parents, teachers, and anyone who cares about the future to do everything they can to ensure that every youngster has the kind of support I was lucky enough to have.

As with everything else in my life, if I've accomplished my goals with this book it is because I had help.

I am indebted to Phil Goldberg, who turned what seemed to be an insurmountable task into a pleasure and helped me find the right words to express my thoughts and feelings. I'm grateful as well to Lynn Franklin for seeing the possibilities in the book and helping me through the publishing process. And I'm grateful to Eric Major for his editorial guidance and enthusiasm.

Many people were generous enough to help fill in the gaps in my memory. Thanks are due to Joan Andersson, my uncle Leonard Anderson, Ed Arnold, George Atmore, Dick Bank, Shirlene Baxter, Bill Bright, Tom Brokaw, Carly Cady, Vern Chesbro, Don Cohen, Craig Dixon, Rose Drake, Braven Dyer, Jr., Karl and Julie Finley, Joel Finley, Al Franken, my nephew Brian Gibson, Bud Greenspan, Barbara Hopkins, my aunt Bobbi Johnson, Calvin Johnson, Dawna Kaufmann, Ethel Kennedy, Stan King, Bob Liebowitz, Ed Mascarin, Pauline Mathes, Bob Mathias, Erwin and Betty Ohannesian, my aunt Roenna Richardson, Stu Robinson, Mike Roth, Eunice Shriver, Gloria Steinem, Peter Ueberroth, Wei Chen-wu, David Wolper, John Wooden, C. K. Yang, and Frank Zarnowski.

Thanks also to Dick Van Kirk and the staff at Special Olympics of Southern California, especially Melissa Trent and Mikkole Albano; to Anita DeFrantz, Wayne Wilson, and Michael Salmon of the Amateur Athletic Foundation; to Becky Adler and Angela Lomas for their help in transcribing tapes; and to Lori Deutsch and Dee Leroy for their valuable feedback on the manuscript.

Above all, I want to express my deepest gratitude to my family: my wife, Betsy; our children, Jenny and Josh; my brothers, Ed and Jim; and my sisters, Erma and Dolores. Without their help, support, and encouragement I could not have written this book, nor had a life worth writing about.

INTRODUCTION
by Tom Brokaw

WHEN I WAS a young man growing up on the prairies of South Dakota, a long way from the major sports capitals of the world, when winter gave way to spring my friends and I would organize informal competitions around track and field events. We'd pole vault and high jump into pits filled with sawdust still frozen from the lingering cold, race around a one-mile loop in our small community, jump hurdles. Even the best among us were pretty pathetic, especially when we'd read the records of other young men in far-off places.

In various sports publications I began to read about a new California high school sensation, one who was challenging the records of Bob Mathias, another Californian, who had won an Olympic gold medal in the decathlon when he was only seventeen. The new star was someone named Rafer Johnson.

By 1960 Rafer was the favorite to win an Olympic gold medal in Rome. He was featured on the cover of *Time* magazine. I vividly remember that issue. I was in awe of his individual marks: In one event after another he was posting times and reaching distances reserved for specialists in those events. Then, as I read on, I realized he was almost too good to be true as a citizen as well as an athlete: a modest, church-going, studious young man who took his duties as UCLA student body president as seriously as he did his commitment to track and field. I had a new hero.

As fate would have it, a few years later we were colleagues, both employed by KNBC, the NBC-owned television station in Los Angeles. When we met I gushed something about how I'd always admired his Olympic performances and his values. He was genuinely embarrassed by the attention.

We became friends and in the course of our friendship I came to know that Rafer's essential decency and modesty had been understated. Moreover, as a friend—especially as a friend who was that famous and celebrated—he was as true as the one-hundred-meter straightaway. Conversations were never about him or his childhood. More likely they were about something in the news or about the difficult little tricks of broadcasting that he was eager to learn.

His career was just hitting its stride when his friend Robert Kennedy asked him to join his 1968 presidential campaign. Rafer and I discussed it at length. I could see he was torn. He was looking for a career but Bobby obviously meant so much to him. Characteristically, in the end Rafer placed a higher value on his friendship and admiration for Bobby than he did on his own career. He went on the campaign. He was at his friend's side for the closing days of his life.

In this book you will read a great American story of a man, his family, the people who befriended them, and their pride in what they have achieved. Race is indisputably an element in this book as it is in Rafer's life but he measures racism in America the same way he measures the grueling final event of the decathlon, the 1500-meter run. It is a struggle to be overcome by doing your best, one long step at a time. It is not vanquished by whining and pouting. I cannot imagine Rafer doing either.

It is not an exaggeration for me to say at this stage on our lives that Rafer Johnson remains a model by which I judge many people I encounter. He is, for me, an icon of dignity and determination.

When he took the torch to light the flame at the Los Angeles Olympic Games in 1984, I was watching the opening ceremonies on television in a Montana motel room, grimy and exhausted from a long, difficult backpacking trip through a vast wilderness area. As my friend ascended the steep steps in the Los Angeles Coliseum, his great athletic frame still fit at age forty-nine. I dissolved into tears of pride—and gratitude that the rest of the world would at that moment have a small sense of a long journey in which he never faltered. It was the perfect symbolic act for this quintessential American hero: a torch held high, a steady, difficult climb, and the lighting of a flame that is emblematic of human excellence and achievement.

That is the life you will read about in this book.

The Best That I Can Be

1

THE STARTING BLOCKS

Home is where one starts from . . .
—T.S. Eliot

THE FIRST THING an athlete learns is the importance of a good start. As a sprinter, I honed the ability to settle comfortably into the starting blocks and focus my attention radar-like, ready to explode the instant I heard the starter's gun. If I hesitated for a split second I might be too far behind to catch up; if I was overeager and tried to anticipate the gun, I might bolt too early and have a false start. In the decathlon, a good start also means scoring well in the first of the ten events, the hundred-meter dash. Because it sets the tone for everything that follows, the race can have a disproportionate impact on the outcome of the decathlon as a whole.

My start in the race of life had mixed results. By all objective standards, growing up black in Texas in the late 1930s and early 1940s would not be considered a good beginning. It was as if the starting blocks had been rigged and the running track in my lane was ploughed up and uneven. Still, I somehow acquired the necessary tools to take advantage of the opportunities that life would later present. Will I ever fully understand what made me a disciplined youngster and a determined adult? Looking back, I marvel at how I learned to give all I had to every challenge; to compete hard and try to win, but to play the game honestly and fairly.

I was born in Hillsboro, Texas, a tiny town in a flat expanse of land about sixty miles south of Dallas. With rich soil for growing crops and strong bodies to pick them cheap, the area's economy revolved around farming. Most people lived and worked on farms; the rest provided services for the farmers and hired hands. My father, Lewis Johnson, was one of those farmhands. Six foot six, lean and handsome, he had learned at an early age to go wherever there was a day's pay to be earned—something that was not easy to come by during the Great Depression. As a young man, he mostly picked cotton. People always described him as a hard-working, responsible, generous man who loved to have a good time.

While working the fields around Hillsboro, he met a girl with cheerful eyes and a round, endearing face with prominent dimples. Alma Gibson was three years younger and a foot shorter than her beau, and his equal when it came to hard work. When they got married, in 1932, unemployment was at an all-time high, the Dow Jones Industrial Average was at an all-time low, and candidate Franklin Delano Roosevelt was pledging a "New Deal" for hard-pressed Americans. Dad was twenty, Mom was seventeen. Their first child, a daughter, became seriously ill as an infant and did not survive. I was born next, in 1935. My father named me after a childhood friend of his who had died in grade school.

For the first two years of my life, we lived in Hillsboro in the home of my father's parents (my mother's parents had passed away before I was born). It was a good-sized house, but with five of my father's nine siblings living at home, it was crowded. Built on a corner property on the outskirts of town, it was an old wooden structure with front and back porches and a large back yard dominated by a vegetable garden. With no electricity or running water, we used oil lamps and an outhouse and pumped water from an outside well. Nearby was an open field and a network of dirt roads on which children could ride bicycles, run loose, and kick up storms of dust.

A railroad worker in his younger days, my grandfather was forced to retire early when he fell from a train and suffered disabling injuries. To sustain the family, his children worked the cotton fields, chopping and weeding in the spring and picking in the fall. My grandfather was a deeply religious man who had read the Bible to his children on a regular basis. By the time I knew him, though, his children were reading to him, for he had gone blind from glaucoma. I used to marvel at how this sightless man could work tirelessly and flawlessly around the house and in his vegetable garden. The family work ethic was reinforced by my grandmother, a strong, warm, loving woman who took care of everything and everyone—including me, her infant grandson, while my parents worked long hours in the fields.

Drawn by the demand for farmhands as New Deal programs put some money into the pockets of hungry Americans, my father moved us briefly to Oklahoma. He picked sugar cane; my mother cared for me and gave birth to my brother Ed. When I was three and Ed was two we moved back to Texas, settling in the Oak Cliff section of Dallas. There my brother Jim and sister Erma were born. My youngest sister, Dolores, was born in Houston, where we spent part of every summer at the home of my mother's aunt, Dollie Ann, and her husband, Aubrey. Aunt Sweet, as we called her, had raised my mother after her own mother died, and she raised Dolores as well until we relocated to California. As a child I did not understand why my baby sister did not live with us in Dallas. I assume now that it was because four kids and long working hours were about all my parents could handle at the time. It's an enigma that still lingers.

An all-black neighborhood west of downtown Dallas, Oak Cliff was nestled in a little valley formed by the Trinity River. Most of the hard-working people who lived there had jobs in oil companies, filling stations, or the paper plant nearby. Others did domestic and yard work in the white sections of town. Still others labored on construction sites. There was a lot of work in Dallas as the depression lifted and mobilization for World War II increased the demand for oil. The poor families of Oak Cliff struggled and scraped, but they always put food on their tables.

Except for the main arteries that ran to other areas of Dallas, the streets of the neighborhood were unpaved and without sidewalks. We constantly dragged either mud or dust into the house on our shoes. The fragile wooden homes in the neighborhood were built close together on small lots. During the six years we lived there, we rented three different houses. One of the moves was forced by a fire, which began in our wood-burning stove. I remember the terror I felt as my parents scrambled to rush us out of the inferno, and how heroic my father was when, out on the street, he realized someone was missing and ran back inside. A few heart-stopping minutes later he emerged, dragging my sister Erma by her nightgown.

My father worked for a man named John Eastman, who owned a company that made drilling implements and other equipment used by the oil industry. Dad was basically an all-purpose handyman. He worked on Mr. Eastman's cars, cleaned up around the office, did some work in the fields, served as a chauffeur, and helped out—as did my mother—at the Eastmans' private parties. By all accounts, he was fond of his employer and liked his job. Apparently he was well liked in return, and was paid a decent wage. As my uncle Leonard put it, "If white people in Texas didn't like you, they'd let you know. If they liked you, they'd go the limit for you."

In addition to helping out the Eastmans on occasion, my mother supplemented the family income by doing domestic work and sometimes wrapping gifts at a downtown department store—all the while caring for her children and making sure we were properly fed, clothed, and educated. Like most kids, I took it for granted at the time, but I came to marvel at her selflessness and indomitable strength.

I'm told by older relatives that we were somewhat better off than most families in Oak Cliff. For example, we owned a shiny Model A Ford. I remember a drive to Houston when I rode with my uncle in the uncovered rumble seat that folded open just above the trunk. It was a bone-rattling journey but it seemed like a great adventure to me, and surely preferable to squeezing into the front seat with my parents and my brother Ed.

The house I remember most seemed big to me as a boy, but was actually cramped. My brothers and I slept in the same bed, with Ed and me pointed in the usual direction and Jimmy between us facing the other way. We did not have electricity or indoor plumbing. I don't think anyone in Oak Cliff did. We carried buckets from a well for my mother to cook with, and used a dipper to fill our drinking glasses. We bathed in a metal tub, which was placed in the middle of the kitchen floor and filled with steaming water heated in the stove. That stove also provided heat in the winter. Kerosene lamps supplied light. Blocks of ice were hauled to our icebox for refrigeration. We trudged to the outhouse in all kinds of weather. I remember that outhouse well because Ed locked himself inside one day to escape punishment after he knocked Erma off the gate we used to swing on and bloodied her head. Erma still has the scar from that fall.

One of my most vivid memories is the time I nearly burned down the house because my desire to help out got the best of me. Our wallpaper was ancient and frayed. I thought I might be able to improve its appearance by burning off the frayed edges that curled out from the wall. I'd light a strand with a match and watch it burn, enchanted by the pretty flame and intrigued by the acrid smell. Then I'd snuff it out. At one point, I failed to act quickly enough and the flame climbed up the wall beyond my reach. I ran to the kitchen for a dipper of water. When I came back, a large section of the wall was on fire. I stood as close as I could and flung the water. There was a hiss. Smoke billowed and filled the room. The flames were dead. I felt as proud of that water toss as I would later feel after an exceptional javelin throw. Naturally, my parents saw it another way. I had taken the precaution of hanging my mother's coat over the damage, as if that could hide a huge black patch in the middle of the wall. I got beaten within an inch of my life.

As kids, of course, we didn't know we were poor. No one told us we were deprived, and as far as we could tell, Mom and Dad made sure we had the basic necessities of life. Besides, we had steep hills to ride our wagons down, riverbanks to romp along and swimming holes to dive in, vines to swing from and trees to climb, fields to play baseball in and chase each other through, and even a cemetery through which to run at night and scare one another out of our wits. And we had each other. Although everyone—even we kids—had to work hard, we had fun at home; the love in our household was as tangible as the furniture, just as it is now whenever I'm with my brothers and sisters.

• • •

Every morning my mother would prepare a big breakfast—typically eggs and bacon or sausage—and then Dad would go off to his job. After helping the younger kids get ready for school, Mom would walk to the end of the block, cross Tama Street, then continue through an open field and up to the top of a hill; there she caught the streetcar to the home of some white family where she did day work. After school, and all day long during vacations, we kids were more or less on our own, although certain neighbors would keep an eye on us.

It was long before television, of course, let alone video games and computers. In our neighborhood we didn't have clubs or gymnasiums with structured activities. We had no organized sports either. I remember playing informal baseball games in the open field behind the church, but strangely enough, no football or basketball to speak of. We had roller skates, wagons, homemade scooters, marbles, secret hideouts, open fields, and all the indispensable ingredients of childhood fun: energy, friends, and imagination.

I loved to play, and I loved to compete. Maybe I was simply born that way. I wanted to be the fastest kid on the scooter and the first to reach whatever we were running to, whether the swimming hole or the candy store or the schoolyard fence. I spent long hours shooting marbles in a circle and felt great when I went home victorious, with my precious marble bag a few ounces heavier than it had been when I started out—and I felt awful when I trudged home with an underweight bag.

To say I did not like losing is an understatement; it felt like a kick in the stomach. But my desire to win was balanced by something I must have learned at home: Always play by the rules. Somehow I knew that there were consequences to playing unfairly, and that winning would not be satisfying if it were accomplished by cheating. Wherever it came from, this attitude stayed with me throughout my athletic career. For example, trying to guess when the starter would pull the trigger on the starting gun was a common practice, but I considered it a form of cheating and I often saw it backfire when an overeager sprinter was penalized for bursting from the blocks too soon.

Another lifelong philosophy was mysteriously transmitted to me in childhood: What matters even more than winning is to approach every challenge with total and complete effort. I learned never to give undue attention to the score or to my competitors. Instead I focused on being the best that I could be. Later in life, that attitude would be reinforced and put into words by gifted coaches; but from as far back as I can remember, it's what drove me. I did not lose often, and when I did it was a big disappointment. But if I worked as hard as I could, and did everything in my power to win, I was able to live with defeat. I would feel let down, but not down on myself.

That attitude did not diminish by one iota my desire to win or my hatred of losing. It simply made me a stronger, more focused competitor. It motivated me to prepare hard for each competition, and to push myself when it would have been perfectly acceptable to ease off. I believe it also made me a better sportsman. I was able to root for others to do their best even when I was trying to defeat them. Without that attitude, I would not have been able to form durable friendships with teammates and opponents alike, something I treasure more than all my trophies.

Apparently I showed signs of exceptional athletic ability as a child. My father once told *Sports Illustrated,* "He was awful good at running and throwing. Just his movements made you know he was good at them." (My mother, on the other hand, used to tell people that she could outrun me.) If I did have a gift for running, it must have been displayed on many occasions: when I had to chase down one of my brothers because he had misbehaved, when we raced through the spooky cemetery

(I was always the first one out), or when I galloped on my stick horse. This was essentially a broomstick I imagined to be a dependable horse like the Lone Ranger's Silver. I was a fast stick-horse rider, but I never attributed that to personal talent: I just thought I had the swiftest horse around.

There was at least one moment when my throwing ability raised eyebrows, literally. A family of brothers who lived up the hill had a fondness for picking on Eddie and Jimmy. One day Eddie came home crying. Like a two-man posse, Jimmy and I jumped on our stick horses and rode off to avenge him. We found the thugs at home alone and held them hostage, throwing rocks at the house for half the day and threatening to use our slingshots if our enemies dared to show their faces.

Having made our point—and getting very bored—I called out, "Don't you ever put your hands on my brother again!" We started to leave but one of our enemies emerged from the house and taunted us. I wheeled and hurled a round, flat rock at him. It landed with a thwack just above his eyebrow—and stuck there. The rock lodged in his forehead. Blood ran down his face. Amazed and horrified by the gruesome sight, I galloped away on my stick horse with my brothers at my heels.

Someone with an eye for talent might have seen that throw and marked me as a future discus champion, quarterback, or rifle-armed third baseman. At the time, it was enough to know that those boys would never bother us again.

Our unsupervised times were not all play, not by a long shot. My brothers and I had responsibilities that had to be fulfilled before our parents got home. On any given day we might be asked to straighten up the house, sweep the floors, make the beds, or clean up the yard. Some of our chores were pretty grown-up, now that I think of it. To do the dishes, for example, we had to pump water from the well, carry it inside, light the wooden stove, heat the water, and fill the wash pan. We also had to look after our baby sister, Erma.

As the oldest I was naturally in charge. In part, that meant riding herd on my brothers to make sure the chores got done. I believe that a lot of my future success can be traced to the self-discipline I gained from being given responsibility at a young age. To the extent that I developed leadership qualities, I can thank the lessons I learned from those duties. Without them, I doubt if anyone would have made me a team captain, or student body president, or flag bearer at the Olympics.

When necessary, I could be a stern taskmaster. "If we didn't do what we were supposed to do, Rafer would put his finger in our face," Ed recalls. I seldom had to get tough with the younger kids, but when I did it was for their protection and my own self-preservation: If we didn't complete our chores, we'd get our tails whipped. Our parents believed in seat-of-the-pants discipline. If you were told to do something, to be somewhere at a certain time, or to act in a certain way, you had better comply or it could be whipping time. Dad would do it with a belt; Mom would use a switch. Both hurt, and both made their point. But if I had to be punished, I preferred to have my mother do the job. When she lashed me, I felt as much love as I did pain. It was like taking bad-tasting medicine sweetened with sugar. I was getting what I deserved; I was being taught a lesson and justice was being served.

Dad hurt me a lot more than Mom not only because he was stronger and his belt was fiercer than her switch, he also often seemed excessive. The punishment didn't always match the crime. Whereas my mother's strokes felt reluctant, like she hated having to do it, Dad's lashes had anger behind them. Sometimes he seemed to relish it; I thought he might even want to hurt me. I realize now that he was venting his own frustration and anguish, but at the time, all I felt was his rage. I was afraid he might someday lose control and do some real damage.

Although I've never laid a hand on my own children and would never condone abuse in any form, the whippings I received paid off in their own way. I was able to turn the experience to my advantage once I realized something crucial: Pain was temporary, and I could handle it. While I was being punished, I would think, "My father can hit me as long as he wants, and tomorrow it won't even matter." I even said that to his face when I felt defiant.

The ability to endure pain and still perform at a high capacity gave me a competitive edge. Sports is always referred to as character-building; a major part of that is learning to withstand sprains, twists, aches, bruises, cramps, spasms, soreness, cuts, scrapes, and unimaginable fatigue, while yet coaxing your body to do its best. Every sport entails physical and mental travail, but the decathlon is a veritable factory of pain. I never competed in one in which pain was not a factor. But I knew that an injury was an obstacle to success only if it prevented me from executing properly—that is, if I could not move my legs, arms, or torso the way I had to. During my career I had to endure grueling rehabilitation from injuries, and sometimes run and jump through searing pain. My only fear was that continuing to perform might cause permanent damage. The pain itself I could deal with.

Without my ability to withstand pain I could never have done what was necessary to set world records and win a gold medal. But long before I ever dreamed of becoming an athlete, I put this ability to good use. I saw that my younger brothers and sisters could not handle pain as well as I could. It hurt me more to watch them get whipped than to be whipped myself. So one day, when my father took the belt to one of them, I told him to punish me instead. He responded by thrashing both of us. Thereafter, I shielded my siblings by taking the blame for some of the things they did. That way, I'd get the belt instead of them.

Knowing I could handle pain also made me unafraid of fights. In trying to protect Ed and Jim from harm, I got into several scrapes. In most instances I was able to use either the threat of force or fast-talking diplomacy to settle conflicts before things got out of hand. "He was a peacemaker for other kids," my mother once told an interviewer. "When they got into fights, Rafer would stop them." I think my attitude toward pain gave me the upper hand in negotiations.

One day, before going to work, my father put some money on top of a dresser and told me to pay the bills when some merchants came by to collect. I followed his instructions, but somehow ran short of cash. When someone who did not get paid complained to my father, Dad got enraged. I told him that I hadn't done anything wrong and did not know where the money had gone. He wouldn't listen. He nearly tore my rear end off with his belt. It was the first time I was beaten for no good reason. Not only did the punishment not fit the crime—there *was* no crime.

Small as I was compared to this gigantic man, I warned my father to never again beat me for nothing. My reward for speaking my mind was another whipping. Later, Dad discovered the missing money behind the dresser. It had fallen during the course of the day. He never apologized. The sting of that undeserved punishment stayed with me. It not only made me tougher, it taught me the importance of justice. I began to look at everything in terms of fairness and proportion, always asking myself if my response to someone else's actions—and their reaction to mine—was equitable and reasonable. To this day, nothing upsets me more than being accused of something I didn't do, or seeing someone else get penalized unfairly.

Just as I was too young to be conscious of our poverty, I was too young to understand discrimination or to know that our chances in life were limited by the color of our skin. Texas was not Mississippi or Alabama, but Jim Crow was alive and well there. Segregation was a way of life where I lived; it was accepted in most of the country, even in the armed forces that were fighting fascism abroad. The only white person I saw on a regular basis was Mr. Emmett, the proprietor of the grocery store on our street, where my mother picked up the staples for our kitchen and we kids spent our pennies on candy. Mr. Emmett was a pleasant, friendly man who treated everyone well. At the downtown shops we would run into white people, but I did not know any white boys my age and I can't remember exchanging meaningful words with any white adult besides Mr. Emmett while we lived in Texas. Neither can my brothers and sisters.

Nor do I remember any racial incidents of the type that we associate with the South of that time: no Klan rallies or cross-burnings, no lynchings, no one beaten up or humiliated by rednecks, no slurs or insults, no rigged trials. I'm sure such things occurred, but I was too young and too isolated to know about them. I *do* remember separate drinking fountains, with signs reading WHITE and COLORED. I remember being led to the back of the streetcar on trips downtown, even though there were plenty of seats up front. I remember separate sections (Negroes upstairs, whites downstairs) at the movie house, and separate bathrooms as well, but on those Saturday afternoons we spent in the darkened theater my only concerns were the cartoons and the serials with characters like Flash Gordon and the Lone Ranger.

I don't remember thinking how absurd the racial division was, or realizing the indignity that was implied by it: that one group, the one I belonged to, was inferior to the other. Not that I was totally in the dark about racism. My parents and other elders told us kids about the legacy of slavery, and made sure we knew about great African Americans like Booker T. Washington and Frederick Douglass. Not to mention Joe Louis. In those days, Joe was a god to us. I remember sitting around a radio on someone's front porch, listening with my father and his friends to the broadcast of heavyweight championship battles. We suffered with every blow Joe received and we rejoiced in every punch he landed. We celebrated his knockouts as if we'd slain a wicked slavemaster ourselves. The fact that Joe's victories were victories for black people as a whole was hardly lost on me or the other kids.

For the most part, we paid little mind to racial issues. In that time and place, segregation just seemed normal; it was the way things were, and that was that. Kids like me assumed that the whole world was that way, and the grownups chose not to challenge the status quo. Recently I asked an older relative about those days. "We minded our business and tried to take care of our own," he said. "We left the white people alone and they mostly left us alone."

While black adults endured their lot in life with strength and quiet dignity, racism infected their spirits like a virus infects the cells of our bodies. I'm certain it contributed to the one dark shadow that hovered over my home life: My father drank as hard as he worked. Alcohol might have been his medicine, his way of alleviating the daily indignities he faced—even at a job where he was treated decently—and the frustration of knowing he could never live up to his potential or lift his family's prospects above the low ceiling that was set for people of color.

During the week our home life was smooth, harmonious, and peaceful, but I came to dread the weekends. I never knew when my father would decide to blow his paycheck on booze and set the place in an uproar. It was as if there were two of him: The kind, hard-working family man who showed affection for his wife and children, and the hell-raising drunk who would stay out till all hours and come home with a chip on his shoulder, slamming doors and roaring at the top of his lungs, ready to pull my mother out of bed and beat her at the slightest provocation. Sometimes he didn't return until Sunday.

To us kids, Dad's behavior was terrifying. He never unleashed his drunken rages on us, but time and again we felt the stable foundation of our home being shattered as if by earthquakes. We felt our mother's agony too. No woman deserves to be abused, least of all someone like Mom. They called her "Dimple" because of the cute little craters that formed on her cheeks when she smiled. And she smiled a lot. She was an upbeat, cheerful, outgoing woman, who seemed almost always to be happy. As strong as she was well-liked, she was extremely protective of her children, ready to pounce like a lioness on anyone who wronged us. She was, in every way, a good woman and a wonderful mother. My inability to protect her from my father's tantrums was agonizing. I felt helpless. It was not until my brothers and I were old enough to stand up to Dad that we were able to put an end to it.

My father's weakness for alcohol and the turmoil it caused made a deep impression on me. It was a powerful lesson in how not to be a man, and I vowed early on never to succumb to such self-defeating, hurtful behavior. I have always respected my body and treated it with care. I think I could fit all the alcohol I have ever drunk into three glasses.

Aside from his drinking, my father was a fine role model. No matter what had occurred over the weekend, come Monday morning he was up early and at the breakfast table. Often he'd look contrite and even apologize. Unfailingly he'd get to work on time, ready to give an honest day's labor. Once again he was good old Dad, and he'd stay that way all week. Come Friday, though, anything was possible.

My mother was a model of consistent goodness. To my mind, her ability to remain warm, loving, and joyful in the face of the harsh realities of her life was a greater achievement than anything I ever did in sports. My way of honoring her was to push myself to be all I was capable of being, and to do so with the kind of integrity she valued. It was one way of giving something to the woman who gave me so much.

The N. W. Harlee School was a rectangular brown brick building, two stories high, with a scruffy schoolyard spread out behind it. All the students, maybe fifteen to twenty per class, were black, as were all the teachers. The ten- or fifteen-minute walk from home took us over some open fields, across a small bridge that spanned the Trinity River, and through the cemetery.

Everyone in my family remembers me as an eager student who loved to read and was diligent about his homework. I didn't start out that way. Like most of my peers, I valued the streets and playing fields far more than the classroom. That changed in the third grade, thanks to an exceptional teacher. Miss Bailey was a stout, dignified woman with great concern for the welfare of her pupils. With dedication and persistence, this gifted teacher stressed the importance of working hard and using one's full potential. Miss Baily instilled in me a love of learning and a desire to do well academically. The spark she ignited stayed lit all the way through college, and in many ways remains lit to this day.

I had a friend named Curtis who was a good athlete and a mischief-maker. To say he was an indifferent student is putting it mildly. He never did homework and hardly paid attention in class, finding every opportunity to disrupt a lesson with a joke or a prank. I sat next to him, and I enjoyed it. He brought out the naughty, fun-loving side of me that balanced the earnest, disciplined side.

Curtis was the kind of kid an adult would call a "bad influence." I hesitate to call him that, since I joined him happily and even initiated some of the troublemaking myself. The problem was, Curtis had a way of going too far. I'd go along with him, only to find that our innocent fun had turned into trouble. Once, for example, he got me to climb up onto the roof of our house. Then he decided that we should jump to the ground. Foolishly, I followed him, only to land on a board and end up with a nail piercing my foot from bottom to top.

It was clear to Miss Bailey that Curtis would not have a positive impact on my future. One day she told me point-blank that if I wanted to do well in her class I would have to stop doing the things my friend was doing. When the warning didn't sink in, she split us up by making Curtis repeat the grade.

Miss Bailey knew how to use rewards to reinforce good habits. For example, she would take students who did well on special trips. One glorious night a few classmates and I were rewarded with a trip to the Cotton Bowl to see a fireworks display. I remember it as a gray evening, with dazzling bursts of color lighting up the night sky. I also remember being frightened by some thunderous claps of sound, and Miss Bailey covering my ears protectively. Mostly I remember feeling very grateful for the chance to be there, and proud of having done well enough to be in that select company.

By showing me the pleasure of learning and by rewarding good work, Miss Bailey convinced me that it paid to study hard. That, plus my parents' encouragement (they made sure I always did my homework), turned me into a good enough student to eventually win an academic scholarship to UCLA. I believe that good learning habits helped me in everything I did. In sports I always felt there was more to learn, and I looked for information wherever I could find it—from coaches, teammates, even opponents. Good study habits also helped me concentrate on the field; I could block out distractions and stay focused on what I had to do at every moment, no matter what was going on around me or what had happened a few minutes earlier. This was invaluable in a two-day, ten-event competition like the decathlon, especially in the glare of an international spotlight. Sometimes I wonder if I would ever have gained those advantages if not for Miss Bailey.

Life in our close-knit community centered around the Baptist church. The house we lived in during most of our time in Oak Cliff was actually connected to the church grounds. Every Sunday morning we would stroll there down a narrow dirt path between two of our neighbors' homes. After services, we kids would go from chapel to Sunday School. I looked forward to that time; it felt less like a school than a social club, a gathering place for all the kids in the community. We would start out all together in a Bible class, then break up into different age groups and spend the better part of the day playing games, reading stories, and singing religious songs. Later we'd return with our parents for evening services and, usually, more social time with our friends.

It was not until high school that I understood the deep spiritual significance of Jesus' life and became a committed Christian. But even as a child, church had a major impact on me. I remember three things in particular about those Sundays. First, the music. The awesome power and passion that surged through the church when the choir sang spirituals and hymns was inspiration to the soul. Second, the sermons. I can't recall the preacher's name, but the clear conviction in his voice and the spirit of his message are still fresh in my mind—the message being that life should not be, and did not have to be, the way it was for people of color; that spiritual redemption could be found; and that betterment in the here and now could be had through proper actions.

Third, I remember the community itself. In retrospect it is clear to me that the people of Oak Hill tried to make up for the obstacles in their path by looking out for one another. My siblings and I experienced it firsthand; our parents were at work all day, but the neighbors made sure we never felt ignored, alone, or endangered. It was understood that life could be better for all if everyone took responsibility for each other, and that our own needs are best served when we contribute to the good of the whole. These became core beliefs of mine. Wherever fate has taken me, I've always tried to recreate the sense of community that we had in that small Baptist church.

Did I get off to a good start in Texas? If those years were the equivalent of the first decathlon event, I would say that, thanks to a strong support system, my score was better than it might have been considering the obstacles in my environment. Some mysterious combination of genes, upbringing, and community enabled me to compensate for my disadvantages, just as a gritty sprinter might make up for lost ground with extra effort and a well-timed lunge at the tape. But my prospects for the rest of the competition would not have been considered bright. From what I've been able to gather over the years, most of the boys I grew up with went on to lead good, decent lives, but were severely constrained from reaching their full potential by bigotry and inequality of opportunity. Others became small-time hoodlums. At least two died in prison. Another was stabbed with an ice pick during a brawl. Curtis, my best buddy and the class clown, was shot to death.

I was lucky. When I was nine my family moved to California, where conditions for the next phase of my life were exceptional. To my everlasting gratitude, I was given the tools I needed to make up for the slow start.

2

THE LONG LEAP FORWARD

Don't look back. Something might be gaining on you.
—SATCHEL PAIGE

DECATHLETES learn to live one event at a time. No matter how well or how poorly you do in the hundred meters, you have to put the race behind you as soon as it's done and focus your attention on the next event, the long jump. If you've done well in the first event, you're eager to move on and keep your momentum going. If you've performed below expectations, it's only natural to try and figure out what went wrong. Some athletes take that to an extreme, carrying the disappointment with them like excess baggage. They might even berate themselves or worry that they're destined for a bad day all around.

Dwelling on negative thoughts paves the way to failure. You have to save the analysis for later and tell yourself that you'll do better in the next event. I was lucky enough to get that message early on. I was able to completely forget the previous event and focus on the challenge at hand.

"I don't care if I never see Texas again," I told *Time* magazine before the 1960 Olympics. "There's nothing about it I like. If my family had stayed in Texas, I not only wouldn't be representing the U.S. in the Olympic Games—I wouldn't even have gone to college." Like most young people I was prone to exaggeration, but at the time I meant it. In truth, there was a warm place in my heart for Texas. It was my birthplace, a source of beautiful memories, the home of relatives I loved and continued to visit. But I knew that my life would have been very different had my family stayed in the segregated South instead of moving to California, where we found excellent conditions for a long leap forward.

In the war years, word spread through the cities and towns of the South that there were jobs to be had up north and out west. For African Americans, that meant not only higher pay and greater opportunity but freedom from institutionalized segregation. Word of a better life filtered back to Texas from men and women who had relocated and sent letters home or returned to visit their families. Representatives of large companies would come around recruiting; some even paid the transportation costs for willing workers.

My father's strong desire to provide a better life for his family led him to California, where his sister and brother-in-law had already moved. He liked his work in Dallas, and was treated well by his employer, Mr. Eastman, but he knew the grass was greener in the Golden State: better jobs, less discrimination, better weather, and abundant food. "I saw I had good boys growing up," he told *Sports Illustrated* in 1959, "and everyone knows California is the land of opportunity."

He ventured alone to Oakland in 1944, landing work in

the booming shipyards that fed the American war effort. Later he painted ships on Treasure Island in San Francisco Bay, probably the most picturesque military base in the country. In 1945 he summoned the rest of the family to join him. Among my memories of our last days in Texas was hearing on the radio that Franklin Delano Roosevelt had died. From the sad, ominous mood of the adults around me, I thought the world was about to end. A few weeks later, another radio report drew the opposite reaction: The war in Europe had ended. I understood that a bad man named Hitler had been defeated and the victorious American troops would be coming home.

We traveled by train for two and a half days, then crammed into the three-bedroom house of my Aunt Novella and Uncle H.B. in Oakland where my father was living. A month or so later, with defense workers being laid off, my father took us to where the work was, in the San Joaquin Valley.

Thanks to the Central Valley Project, which had irrigated hundreds of thousands of acres, the land in that part of California was producing abundant crops. Farm workers were needed to feed the energetic men and women who were creating families and building a new prosperity. We settled first in the town of Chowchilla; then we moved south to Madera and then, for a short spell, to Fresno. In the first two locations we lived in meager houses provided by Dad's employers; in the third we lived in a canvas Army tent like migrant workers. Dad worked as a foreman on a cotton-picking crew.

Fourth grade was divided between schools in Chowchilla and Madera. For the first time, my classmates were not all African Americans. In fact, I don't recall *any* black students, although there were some Asians and Latinos mixed with the predominantly white population. It would have been only natural for me to have been self-conscious. But I don't recall anything more than the jitters any new kid in school might feel. My most vivid memories are of long solitary walks to and from school through the broad, fertile fields, and of Mom cooking while the rest of us tried to keep rainwater from flooding the tent in Fresno. That, and picking cotton.

My brothers and I worked the fields after school, on weekends and holidays, and all summer long. Alongside my father and mother, we did something called "taking rows." With sacks strapped to our backs and dragging behind us, we would walk in the space between crop rows and pick the cotton on both sides. Dad was so tall and rangy he could reach *two* rows on each side. I looked forward to being big enough to do that myself. Fortunately, I never had to.

When your sack was full you would shake the cotton balls to the bottom and carry your load as much as two hundred yards to the scales. After your bag was weighed, you would haul it up a ladder and dump it into a trailer, where other workers would stomp on it to flatten the load. We got paid by the pound. My father might pick six or eight hundred pounds on a given day, and the rest of us together might duplicate that tally.

If I had anything good to say about picking cotton it would be this: It was a great workout. In later years I did other physical work. Every summer, at Aunt Sweet's house in Houston, I earned money baling hay and stacking the bales. In California I mowed lawns, hauled boxes in a cannery, worked under hoods at a car dealership and on a garbage truck. I fully believe that the labor made me strong and prepared me for the discipline I'd need as an athlete. But thinking about picking cotton brings tears to my eyes to this day, just from remembering how hard my parents had to toil to earn a meager living.

On route 99, at about the exact midpoint between Los Angeles and San Francisco, forty miles west of the snowy peaks of the High Sierra, sits the town of Kingsburg. When the area around it was discovered by European explorers searching for a route to the Pacific Ocean, it was a desert. With irrigation, the leveling of land, and the expansion of the Southern Pacific Railroad, a small settlement grew. Originally named Wheatville, the town began with just a switchyard and a shed. Then came a general store, a blacksmith, a hotel, and other essentials. The principal products were wheat and sheep, neither of which needed much water. For quite a while, Kingsburg had a reputation as a "wide-open town" of hard-drinking, tough hombres. Then, in the late 1800s, there was an influx of sober, industrious Swedes who had left their homeland for economic opportunity and religious freedom. Before long they turned a red-light district into "the City of Churches."

Until the 1930s, when the region attracted workers from parts of the country hard hit by the Great Depression, 94 percent of Kingsburg's population was of Swedish extraction. By the mid-1940s there were plenty of Latinos, Japanese, Armenians, and Italians, but Kingsburg remained so Swedish that signs along Route 99 still urge tourists to stop and see the "Swedish Village." I'm sure that in 1946 no one thought twice when they heard that another family named Johnson had moved to town; it was the most common name in Kingsburg. No doubt everyone expected the newcomers to have blond hair and blue eyes like all the rest. There were no other African Americans within the city limits.

My father had lined up a job as a section hand for the Southern Pacific Railroad. We took up residence in a small colony of "section houses" that the company provided for its workers on a parcel of land adjacent to the Del Monte cannery. When I became well known, virtually every article written about me said I had been raised in a boxcar. That wasn't exactly true. The housing units were the shape and approximate size of boxcars but they were built to be homes, with regular doors and windows. Our house was actually one and a half units joined together, with a sitting room, a kitchen, three small bedrooms—one for the girls, one for my brothers and me, one for my parents—and a tiny front porch. The toilets and showers were outside and shared by other families.

The railroad tracks were so close that at night the train's lights would shine through the windows, casting spooky shadows on the walls and ceilings. The harsh blast of the whistle and the rumble of steel wheels would shatter the rural silence and shake the house so much you'd think that Kingsburg was the epicenter of an earthquake. Years later, in fact, when we lived in a different part of town, an earthquake did rock the area in 1952, and at first I thought it was the train again.

In a 1961 television documentary produced by David L. Wolper, Mike Wallace called my hometown a quiet, unassuming place. "People work hard, watch their youngsters go to school, grow up, get married, live and work here in Kingsburg," he said. "They talk mostly about crops, local gossip and the weather. What people do around here rarely matters to the outside world." He also said that Kingsburg was "just another truck stop on Highway 99" until Rafer Johnson put it on the map. But as far as I'm concerned, it was Kingsburg that put Rafer Johnson on the map.

When I tell people that we were the only blacks in a town of about 2,500 people, they invariably get ready for a horror story. The truth is more like a Frank Capra movie.

When I entered fifth grade in my new school, I got into a few scuffles, but only one had racial overtones. A boy who was trying to act tough hurled what we now call a racial epithet at me. I decked him. The other fights were of the boys-will-be-boys variety. New kids are often tested, especially when they're different in some obvious way. Fortunately, most of the young people of Kingsburg were innocent enough to treat me and my siblings like any other kids. Children notice differences like skin color, but unless they've been taught otherwise they see it in the same light as tallness and shortness, thinness and fatness, hair color and style of dress—just another way to distinguish one person from another.

One fight was a turning point in my assimilation to my new environment. A big bully was picking on a smaller boy. I tried to stop him and he hit me with a sneak punch to the face. Once I regained my senses I launched a counterattack, but a teacher came between us before I could do any damage. The brief battle was painful and frustrating, but the reaction to it was amazing. Here I had fought with a white boy, yet *he* was suspended from school and I was treated like a hero. I suddenly had the respect of my peers and a reputation as a peacemaker that would last a long time. Young as I was, I knew I was no longer in Texas.

The only antagonism my family faced came from the police chief. It seemed that every time something was stolen or vandalized in Kingsburg, the chief made the Johnson boys his prime suspects. He came straight to our house, probably hoping to find evidence of wrongdoing or to bait my father into doing something rash so he'd have an excuse to arrest him. I distinctly remember one of the chief's visits. Some bicycles had been stolen and he wanted to look around our house to see if the bikes, or their parts, were there. Indignantly my father asserted our innocence and told the chief not to come back if all he intended to do was accuse his boys of stealing.

Time magazine reported that when my father left the railroad to work for Fishel Products, and my mother was hired as a domestic by the Fishel family, the chief tried to pressure the Fishels into firing them. If *Time* was correct, the chief must have thought it was okay for us to be in section houses, but not to work for a prominent family and live in a house on that family's property. That would make the black Johnsons almost as visible as any of the white Johnsons. The magazine said that the chief threatened my mother with these words: "I don't want to see the sun set on any niggers in this town." In fairness, the chief was said to be deeply hurt by the allegations. His family claimed he was not a prejudiced man. Perhaps the reporter was in error, but my mother would not have made up such a story.

To their everlasting credit, the Fishels told the chief what he could do with his opinion, and went on to treat my family like part of their own. The same is true of Wilbur and Edith Shannon, who owned a car dealership and gave me my first real job when I was in high school. After class, on weekends, and during the summer, I'd wash cars, clean up, run errands, and even do some minor mechanical work. Apparently some customers tried to get the Shannons to hire a white boy instead. The Shannons said they'd hire whomever they pleased.

For the most part, whatever prejudice individual citizens may have harbored they kept to themselves. As one of my friends put it when we had grown up, "Years after somebody died you would find out they were a racist." Remarks had been muttered by people who did not like African Americans shopping in the same stores they shopped in or going to school with their children. And when my brothers and I became teenagers, some white parents were terrified that we might get interested in their daughters. But I don't remember any incidents of overt racism, and neither can anyone I've spoken with. I remember Kingsburg with great affection as a Norman Rockwell painting come to life, a peaceful, harmonious place where people were treated with decency and "Live and let live" was the motto. As far as we could tell, my siblings and I were treated like all the other kids in town, and were given the same opportunities for education and recreation. No Kingsburg child was shortchanged if the community could do anything about it.

• • •

At the time my family was settling in Kingsburg, lynchings were still common in the South, military units in the just-ended war were segregated, our national pastime was still as white as snow, the civil rights movement was just a dream, and Martin Luther King, Jr., had not yet been ordained a minister. How was it that the town could absorb a black family so gracefully? It's probably due to a combination of factors.

I'm sure it helped that we were the *only* African-American family within the town limits and one of very few in the area as a whole. Unlike people of color in larger cities, we may have been seen as individuals rather than as representatives of a group. There was no ghetto, no legacy of slavery, no history of Jim Crow laws, no built-up animosity, resentment, or tension. The whites of Kingsburg had never had a reason to draw racial lines or to teach their children to hate or feel superior to blacks.

Kingsburg's Swedish origins may have had something to do with it as well. Swedes have always had a reputation as a progressive and tolerant people. Also, the original settlers had left Sweden as religious dissenters and were treated as second-class citizens when they first arrived in California. Perhaps this heritage had cultivated in Kingsburg's Swedes a tolerance for differences. And I suppose it didn't hurt that Johnson is a Swedish name.

Ed Mascarin, my friend since the fifth grade, points out that the town was actually quite multiethnic. There were prominent citizens, working-class families, and poor people of many different backgrounds. All the children went to the same schools and played in the same playgrounds. This mingling of classes and ethnic groups may have contributed to the tolerant atmosphere.

Kingsburg historian Pauline Mathes notes that the townspeople had just had an encounter with racism when my family arrived. Japanese families of long standing in the community had spent the war years in internment camps. A Japanese school and church had been burned by angry bigots. But other citizens had spoken out against internment and a doctor had protected a pregnant Japanese woman from a group of men who wanted to send her away. Perhaps the chance to witness discrimination firsthand had softened some hearts and opened some minds.

One factor I don't want to neglect is religion. Virtually every denomination was represented in Kingsburg. Services were well attended, and much of the town's social and civic life centered around its religious institutions. Certainly, church-going is no guarantee of tolerance; some of the most virulent racism has been instigated by bigots who called themselves Christians. But the faithful of Kingsburg were, with very few exceptions, Christians in the truest sense of the word. That hadn't always been true. At one time, Roman Catholics had to travel to other towns to worship because they couldn't get a church built in town. But in a town that small, time and every-day encounters can eventually heal longstanding prejudices. The Catholic community became one of the most well-respected and influential in town.

People have suggested that my prominence as an athlete helped grease the wheels of my family's acceptance. My siblings may have received more favorable treatment, and my parents more acceptance, because I was a local hero. But all that began when I was in high school. It doesn't explain our first five years in town. Besides, people can treat sports heroes as celebrities without really respecting them. If I was a trailblazer for the rest of the family, as my brothers say I was, it was probably just as important that I was known as a good student and responsible citizen.

The character of my parents also had a lot to do with our acceptance. They were personable, honest, good-humored, and hard-working. People tended to like them. True, I don't know what might have happened had they tried to move to an all-white street, or if my father had attempted to join an organization like the Kiwanis Club. Their social life in the early years in Kingsburg centered around black friends and relatives in nearby towns. Their kids, though, made friends in town quickly and were made to feel at home right from the start.

Whatever the reasons, I've always been grateful for the way my family was embraced by Kingsburg. We had been part of a strong community in Dallas too, but it was segregated and isolated. Its children faced a future handcuffed by oppression, poverty, and hate. In these optimistic postwar years, with the American economy booming, the people of Kingsburg faced the future with high expectations and passed that feeling along to my generation. They could afford to give all of its children hope, opportunities to grow, and the resources to help them be all they could be.

I believe we are what we come from, and Kingsburg gave me a new and different place to be from. I wasn't there long before I knew it was special. I wished that the kids I'd left behind in Oak Cliff could join me. I still wish that had been possible.

In addition to Aunt Sweet's home in Texas, I'd spend a portion of each summer in Sacramento with my Uncle Walter and Aunt Bobbi. When I wasn't working with my uncle on their property, I'd spend time by myself. "Rafer would get a lot of books and read all the time, and bang on a typewriter," Aunt Bobbi recalled. "We'd try to get him to go to a show or something, and he wouldn't want to. He was the quietest child you ever saw. And he always wanted to eat spaghetti."

My Kingsburg friends would agree with the spaghetti part, but they would shake their heads if they heard me described as quiet. I tended to be sociable and was often the center of attention. But I also had an introspective side. I enjoyed solitude, and I loved to read. My competitive nature may have contributed to that. The teachers in Kingsburg held summer reading contests. They would give us a list of acceptable books, and the student who read the most would win. Coming in first one year reinforced my love of reading.

Summers in the San Joaquin Valley were long and steamy, with temperatures often exceeding a hundred degrees in the shade. On weekends when my father was sober, we might spend all day fishing and cavorting on the banks of the Kings River, devouring one of my mother's magnificent picnic lunches. Or we might pack up the car and go to Fresno. My folks would drop us kids at a movie and pick us up after the show for Chinese food. Afterward, we would get some ice cream and drive around with the radio on, taking in the sights of what seemed to us like a big city.

Other days, I might be delivering newspapers or mowing lawns for pocket money, or riding my bike. I considered the whole town and its outskirts my playground. Kingsburg had very little traffic then—even Highway 99 was just a two-lane road—so I was able to bicycle up and down the shady streets, along the marshes and riverbanks, through endless fields of grapes, peaches, and every other fruit and vegetable that Americans eat. I wandered by foot along the railroad tracks and around the downtown district with its Swedish-style buildings, the drugstore with the old-fashioned soda fountain, the small restaurants with the smell of coffee and hamburgers wafting through the doors, the movie theater that showed new films every week, the bowling alley, the park, the City Hall, the jail, and the appliance store where I saw my first television set. I remember standing in front of the window, transfixed by the moving images, never dreaming that one day millions of people would watch me on screens like that one.

Much of the time I could be found playing with my brothers and friends. On scorching days we'd go down to the river to fish and swim and lay around dreaming. As Jimmy once put it, life was "like a slice out of *Tom Sawyer.*" In fact, one memorable day Jimmy had an adventure worthy of Mark Twain. A bunch of us went to the swimming hole we called "the second drop." This was where an irrigation ditch dropped from one level to another and the water backed up to form a pool. Swimming was not allowed, so when a car came by we would scamper into the grape fields to keep from being seen. One day, when we ran to hide, I lost sight of Jimmy. Since he was three years younger than me, it was my job to keep an eye on him. I dashed back to the ditch. He was nowhere in sight.

He had fallen into the pool, banged his head on the concrete walkway, and gotten caught in turbulent water. Unable to find his way back to the surface, he felt he was close to dying. For some reason, he didn't panic or flail about. Instead, he told me later, he felt mysteriously peaceful. Meanwhile I was looking for him, not knowing whether he was in trouble or just being mischievous. Then I spotted him bobbing toward the surface. I jumped into the water. He says he saw my face go in and out of focus as I came closer. I grabbed him and threw his arms around my neck. He clasped his hands together and held on tight.

With the help of our friends, I pulled him out of the water. I'd seen artificial respiration in movies, so I started pressing on his chest, praying that I was doing the right thing. When he burped up water, I knew he'd be okay.

For my brother and me it was a turning point. On a documentary that NBC aired during the 1996 Olympics, Jimmy told Bob Costas that as a boy he'd always looked up to me, but after I saved him I became his hero. I didn't feel like a hero, I felt relieved. As I pressed on Jimmy's chest, all I could think of was how Mom and Dad would feel if something awful happened to their youngest son.

After that, I would look at Jimmy and remember that I'd saved his life. Even when he was playing cornerback for the San Francisco Forty-niners, I would think, "He wouldn't be there if I hadn't pulled him out of that swimming hole."

Oddly enough, a few years later I got to save my other brother. Eddie and I were fishing in the Kings River one day when the water was so low you could wade across without getting your face wet. As he searched for a good place to throw his line, Eddie stepped into a deep crevice and sank. He couldn't swim. I had just taken a junior lifeguard course at the YMCA, so I put my training to use. I dove after him and hauled him a few yards to where we could stand. He was never in serious danger of drowning, but that didn't stop me from teasing Eddie from time to time that I had saved his life.

My capacity for turning all of Kingsburg into a playground once led to a crisis that could have put an end to my chances of an athletic future. Adjacent to the section houses where we lived was the Del Monte cannery, the biggest employer in town. To my brothers and sisters and me, the conveyor belt was like an amusement park ride. We'd climb a chinaberry tree, jump onto the elevated belt, and roll along with—or inside of—the empty boxes. After traversing about fifty yards, we would grab the branch of another tree and hop off.

On one ride, when I was ten, I was laughing so hard I missed the second tree. I could have jumped the nine or ten feet to the ground, but the yard was strewn with berries that were as hard as stones and I didn't want to land on one. Instead, I rode the belt to the spot where the boxes were picked up by motorized metal rollers to be carried to the loading dock. When the belt doubled under and began to loop around, I could leap over the rollers onto an elevated wooden platform. I waited a split second too long. My left foot was dragged down and forward, and wedged between the belt and the metal rollers. The scraping of the rollers burned the top of my foot, and the rough conveyor belt rubbed the underside, tearing loose my entire instep. A flap of skin hung grotesquely, like the sole of a shoe that had come unglued. I had never felt such pain before, and I never would again.

I yelled and screamed. My brothers and sisters ran to get help. Someone pushed a button and the belt ground to a halt. Several men ran over to help. As they tried to figure out how to pry my foot loose and stop the bleeding, workers in another part of the plant, unaware of what had taken place, started the belt rolling again. The agony returned. I screamed as my brothers raced through the cannery to stop the belt once more. Finally, the men lifted the metal rollers with a wrench and freed my foot.

Surgeons sewed the flap of skin back into place. I was in the hospital for two weeks. For most of that time, the pain of blood flowing to the sewn-up sole was so unbearable I had to remain in bed with my leg elevated. On top of that, the wound somehow got infected. I heard doctors tell my parents that I might never again walk on two feet. They might have to amputate. All I could do was lie there and imagine living the rest of my life with one foot. It was years before I would dream of the Olympics; all I wanted then was a normal kid's life. I was terrified, but my mother said she believed I'd be able to run and jump again, and that was good enough for me.

The doctors saved my foot. The recovery process was long and tedious—I was on crutches for eight weeks—but sometime that fall I was able to remove the cast and walk again. From that moment on, my left foot has been a constantly annoying presence. Throughout my athletic career, I was unable to compete without it hurting. Since it was my take-off foot, I had to make adjustments in order to compete in the high jump, long jump, and pole vault. Wearing cleats was difficult too; I would always feel unusual pressure on the left foot. To this day, the big toe remains rigid and basically without feeling, and the sole of the foot is so sensitive it hurts when rubbed. I can't walk barefoot, even on a sandy beach; if I were to step on an uneven surface, or on a rock or pebble, it would hurt.

My ability to endure pain, which I'd learned the hard way from my father's beatings, helped me overcome that injury. And the memory of my recovery gave me added faith in my ability to recuperate. Later, when I incurred serious, career-threatening injuries, I would think, "This is arduous and painful, but it's nothing like the conveyor belt."

When I regained the use of my foot, I hit the playing fields of Kingsburg with a vengeance. Soon I was old enough to participate in the abundance of organized sports that the community had created for its youth. With clubs and service groups sponsoring teams, forming leagues, and putting on tournaments and special events, there was ample opportunity for every child in town to compete in the sport of his choice.

My choice was pretty much everything. I got involved in baseball, touch football, basketball, and track. By the time I got to the seventh grade, there was a buzz around Kingsburg and neighboring towns—not just about the Johnson boy but also about other outstanding athletes in the same age group, like Guy Troisi, Eddie Mascarin, Daryll Creed, Bob Wiley, and Monte Clark (who went on to play and coach in the NFL). Each town in the valley supported its high school teams with a passion. The Kingsburg Vikings had never been known as a powerhouse team, but now word was out that the crop of youngsters coming along might just write a new history when they came of age.

By now my family was settled in our new hometown, and I could feel my personality beginning to emerge like a sapling planted in nourishing soil and given plenty of loving, knowing attention. I was one of a small group of kids who gravitated to leadership positions. I ended up getting elected president of the student body at Roosevelt Elementary School. I count myself lucky that my peers singled me out. The acceptance drove home how good it was to be allowed to do what any other kid could do.

With the memory of Miss Bailey fresh in my mind, I worked as hard at my studies as I did at sports. We had terrific teachers; dedicated and skilled, they had all the support they needed to do their jobs well: adequate funding, well-equipped facilities, parental involvement, and small classroom sizes. I've accumulated a ton of memorabilia over the years, ranging from my first airplane ticket to my Olympic gold medal. One item I cherish as much as anything else is a letter from one of my teachers to my parents, praising my "scholarship and good behavior" and congratulating Mom and Dad for the "careful supervision you have exercised over his development." He signed it, "Rafer's friend, Richmond Fowler."

The African saying that Hillary Rodham Clinton made famous is true: It does take a village to raise a child. The village of Kingsburg was filled with people like Mr. Fowler who played an active role in the development of all its youngsters. With few exceptions, Kingsburg adults were also shining examples of how people should behave toward one another. The men and women I came in contact with as a child—in school, shops, church, and the homes of my friends—were models of decency.

Two families stand out in my memory, the Fishels and the Shannons. Ed Fishel, the owner of a company that produced animal feed and dog food, hired my father as a handyman. Later Dad joined the crew that mixed and packaged the food, and he eventually became a foreman. Mr. Fishel's wife, Toby, hired my mother to do domestic work at their home. The Fishels also purchased a house and moved it to their property for us to live in. It was a small clapboard structure, probably less than a thousand square feet, but it was a mansion compared to the section house, with a gas stove, an indoor bathroom, and more privacy for everyone. Later Dad built an extension onto the back of the house, enabling me to have my very own room.

The Fishels—including their son, John, who helped run the plant, and his wife, Beverly—were fair to their employees and generous to us. When I was away, I would write to them as if I were corresponding with a close aunt and uncle. They were as proud of my accomplishments as any relative could be.

The other couple with a special place in my heart are Wilbur and Edith Shannon, who hired me to work at their Dodge–Plymouth dealership. When I think of them and the Fishels I sometimes get tearful—not just because my memories are so precious, but because they stood up for what was right when pressured to fire their black employees.

Kingsburg Joint Union High School was a one-story, Spanish-style building with white stucco walls and a red tile roof. The total student body was less than 400, most of whom had traveled through their school years together. Almost from the start I found myself at the center of student life. Most of that prominence I owed to sports. As my confidence and skills grew, and my body reached six foot one and 185 pounds, I started doing things no one in that part of the world had seen before. I excelled in four sports, became team captain in three, and earned eleven varsity letters.

In baseball I was a third-baseman until a sharp ground ball ripped the nail off my big toe. After that, I divided my time between first base, where my size and reach came in handy, and centerfield, where I could take advantage of my speed. Legend has it that I was asked to stop hitting the ball so hard because I was breaking too many bats. I *did* break a lot of bats at first, but I think it was because I gripped them cross-handed, causing me to connect either on the handle or the insignia. After I corrected that quirk, I broke fewer bats. I did hit for power, though my greatest asset was my speed; I could leg out infield hits on weak ground balls. One season I parlayed that skill into a .500 batting average.

In basketball, playing forward, I averaged seventeen points a game and became known as a fierce defender and rebounder. Our team won the league title each year, and I was named to the all-league team three times.

In football I played running back on offense and safety on defense. I also returned kicks and kicked off, taking great pride in booting the ball into the end zone. I loved running with the football. The thrill of busting through the line for long yardage, or breaking into the open field and outrunning my pursuers down the sideline, made me want the ball even when the other team knew I'd be getting it. One year my coach used a spread formation, in which the snap would come to me and I would decide whether to run or pass. As a senior, I averaged more than nine yards per carry and was named to the All-State team. More important, by the time my teammates and I graduated, the Vikings had won two consecutive championships.

Yet my greatest love was track and field. There was something pure and innocent about the sport: You ran, you jumped, you threw things, just as young men had done since the dawn of civilization. Whoever got there first, jumped the highest or longest, or threw the farthest, was the winner. There was a unique sense of camaraderie among track men, perhaps because the sport did not involve one-on-one physical confrontations or attempts to do harm to opponents, and because track meets gave athletes a chance to get to know each other. In track, I felt, you could be a true sportsman. This appealed to me greatly.

Before long I earned a lot of notoriety in track. I remember overhearing a fan from another town tell his companion, "I'm really looking forward to seeing this Swedish boy, Rafer Johnson." Imagine his surprise when he saw me line up in the starting blocks. Friends say that at track meets held at night, when I ran down the back stretch where the stadium lights were dim, all they would see were my white socks moving past the pale bodies of other runners. It sounds like the kind of memory that gets exaggerated over time. But I do remember being so confident as an anchor runner on relay teams that I felt I could catch any opponent, no matter how big a lead he had.

It was about this time that I started hearing comparisons to other African-American athletes. Like most Americans, I was well aware of Jackie Robinson's magnificent talent and his heroic struggles in breaking baseball's color bar. I also knew that Jackie had been a four-sport star at UCLA and might have made the 1940 Olympic team had the Games not been cancelled because of the war. To be compared with him was an awesome compliment. So was being mentioned in the same breath as another hero of mine, Jesse Owens. I had known about Jesse since I was a boy and had long been inspired by his incredible performance at the 1936 Berlin Olympics, where he won four gold medals and crushed Hitler's attempt to prove the superiority of the Aryan race.

I was flattered beyond belief when people said I could be like Jesse or Jackie. I didn't think I was *that* good in track. In my freshman and sophomore years I did well as a sprinter in local meets; but when the base of competition expanded to include athletes from other areas, the outcome was different. I had to fight for my life to qualify for statewide meets, and I never did beat some of the great sprinters from the Central Valley, like the Hall brothers from Fresno and Leamon King from Delano. (Leamon went on to break the world record in the hundred meters and win a place on the 1956 Olympic team.)

Had I stuck with sprinting, I might never have become anything more than a high school star and a competitive track man in college. Football might have been my calling. But my coach, Murl Dodson, realized that my potential as a sprinter was limited. He turned me in a direction that altered the course of my life.

Coach Dodson was the first of several coaches whose wisdom and support I've always cherished. He was not very sophisticated in terms of technique, but he learned whatever he needed to teach me, and he provided me with crucial building blocks in my developmental years. He cared about me, devoting time and energy beyond the call of duty to help me progress—and not just in sports. Because of his involvement with the YMCA, I got involved in a number of community activities that expanded my horizons.

Athletically, the most important thing Coach Dodson did was to urge me to become a multi-event man. Believing that I had the physical requirements, the ability to learn, the discipline to master several skills, and the motivation to excel, he suggested that I add other events to my repertoire. Soon I was doing the high and low hurdles, the high jump and the long jump. Within weeks I won three of those events at a meet in San Francisco. Not long after that I won the state high hurdles championship and came in second in the low hurdles. Soon I was putting the shot and throwing the discus as well.

In July 1952, before my junior year, Coach Dodson drove me twenty-five miles to Tulare to see the Olympic decathlon trials. They were being held in that small town because Tulare was the home of Bob Mathias. A superb athlete, Bob had won the gold medal at the 1948 London Olympics at the astonishing age of seventeen. Now, a month shy of *my* seventeenth birthday,

I was going to watch this local legend in his quest for a second decathlon gold medal, a feat no one had ever accomplished.

It was the first decathlon I ever saw. Watching athletes compete in ten different events over two consecutive days was thrilling. I couldn't imagine a greater challenge. At the same time, I couldn't help thinking that I could do what the athletes on the field were doing. In fact, while it may sound arrogant, I honestly felt that if I had prepared for the event, I might have finished in the top three—and the top three qualified for the Olympic team.

Coach Dodson was way ahead of me. The trip to Tulare was part of his plan to get me to take up the decathlon. His strategy got a big boost when Mathias, urged on by the hometown crowd, broke his own world record. A new universe had opened up to me. On the way home, Coach Dodson said that if I were to devote myself to the decathlon I could be the next Bob Mathias. This appealed to me greatly. My athletic ambition had been burning, and I'd been hoping to find a specialty in which I could be the best. But my coach still had a lot of convincing to do.

A virtual track and field meet in itself, the decathlon is called the most grueling of all competitions. It's unique in that performance in each of the ten events is measured against an abstract standard of excellence—scoring tables based on complex formulas—not on who wins or loses in direct competition. The total score in the ten events determines the order of finish.

What really distinguishes the decathlon, though, is that it requires a remarkable combination of skills and attributes: speed for the sprints and hurdles, quickness and upper body strength for launching heavy objects through the air, agility and spring for leaping high and far, endurance for long-distance runs. I have never liked the term "world's greatest athlete," but it's easy to see why the best decathlete has traditionally been called that.

To excel in this new discipline I would have to become competent in skills that were unfamiliar to me. I had thrown the discus and put the shot, but only at the lighter high school weights. I had never thrown a javelin, and had only toyed with the pole vault. But the real obstacles were the long races—the 400 meters and, especially, the 1500. Running laps had always been part of my conditioning program, but I loathed it. "I had to talk like a Dutch uncle to get him to go into it," Coach Dodson said in an interview. "He didn't like anything beyond about 220 yards." The coach predicted my attitude would change, and he was right. When I started out I despised distance running; eventually I grew to only hate it.

I made a commitment to the decathlon. Coach Dodson's logic was convincing, and his belief in me was contagious. So was the air of celebration and pride that spread through the San Joaquin Valley when Bob Mathias won Olympic Gold in Helsinki and again broke the world record. When I returned to Tulare to see the huge parade that greeted Bob's return, I had no way of knowing that I would be the one to break his record three years later. But I did dare to dream that I too would be an Olympic champion. From that moment on, that goal became the driving force in my life. "I never saw a boy get so wrapped up in one thing so quickly," said my mother in a television interview. "He liked all sports, but after he saw the parade for Bob Mathias, the track was all he lived for."

Within weeks, Coach Dodson took me to San Francisco to compete in an invitational decathlon for high school students. Thankfully, the distance run was only 800 meters long, not the usual 1500. I came in first, setting a new record for the meet. If I needed any more convincing, that was it. With my coach's dogged assistance, and encouragement from family, friends, and townspeople, I spent hours every day trying to master the new skills—even when the new school year began and I was playing football, studying, and involved in extracurricular activities.

The hardest of the new skills was the pole vault. Coach Dodson taught me everything he could, but there was a great deal he didn't know. I wasn't progressing quickly enough. Then one day he took me to meet Cornelius "Dutch" Warmerdam. A former world-record holder and the first vaulter to break the fifteen-foot barrier, he was then the track coach at Fresno State. I spent an entire day working with Coach Warmerdam on the fundamentals of vaulting, which requires a tremendous amount of technical proficiency. He showed me how to coordinate the various moves and corrected a glaring weakness: I was not swinging my feet high enough over my head on the way up. By the time I left Fresno I had a new feel for pole vaulting. On my last attempt, I vaulted 11′6″, a full two feet higher than my previous best.

The following spring I came in first in the state high school decathlon championships, an accomplishment I would repeat the following year. Soon after graduation I entered my first non-scholastic competition. Now I was putting a sixteen-pound shot, not the twelve-pound high school weight, and hurling a 4.5-pound discus instead of a 3.9-pounder. I was also up against experienced, accomplished athletes. This was the annual Amateur Athletic Union (AAU) decathlon, a big-time event at a major venue with a national press corps on hand. Had it been an Olympic year, this would have determined who made the team.

That year, the AAU competitions were held in Atlantic City, New Jersey. The generous people of Kingsburg put up the money for Coach Dodson and me to make the trip, just as Tulare had done for Bob Mathias in 1948. I had never been on a plane before. Aside from the competition, what I remember most about the trip was walking on the famous boardwalk and noticing how much darker and grayer the Atlantic Ocean was compared to the Pacific.

I finished in third place. The winner was the Reverend Bob Richards. People remember Bob for his two Olympic gold medals in the pole vault (in 1952 and 1956), and for his image on the Wheaties box. But he was an excellent decathlete as well, winning three national titles during the 1950s. He was a fine gentleman too. I had actually met him the previous year, when he came through the Central Valley on a speaking tour. He delivered an inspiring speech at a father–son banquet, and then surprised us by removing his coat and tie and taking the athletes outside for pole-vaulting tips. One thing that he said reinforced my desire to become an Olympian. Pointing to his steel pole, he said, "Most people see this as just a sixteen-foot pole, but to me it's been an opportunity to see the world."

Despite my respect for Reverend Richards and Aubrey Lewis, who came in second, I hated to lose. Coach Dodson was quick to put things in perspective: Coming in third in a field of high-caliber athletes was a great accomplishment for someone fresh out of high school. Had it been an Olympic year, he pointed out, I would have made the team. He was right. Now I had a clear and realistic objective: the 1956 Olympics in Melbourne, Australia, only two years away.

Determined to do as well in class as I did on the field, I had to work very hard in high school and to organize my time efficiently. I made a key decision: to study with the smartest kids in every subject. I had already discovered that working out with others keeps you motivated, reverses your weaknesses and firms up your strengths, and I figured if it worked in sports it ought to work in academics. So I studied with Eddie Mascarin, who went on to Berkeley, became an engineer, and now owns a big heavy-equipment company; Don Wedegaetner, who heads the chemistry department at the University of the Pacific; Dale Bengston, who became a theologian; and Calvin Johnson, who is now an orthopedic surgeon.

My friends understood the importance of studying hard and making the process enjoyable. At times we stayed up till two or three in the morning, preparing for exams or working on a class project. "Rafer was very disciplined and made the most of the time he had," Calvin recalls. "We just helped him apply his natural intelligence." I learned an awful lot from my study mates, and I like to think I helped them as well—at least by contributing some comic relief and an occasional song.

The teamwork strategy paid off handsomely. I received all A's in high school, with two exceptions. Ironically, my two B's came in Physical Education. The teacher, Walter Sefton, was also the head coach in basketball, football, and baseball. A traditional man with strong convictions, he believed that no one deserved an A in Phys Ed, not even a student who starred on every team he coached. The highest grade he gave out was a B. So, although I did not officially get straight A's, I can say I got the highest grades possible.

While academics and sports were a close one-two in Kingsburg, extracurricular activities were not far behind when it came to community support. I sang in a quartet and strummed a decent guitar at sing-alongs. I satisfied the ham in me by acting in "Our Town" and "Arsenic and Old Lace." I was president of my sophomore class, and in my senior year was elected student body president. I took these honors seriously, and I'm proud to say that I was regarded as a fair and competent leader.

I also spent a great deal of time in two organizations that Coach Dodson was involved with. The California Scholarship Federation (CSF) was a merit society for students with good grades. I became a lifetime member, and president of the Kingsburg chapter. The second group, Hi-Y, was a YMCA character-building program for high school students. One of its major activities was a summer camp for children, including many from underprivileged backgrounds. I spent one summer at the camp in Sequoia National Forest as a counselor, enjoying the cool, pure mountain air and the incomparable beauty of the giant redwoods. Our chapter also organized projects that benefited the community. By showing me how rewarding it is to make a difference in others' lives, Hi-Y was, for me, the beginning of a lifetime of volunteer work.

Probably because they felt more comfortable there, my parents went to a black Baptist church in Fresno. The whole family would drive there just about every Sunday morning. After we'd been in Kingsburg a few years, though, we kids started going to local services with our friends. When I was in high school, Calvin Johnson invited me to the Mission Covenant Church, where his father was the minister and many of my friends were members.

Covenant was one of the largest churches in Kingsburg, and its congregation was mostly of Swedish ancestry. Needless to say, I stood out among all the blond hair and fair skin. But if my presence was a problem for anyone, this was never made public. I can't imagine any newcomer being welcomed more graciously. After a while I joined the choir and began taking part in church activities—Sunday School, trips to the mountains, parties, fund-raisers, and a variety of social events.

At first it was the social aspect of the church that kept me coming back. But I was powerfully and lastingly affected by the spiritual component. Mission Covenant is an evangelical church, meaning it upholds the literal truth of the scriptures. As Calvin explained it, "We believe in the virgin birth, that Jesus Christ was the Son of God, that He lived a sinless life, died for our sins and was resurrected, and the only way back to the Lord is through acceptance of Jesus."

I made that leap of acceptance at a Youth For Christ banquet on October 30, 1953. I had heard many preachers before, but the speaker that night, Reverend Hoffman, seemed to be talking directly to me. Small in stature, he had a loud, clear voice, and I knew that the Jesus he spoke of could make my life more complete. At home that night I thanked God for being so good to me and promised to do something in return for my many blessings. Here's how I described the event in a 1959 article: "Even with all of my church activities, sports and school work, I knew there was something missing in my life. I found out what it was when I took Christ as my Savior. There was not much emotion at the time, but later when I realized what Christ had done for me the tears really flowed. I felt great."

In that article I said that my favorite Bible verse was Romans 5:6, which reads: "For when we were yet without strength, in due time Christ died for the ungodly." I guess I wasn't too consistent in those days, because at another time I said that my favorite verse was John 3:16: "For God so loved the world, that he gave his only begotten Son, that whosoever believeth in him should not perish, but have everlasting life." I'd be happy to have either verse as my guiding light.

To me, accepting Christ meant turning over my life to Jesus and letting Him steer it. It meant opening up through prayer to divine guidance so that I was more likely to take the right path. From the moment I made my commitment I considered myself in a partnership with Christ. Although I have not always succeeded, I have tried ever since to live the way He would want me to. Prayer became a consistent feature of my life—not just ritual prayer, but an ongoing conversation with Jesus. Before every athletic event, for example, I would pray silently and inconspicuously. I would not ask for victory, just empowerment to be the best that I could be at that moment. My attitude was, win or lose, gold, silver, or bronze, "Thy will be done."

I became very active in Youth For Christ (YFC). Our school's chapter had about 130 members, approximately a third of the student body. We met twice a week for prayer and traveled to other schools for various events. Over one Christmas vacation, about fifty of us took a bus to Los Angeles and boarded a boat to Catalina Island for a statewide YFC conference. I remember spending the night on a cot in a dormitory and not getting a whole lot of sleep. For a sober group of Christians, we had a lot of fun. According to Calvin, I get some of the credit—or blame—for that.

There was an outreach component to YFC activities, and I gave a lot of speeches. For some reason I was never intimidated by public speaking and have been doing it ever since. Perhaps it was due to the strength of my convictions. I was not out to convert anyone or to proselytize for my beliefs. I simply felt an obligation to share with others what I considered a gift. It was as if I'd found some bread and knew that others were hungry.

All of this may sound like an industrious, nose-to-the-grindstone existence for a teenager, and I suppose it was. But I remember those years as a lark. Not long ago I was driving my son Josh around Kingsburg, proudly showing him the old man's roots. As he looked around the sleepy downtown district, he asked what in the world I did for fun. I thought for a moment and realized there wasn't much to say except, "I spent time with my friends." Then I added, "I hope you have friends like the ones I had here."

While the Korean War was raging and Senator Joe McCarthy was riding roughshod over the U.S. Constitution, life in Kingsburg reflected the exuberance we now associate with the early 1950s. For teenagers it was like the movie *American Graffiti,* but even simpler and more innocent. "Rock Around the Clock" would not launch the rock 'n' roll era until a year after I graduated from high school. When my friends and I were tooling around the valley listening to Frank Sinatra, Patti Page, and Hank Williams on the car radio, Elvis Presley was sneaking into black honky-tonks in Tennessee, learning his trade. Sex was something married people did, and drugs was just another word for medicine.

In my first year of high school, I hung out with a pack whose leader went on to command a chapter of the Hell's Angels. Those guys loved to drink beer. I would pretend to drink with them, but I couldn't stand the taste and thought the idea of getting drunk was stupid. One night we were chugging along in a custom Mercury with big fins, tossing beer cans out the window (mine were full), when someone suggested stealing hubcaps. They spotted a car in an open garage, four or five feet from a house. We parked down the street and walked back to get the hubcaps. Then one of the guys raised the car's hood and started removing parts from the engine. As I tried to decide whether or not to stop him, I heard a woman's voice inside the house, asking her husband for something. "It's in the garage," he said. "I'll go get it." That was enough for me. It was probably the fastest start I ever had for a sprint. Before my companions had gotten up a head of steam, I was back in our car.

The kids I grew closest to also traveled in groups, but they did things that adults would call good, clean fun. Today's kids would probably call it boring. To us it was anything but. We all had jobs after school, on weekends, and in the summers. At various times I mowed lawns, polished cars, shined shoes, worked at the cannery or the Shannons' car dealership, and woke up at 4:00 A.M. to haul garbage before school started. But we found time for bowling, skating, movies, dances and parties, sipping sodas and scarfing down deep-dish apple pie at Stan's Drive-In, and excursions to Shaver Lake or Bass Lake. "It was a very simple life and we accepted it," says my friend Karl Finley. "Life just flowed easily."

You could get a driver's license at sixteen, and kids who lived on farms could drive even sooner. In the summer before tenth grade, I bought my first car. I was working at the Shannons' dealership when a woman traded in a 1934 Chevy that had been sitting around doing nothing. That seventeen-year-old green beauty had only 1,500 miles on her. I fell in love, and Mr. Shannon gave me a deal I couldn't refuse.

I cavorted all around the San Joaquin Valley in that car, and drove it west to the ocean at Santa Cruz and east to Yosemite. It came in handy when my friends and I felt mischievous. On Halloween, for example, we would pick up outhouses from rural areas and plop them down in the middle of the business district, or pile up eggs and tomatoes and drive around looking for things to throw them at (a practice that ended the night we inadvertently took aim at a police car). On hot summer nights when the picking was good, we might drive out to a farm and crawl around the strawberry patches, eating the cool, sweet fruit. For some reason, strawberries always tasted better at night. That was about the extent of our mischief, though. In a town that small, if you got into trouble your folks would know about it before you got home.

What most concerned parents of teenagers then, as always, was sex. Even going steady with one person was a cause of some concern, because it could lead to an unwanted pregnancy or inappropriate marriage. They had little to fear from my crowd. To us, kissing was a big deal. "Making out," or touching bare skin that wasn't an arm or a face, was adventurous. "Going all the way" was unthinkable. On the few occasions when we heard it had happened, we were as shocked as our parents would have been. Maybe there was more going on behind closed doors than I realized, but not among the kids I was closest to. I know this sounds prudish to the modern ear, but that's really the way it was.

Because of my race I was especially careful about dating.

My friends insist that everyone was colorblind, but I doubt that applied to the parents of teenage girls. The fact that no crisis ever cropped up was partly due to the fact that my close-knit classmates always did things in groups. Almost all pairing off was done in conjunction with collective activities.

By the time I was in high school, mine was no longer the only African-American family in Kingsburg. When the Mosleys arrived in town with a girl my age and another Jimmy's age, our friends acted as if God had served as our personal matchmaker. It seemed only natural to them that I should date Ann Mosley and Jimmy should date Juanita. There were other Mosley children as well, and my siblings and I became friends with them. But we resisted the romantic pairings. I understood that urging me to date Ann was part of my friends' ongoing effort to make what seemed to be good matches; they might try to pair two Catholics, two chubby people, or two math whizzes. But I was not about to go out with the only black girl in town just because it seemed neat to others.

I did take Ann to a few functions. But we simply weren't attracted to each other, and I decided to date only girls I liked and who liked me, whatever their race might be. The numbers being what they were, I ended up dating white girls (with the exception of one black girl in a nearby town). I can recall only one time this caused a problem, and I can't really be sure that race was the main factor. One night I was driving to my house with my friend Nancy Peterson. We had nothing more in mind than to sit and talk. As we drove past the parking area outside the Fishel company's offices, I saw Nancy's father in his car. There was only one thing he could be doing there at that hour: looking for his daughter. I told Nancy to duck, and we drove the rest of the way to my house—about 200 yards—undetected.

After we sat in the driveway and chatted for about an hour, I checked to see if Nancy's father was still in the parking lot. He was. How would I get her home? Even if I snuck past her father again, her mother was probably home, watching for any sign of me. It felt to me as if we had something to hide. I doubt that I'd have felt that way if I were white, or if Nancy were black.

I went into my house and called my friend Marvin Harrison. We decided that I should drive Nancy to Marvin's house and he would take her home. This meant driving with the lights off down a dirt utility road that ran through the grape fields. Luckily we did not get stuck in the sand. To this day I don't know whether Nancy's father was so vigilant because I was black or just because she was out late with a boy.

In my senior year, I dated someone steadily. It was typical puppy love; she was all I could think about much of the time. Because of the racial difference, I never picked her up at her house for a date. Despite our strong feelings, we spent most of our time together in the company of friends, and we remained as sexually proper as an episode of *Ozzie and Harriet.* When I went away to college I saw her when I came home for weekends, but eventually we drifted apart. I consider her and all my Kingsburg friends a special part of my life. They loved me and I loved them; they looked out for me and I looked out for them. To a large extent, they made me what I am.

Gradually I came to realize that being in the spotlight entails responsibility, not just glory. Because everything I did reflected on my entire family, I felt compelled to carry myself in an exemplary way. I think this made me a better person.

Having a local celebrity for a brother had a bigger impact on Ed and Jim than on our sisters. Because Erma and Dolores were younger and female, they were able simply to be proud of me; my brothers were expected to "measure up." Luckily my parents were smart enough not to pressure them, but other people would make well-intentioned comments like, "Your brother is a great athlete, I bet you'll be just as good."

This affected the boys in different ways. Jimmy says he was inspired by my example. Small and wiry, he was at a big disadvantage in his game of choice, football. But his teammates and coaches would tell him he could be as good as I was, and this, he says, boosted his confidence. Something sure did: He went from being a skinny equipment manager to a Hall of Fame defensive back without ever exceeding 180 pounds.

Eddie was a different story. He and I have always been as close as brothers can be, but I suspect that my fame and popularity may have had an adverse effect on him. Whereas Jimmy had three years distance from me, Eddie was only a year younger and pretty much the same size and weight. The comparisons were constant and the pressure to measure up was unavoidable. Jimmy was told, "Work hard and you can be as good as Rafer," but Eddie had to hear, "Why aren't you as good as your brother?" I believe it got to him at times. He was a super athlete, good enough to star in track and earn a tryout as a pitcher with the California Angels. But he was not as ambitious as I was, or as lucky in his choice of friends. I'm sure Ed would say he wouldn't trade places with anyone in the world, but I think his being stuck in the middle between two high achievers was in many ways a misfortune.

As for my parents, it's hard to say what had the biggest impact on them—my prominence in high school or their working for the Fishels and our move to the new house. In any event, their place in the community changed and their lives became more cheerful and relaxed. My father felt better about himself as a man, and more confident about his family's future. Some of his anger and frustration seemed to dissipate. As industrious, responsible, caring parents, they could have won a prize.

Yet my father could not shake his Achilles' heel. In fact, his drinking continued. It was horrifying and incomprehensible to see this model father—so loving, so proud, so concerned about our welfare—become a monster when he drank. Friday afternoons were tense, as we wondered which Dad would show up. We kids feared for our mother's safety. Seeing her get smacked around was unbearable. I was a senior in high school by the time my brothers and I finally stood up to Dad and told him we would no longer stand for his treating our mother that way. He wasn't too drunk to see that he was outnumbered and could no longer intimidate us. The drinking carried on, but the abusive behavior at home was curtailed, at least when my brothers and I were around.

Dad's behavior made me take even more seriously my position as the oldest son. Not only was it primarily my duty to protect my mother, but somehow I knew that I had to make up for my father's shortcomings as a role model. "My father's drinking had a devastating affect on me," Jimmy said years later. "He let me down in a big way, so I would lean on Rafer, and he would give me the strength to have positive beliefs again." My sense of responsibility toward my family has been an important facet of my life ever since.

When you prepare for the long jump (or, as they called it in my day, the broad jump), you lay out markers along the path of your approach. These tell you when to adjust the position of your feet, build up speed, or shorten your stride. If you hit the markers right, your foot will hit the eight-inch wooden toeboard in exactly the right position at exactly the right speed. If all systems are go, you lift off feeling as light as a bird. You achieve distance by leaping high and extending your legs—or, as most modern jumpers do, pumping them as if you were running in air.

The Kingsburg portion of my life went as smoothly as a perfect long jump. I could not fully appreciate my environment at the time, no more than I could comprehend the obstacles I faced in Texas while living there. Later I would come to feel blessed. No child could ask for better conditions; any barriers I faced were solely within myself. I scored big and gained momentum and confidence for the next events in my life.

I still visit Kingsburg regularly, and still keep in touch with friends I made more than forty years ago. Part of me is always there, even literally: My name is carved above the entrance of Rafer Johnson Junior High School.

3

SHOOTING FORWARD INTO LIFE

Leaving reminds us of what we can part with and what we can't, then offers us something new to look forward to, to dream about.

—Richard Ford

AFTER THE HUNDRED-METER DASH and the long jump, the shotput demands an entirely new set of skills and a different mental approach. Tossing a sixteen-pound ball of metal might look like a matter of brute force, but it's far more complicated than that. The shotputter turns his back to the direction he's going to throw in, bends low, and glides with his feet along the concrete throwing surface while simultaneously turning from the hip and thrusting his arm to release the ball from face level with maximum force. He does all this while maintaining precise timing, focus, and balance. It requires the upper body strength of a wrestler, the explosiveness of a running back, and the agility and balance of a dancer.

The next phase of my life required new skills and a fresh mental outlook as well. After the confined world of the Texas ghetto and the intimate serenity of Kingsburg, I was propelled from adolescence into young adulthood, from small-town hero to international acclaim. It took a great deal of inner strength, energy, and psychological agility to manage the new demands, and a shotputter's sense of balance to keep myself moving in the right direction.

In the fall of 1954, America was bursting with hope and optimism. The full bloom of postwar prosperity was upon us. Jobs were plentiful. Automobiles were affordable, and a gallon of gas cost twenty-nine cents. Color television had just been introduced. The year before, the Korean War had been put to rest. Senator Joseph McCarthy was about to be condemned by the Senate, ending years of national paranoia. In the famous *Brown vs. Board of Education* decision, the Supreme Court had just overturned the doctrine of "separate but equal" and ordered the states to integrate their educational facilities "with all deliberate speed." It was a time when people thought big thoughts and dreamed big dreams.

That fall I was thinking about the new life I was about to begin and dreaming about making the Olympic team in Melbourne, Australia, two years down the road.

As a star athlete and A student in high school I had been recruited by colleges across the country—actually, more for football than for track. Early on I had decided that I would remain close to my family and friends in Kingsburg. I narrowed the choice to three schools: the University of California at Berkeley, the University of Southern California, and UCLA.

I was drawn to Cal Berkeley because of its academic reputation and the fact that its track coach and athletic director was Brutus Hamilton; he was a fine man who had won the silver medal in the decathlon at the 1920 Olympics in Amsterdam, and had coached the U.S. track team at the 1952 Games. Also, some of my friends were headed there: my study partner, Don

Wedegaetner; Ed Mascarin, the quarterback on the football team; and Leamon King, the sprinter from Delano. Eddie and Leamon were asked by some Berkeley partisans to convince me to enroll there. But while Leamon and I wanted to be track teammates, the Bay Area was a little cold for my taste; I felt better and performed better in warm, dry weather.

Of the two Los Angeles schools, USC had more going for it athletically. Its track program was one of the best in the country and its football team was a perennial powerhouse. During my visit to campus, the coaches painted a glorious picture of the Trojan tradition and the prominent role I could play in its future. It sounded great to me. Then I journeyed crosstown to Westwood and changed my mind.

There were five essential reasons why I selected UCLA:

- Some athletes from the San Joaquin Valley had gone there. One was Buck Catlin, a Kingsburg native who had thrown the shotput at UCLA. The other was Bob Seaman, a distance runner from Reedley who plied me with tales about UCLA while we worked at the California Packing Corporation that summer.
- The football coach, Red Sanders, wanted me badly, and he had a distinct advantage: He ran a single-wing offense, just like the one in which I'd excelled in high school.
- UCLA offered me the choice of an academic scholarship or an athletic scholarship. The academic one afforded more prestige and money, and would not bind me to any particular sport. I wanted the option not to play football if I thought it might jeopardize my Olympic chances.
- UCLA had a proud, long-standing commitment to racial equality. Two of my all-time heroes, Ralph Bunche and Jackie Robinson, were alumni. In addition to his greatness as a baseball player and a man, Jackie was—and remains—the only UCLA athlete to ever have earned letters in baseball, football,

basketball, and track. Mr. Bunche, who played basketball at UCLA, had been awarded the Nobel Peace Prize in 1950 for his diplomatic efforts on behalf of the United Nations Palestine Commission.

I was also aware of other black athletes in UCLA's past, like football stars Kenny Washington, who was then in the NFL, and Woody Strode, who had become an actor in Hollywood; there were also current standouts like distance runner Russ Ellis, who had good things to say about life on campus. But the clincher on the racial issue came when I walked into the student union and saw pictures of past student body presidents. One of the faces was black. I had no way of knowing, of course, that I would one day hold that office myself. At the time it was enough for me to realize that the recruiters weren't feeding me empty talk about equality.

• I met Elvin "Ducky" Drake, the UCLA track coach. When I set out for a walk across the UCLA campus with this fine man I was still undecided. By the time I shook his hand to say goodbye, I knew I'd be returning as a student.

Universally respected and admired, Ducky had been improving the Bruins' status in track ever since taking over as head coach eight years earlier. Under his tutelage, every school record had been either broken or tied. But the team had still never won a conference championship or an NCAA title, or beaten arch rival USC in a dual meet. Ducky wanted badly to accomplish those goals, and he felt he could do it with me on his squad. I had no reason to doubt him—he seemed to be a true gentleman, a man of integrity whose word I could trust—and I liked the idea of joining a program on its way up.

In the end, what really did the trick was that Ducky said the magic words: "You can make the next Olympic team." Implicit in that statement was a willingness to help me get there.

And so, that August, I sent letters to USC and Berkeley,

thanking them for their courtesy and telling them I had chosen UCLA. I was not prepared for the wonderful response I received from Brutus Hamilton:

> Dear Rafer:
> It gave me a kind of clean and noble feeling to get your kind and gracious letter of August 20. Only a fine sportsman and a gentleman in the finest sense of that word could have written such a letter. I must admit that your letter also made me a little sad, because I know you are going to achieve great things in all phases of your university life and it is a source of regret to me that I shall play no part in directing you toward those successes. But I am glad that you have chosen a great university to attend, and I am pleased that you are happy in your decision. . . .
>
> I know you will find Ducky Drake one of the grandest men you will ever meet in your journey through life. He not only knows his business, but he is a man of impeccable character and good influence. He takes an interest in his boys above and beyond their ability in sports and I count it a great asset to the coaching profession that such a man is in it. If you have problems, and what university student does not? I would advise you to go to Ducky and get his advice. He will not steer you wrong. . . .
>
> I close this letter with a confession. I was never a good hater, and I never coached my boys to hate an opponent. Amateur sports should be friendly but spirited, and there should be no grimness characterizing the competitions. I shall try to get my boys to honor you with their very best performances against you, and I hope that you honor us with your very best efforts. After the contests we will walk down to the corner drugstore and have a malt and talk over the day's activities. . . . I hope I never become so embroiled in a winning complex that I can't appreciate

> fine performances and the splendid characters of the boys wearing the other colored jerseys. I sincerely hope and believe that you and I will be such friends for many years to come.

I have kept that letter all these years because it epitomizes what an educator and a sportsman should be. Brutus and I never got to stroll to a drugstore after a meet, but we spoke often and remained good friends until he passed away in the early 1960s.

Despite Brutus's gracious letter, Berkeley did not give up on me easily. Not long before I was to leave for Los Angeles, Leamon King showed up in Kingsburg in a last-ditch effort to change my mind. Instead, I drove him to UCLA to change *his* mind. In the end we both stayed true to our original choices, but we finally became teammates in the 1956 Olympics.

As much as I looked forward to the adventure ahead of me, it was sad to say goodbye to Kingsburg. I wasn't apprehensive about moving to a big city, but I knew I would miss my calm, uncomplicated life. Part of me did not want anything to change. If most of my buddies had not been going off to college themselves, I might very well have enrolled at Fresno State and pursued my Olympic dream from the cozy comfort of the Central Valley.

On the morning of my departure, my parents, brothers, and sisters gathered outside the house to help me load my 1934 Chevy. As they hugged me goodbye, their eyes were misty but their smiles were broad and proud. I was the first person on either side of my family to attend college. The future seemed as bright as the sunshine on the San Joaquin Valley grape fields.

My first thought when I arrived at UCLA was: All of Kingsburg could fit on this campus. There were more than 14,000 students in attendance, more than five times the population of my hometown. I've often been asked what it was like to move from a sleepy hamlet to a bustling university in a big city. Was I overwhelmed? Was I nervous? Was I afraid? No, in fact I thought it was great. I had been a big fish in a little pond. I looked forward to losing myself in a big pond where hardly anyone knew who I was.

I guess it was naive to think that a six-foot-three African American could be just another student, especially one with big expectations attached to him. The day I enrolled, UCLA's *Daily Bruin* ran this headline: JOHNSON TOPS LARGE, TALENTED GROUP OF FRESHMEN, TRANSFERS. A Los Angeles paper blared, NATION'S TOP HIGH SCHOOL ATHLETE ENROLLS AT UCLA. Another misnamed my hometown while gushing, "Rafer Johnson, 19-year-old Kingsboro High School student and rated as the nation's all-around prep athlete, may become a second Jackie Robinson at UCLA."

Anonymity was not to be my fate. Not that I'm complaining. I've always felt that fame was a privilege, not a burden.

Arrangements had been made for me to live in a residential co-op on campus, which housed students from all over the world. As soon as I got settled I began working on my twin goals: to do well academically and to raise my athletic proficiency to Olympic levels.

Since the official track season did not begin until spring, Coach Drake had established a fall program to keep athletes in shape and sharpen their skills. It was run by his assistant, Craig Dixon, who also coached the freshman and cross-country teams. A brilliant hurdler for UCLA in the late 1940s (he won an amazing fifty-nine straight races and finished third in a photo finish at the 1948 London Olympics), Craig had been hired by UCLA a year earlier with the express purpose of helping to raise the track program to national prominence. In his first year on campus, he had turned out the best freshman squad the school had ever seen. Now he was determined to do even better.

Craig and Ducky made an excellent combination. As a young coach, Craig had fresh ideas and was up-to-date on technical matters. Ducky was more of a traditionalist. My friend and teammate Stan King once said, "Craig was a coach, Ducky was a coach and a father." Craig focused on the technical aspects of the sport, whereas Ducky was also a master strategist and psychologist.

During that fall our workouts were less formal and less structured than they would be in the spring. They were far more sophisticated than anything I'd experienced before, in terms of the facilities and equipment, the knowledge imparted, and the training procedures. I learned a tremendous amount, especially about hurdling, which was Craig's specialty; and I formed bonds with Craig and Ducky that would get stronger over the years.

About five foot ten with a medium frame, Ducky was a bald, pleasant-looking man with an endearing smile. At fifty-one, he might have been taken for a shopkeeper or bank clerk when he wasn't wearing his trademark baseball cap and warmup jacket. He wasn't a motivator in the Knute Rockne tradition of rousing speeches or the Vince Lombardi school of intimidating discipline. He got things done quietly and personally. A firm but gentle taskmaster, he worked us hard but worked himself even harder, spending as much time on the field as needed. Because—in addition to his coaching duties—he was the head athletic trainer at UCLA, Ducky's athletes were always physically ready to compete. And because he was a master motivator, they were ready mentally as well. His favorite expressions—"A winner never quits and a quitter never wins" and "A moment to compete, a lifetime to remember"—were posted in the training room.

Ducky had an uncanny ability to get inside my head. Both

on the field and off, he seemed to know me better than I knew myself. It's not an exaggeration to say that he became a second father to me. In that respect I had a lot of brothers. Perhaps because he had no children of his own, Ducky treated his athletes as if they were his sons. A deacon in his church, he had deep Christian convictions and he lived up to them. His presence was always calming and reassuring. In his quiet, insightful way, he inspired young men to be the best athletes and human beings they could be. One note that he wrote me contained inspiration I've cherished and tried to live up to ever since: "Be gracious. Be humble. Be true."

Although I tried not to abuse the privilege, I knew that if I needed someone to turn to, Ducky would be there. Not long after I arrived on campus, I went to get a haircut in Westwood Village (this was before Westwood became an entertainment mecca for all of Los Angeles). I entered the first barbershop I saw and took a seat. After a while, I realized I'd been waiting a long time and that customers who had entered after I did had already been serviced. When I finally spoke up, the barber said, "I can't cut your hair."

For a moment I was back in Texas, being denied service because of the color of my skin. All I could think of to say was, "Why?"

Sheepishly, the barber replied, "I don't know how to cut Negro hair." He shook as he said it, either out of embarrassment or fear of being attacked. He had probably been hoping I would leave before he had to say anything.

I told Ducky that I wasn't sure if the barber's action was really based on ignorance, not prejudice. As always, I felt better just talking to him. "I'll find out what's what," he said. He later told me that he believed the barber was telling the truth and that he would make an effort to accommodate black students. I ended up finding a fine black barbershop about a half hour from campus, but when I became active in student affairs I went back to the Westwood shop and made sure they were able and willing to cut the hair of anyone on campus.

I plunged into training and also into extracurricular activities in an effort to replicate the full and balanced life I had in Kingsburg. I joined the Air Force Reserve Officers Training Corps (ROTC), mainly because I didn't want to be drafted after college and jeopardize my chances of going to the 1960 Olympics. The ROTC entailed a lot of marching, some physical training, and lectures on military history and strategy. To satisfy the terms of my scholarship I worked part-time for the university's custodial services, mopping floors, dusting, and doing other light maintenance. I joined the Yeomen, a lower-division honorary society that sponsored discussions and got involved in community projects on and off campus. And I joined the Kelps, a spirit organization and a rousing presence at rallies and sporting events. Wearing blue caps with gold piping, we'd line up in two rows and the Bruin team would enter the arena between us. Then we would supplement the official cheering squads from the stands. I participated whenever I wasn't performing as an athlete.

To give you an idea of what the Kelps were like, for my initiation I had to wade into the ocean at night and gather some kelp. Then all the candidates—about twenty of us—had to sneak into a movie theater on one ticket. Once inside, we had to walk across the stage during the film. After that, some of us had to sit in chairs in the busy intersection of Santa Monica and Wilshire boulevards, while the rest of the group hooted and howled. We ended up in the Beverly Hills police station and were let go when an assistant football coach spoke to the officers.

Sometimes the Kelps would get overzealous. In my sophomore year, at a football game against our arch rival, USC, a Kelp threw an apple at USC's Trojan Horse, causing the mascot to bolt. That led to a brawl in which fists and bottles were thrown. After that we were asked to lower our profile. Despite its rowdy reputation, though, the Kelps were a highly respected group that did a lot for the university. They still do, in fact. Kelp alumni give out scholarships and run a golf tournament to raise money for the school.

On top of all my commitments, I went to Kingsburg just about every weekend that fall. I was somewhat shy then, or so my friends tell me, and I missed the easy camaraderie of my small town and the warm presence of my friends and family. So, on Fridays, I would jump in the Chevy and scoot up Highway 99. I saw more Kingsburg High football games than UCLA games. I loved those weekend visits, but the trips up and back were exhausting and both my studies and training suffered. I realized I was overdoing it when I ran into someone in Kingsburg who asked if I was going away to college. He'd seen me around so much he thought I'd never left.

Finally Coach Drake straightened me out. Before one trip to Kingsburg, he wrote up a workout routine for me. I got so distracted I didn't carry out the program. When I returned to UCLA, I was a few minutes into my first workout when Ducky said, "You didn't do what I told you to do." That's how well he knew me. After that I curtailed my trips to Kingsburg and concentrated on my new life in Los Angeles.

Originally I had intended to play freshman football, but Ducky, Craig, and others urged me not to risk injury on the gridiron with the Pan American Games coming up. I decided to postpone football until after the 1956 Olympics. Little did I know that I would end up injured at the Olympics without the help of football, and that those injuries would prevent me from playing football again.

I satisfied my love for variety and team sports by playing freshman basketball, starting at guard and sometimes playing forward. The *Daily Bruin* praised my "tremendous rebounding and defensive play." But with several games left on the schedule, I had to quit the team. The decathlon meet that would determine the roster for the 1955 Pan American Games in Mexico City was coming up. This was the most important international competition for American athletes outside the Olympics. I felt bad about letting my team down, but freshman coach Deane Richardson eased my guilt by telling the newspaper, "Rafer's loss is going to hurt us, but we know he will make his greatest contribution to UCLA in track."

At the All Comers Decathlon at Occidental College, I earned my berth on the Pan Am team with 7,055 points, the ninth-highest total in decathlon history. This made me feel pretty good at the time, since it was only my second real decathlon and I didn't think I was in top condition. Reporters tried to prod me into saying I could break Bob Mathias's record of 7,887. I wouldn't bite, but I did say that I felt I could improve my performance in most of the ten events.

The opening ceremonies of the Pan Am Games were held in a magnificent new stadium before 102,000 spectators. Runners relayed a torch from an ancient Aztec ceremonial site, a symbolic flame was lit, dozens of doves took wing, twenty-one guns fired a salute, and the games were declared open by the president of Mexico. Unfortunately I missed all that. I also missed a three-day trip to Houston, where the American team had assembled for preliminary training. Not wanting to miss too many classes, I had asked permission to arrive late and leave early.

As I rode through foreign streets for the first time, trying to decipher the Spanish signs, I began to realize I was breathing differently. The air was not only smoggy, it was filled with black particles from the burning of tires to provide fuel. It was also thin. When I arrived at our dormitory at the University of Mexico, I started to hear stories about athletes collapsing on the field. Mexico City is 7,600 feet above sea level. At that altitude, a breath of air takes in 20 percent less oxygen, meaning the muscles and brain receive that much less fuel. Most of the Americans had not had time to acclimate, and the medical staff had not even thought of bringing oxygen tanks. They had to borrow some from other teams. The following week, *Sports Illustrated* would run striking photos of superbly conditioned athletes crumpling, gasping, clutching their sides, and being carried off the field. Some even collapsed during the opening ceremonies.

I began to wonder if I'd made a tragic decision. It's easier to make up for missed classes than oxygen deprivation. It was now Wednesday afternoon. The two-day decathlon grind was scheduled to begin on Friday. Would I be able to adjust in time to perform at my usual level, or even close to it? My chief competitor was Reverend Bob Richards, the pole vault champion who had beaten me in my first major decathlon less than a year before. With all his experience in international meets, Bob had an advantage when it came to adjusting to new and unusual conditions. But I was eight years younger. I might also have been hungrier. Fame and glory lay ahead of me, whereas Bob had already tasted it. I decided to put aside all concerns about the altitude and do what I was trained to do: focus on one event at a time and give it my all.

I came in first to Bob's second in the hundred meters, the long jump, the high jump, and the 400 meters. In the shotput we reversed positions when my best toss fell a foot and a half shorter than his. At the end of the first day, I had tallied 4,213 points to Bob's 3,999. I felt good, but far from comfortable. Some of Bob's best events—the pole vault in particular—were on the second day, and that ruthless 1500-meter conclusion loomed before us like a mountain peak.

The next day, Bob and I continued our neck-and-neck struggle. I finished first in the hurdles and discus, but second in the pole vault and javelin. After nine events I led by a hundred points. To win, Bob would have to beat me by about 16.5 seconds in the 1500 meters. That was not likely. It was not one of his strong events, and he was facing the same adverse conditions that I faced—only with older legs. Still, anything could happen, especially at that altitude.

Then Bob dropped out. Facing total depletion, he decided to preserve his health rather than make a long-shot stab at overcoming my lead. The other competitors were so far behind in points that I could have sat out the race and still gone home with the gold. But the medal would have felt tarnished around my neck. I had too much pride and too much respect for tradition to let anything short of a crippling injury keep me from finishing all ten events.

But I wanted to finish in one piece. Bert Dahlgren of the *Fresno Bee* once wrote, "Track people figure that Satan himself must have thought up the idea of running nearly a mile after having performed in nine other events." And that was at sea level! I sought out the great Mal Whitfield for advice. A two-time Olympic gold-medalist, Mal had just finished fourth in the 800 meters when his legs gave out in the stretch. He warned me that I might be in pain the entire distance, and advised me to set a comfortable pace and stick to it. "There will be oxygen waiting for you at the finish line," he assured me.

I jogged easily at a safe and steady pace, and finished third in 5:47.5. I had added only eight points to my score, but my total, 6,994, was a new Pan Am record. The ovation seemed louder than anything I'd ever heard. As I later told a reporter for the *Daily Bruin,* "When I took the victory stand and saw the American flag raised over the stadium, it gave me my biggest thrill in the great competitive sport of track."

• • •

So ecstatic was the feeling of having excelled at my first international competition that I almost literally hit the ground running when I landed back on U.S. soil. The UCLA track season had actually begun before the Pan Am Games. I had been elected captain of the Brubabes, as Bruin freshmen were called, and the team had been the subject of a lot of preseason excitement. There were no decathlons at college meets, but the coaches intended to use my versatility by entering me in as many as six events, depending on the competition and the scheduling.

Our first meet was an auspicious debut for me and the team. We beat Santa Monica City College 79–43, while I won the low hurdles, high hurdles, discus, and high jump, and finished third in the shotput. The next week, at a dual meet against Mt. San Antonio Junior College, I was entered in six events and won all of them, contributing thirty points to the team's 72–59 victory. My javelin toss, 191′ 11″, eclipsed the oldest freshman record on the UCLA books by over six feet. RAFER RUNS WILD, said one headline.

In the mid-1950s, track and field was far more popular in the United States and Europe than it is today. Television had not yet come to dominate spectator sports. The NBA and NFL were fledgling leagues, struggling to attract a following. Los Angeles had the Rams, but the Lakers would not arrive until 1960; and the Dodgers were still in Brooklyn, where they would remain until 1958. Although baseball was very much the national pastime, there were still no major league teams west of St. Louis. In those days, dual track meets between USC and UCLA were front page news. They would sell out UCLA's Trotter Field and draw over 30,000 to the Los Angeles Coliseum. Special invitational meets would attract as many as 60,000. Now, fewer than

2,000 people attend those dual meets, and the next day you have to search hard to find the results in the papers.

That spring I received more than my share of press attention, and writers were excessive in their praise. Cordner Nelson, publisher of *Track and Field News,* said I was "as great a decathlon prospect as ever lived." Others went further, calling me "track and field's boy wonder" and saying I was "destined to be the greatest decathlon star in history." I even acquired some journalistic nicknames, like "Big Rafe," "Iron Man," and "Rambling Rafer."

Superlatives like "sensational," "spectacular," "remarkable," and "amazing" peppered the profiles. Unfortunately, so did the word "Negro." I was the "Negro youngster from Kingsburg" or the "giant UCLA Negro." The "giant" part I could understand—six foot three and 200 pounds was big in those days—but by now Jackie Robinson was starting his ninth year in the majors, and four of the last six National League MVP's and five of the last six Rookies of the Year had been African Americans. Yet reporters still found it necessary to mention my race.

Comparisons to Bob Mathias cropped up everywhere, with charts comparing Bob's world-record scores with my performance in Mexico. Some writers noted that if I'd done as well in certain events in Mexico as I had at meets in Los Angeles, I'd have broken Bob's record. This failed to take into account the difference between running the hurdles or throwing the javelin in a track meet and doing it as part of a ten-event athletic marathon. Nevertheless, there were those who boldly predicted I would eventually break the record. When asked what he thought of my chances, Ducky Drake would say things like, "He's beginning to give indications of his potential." He would never say anything that might raise expectations or make my head swell.

I even popped up on *The Ed Sullivan Show.* Ed came to campus to shoot a segment about a gala premiere of the film version of *The King and I,* which was to benefit the UCLA Medical Center. Along with Susan Hayward, Gregory Peck, Rhonda Fleming, Robert Stack, and other celebrities, some UCLA athletes appeared on camera. At one point the script called for Ed to turn to me and exclaim, "Rafer Johnson! How's the big decathlon winner of the Pan American Games?" To which I reply, "I feel great. Ready to take on all comers at the Olympics—if I make the team."

"You will, boy! Don't you worry," says Ed.

More meaningful than Ed Sullivan, or magazine profiles, or even the admiring handshakes I received every day on campus, was the reception held in my honor in Kingsburg. Because of Bob Mathias and me, the sports fans of the San Joaquin Valley probably knew more about the decathlon than anyone outside of Europe and Russia. The people of Kingsburg were so excited about my being at the Pan Am Games that the local radio station, KRDU, stayed in contact with Mexico City by phone throughout the two days so the results could be broadcast immediately. Al Nehring, the sportscaster who headed the KRDU effort, told a funny story to *Sports Illustrated* about how they converted the throwing and jumping scores from meters to feet and inches: "We strung out Si Tyler's measuring tape in the studio. It had meters on one side, and we could flick it over and read off the feet on the other. We wound enough tape out in the studio to read distances for the shotput, then we strung it on out into an office for discus distances, and wound it back and forth until finally in the reception room we got to the javelin. If Johnson had done much over 190 feet in the javelin, he'd have put us in the washroom."

When I won, someone sounded the fire alarm to notify the town. Police and firemen rushed to the scene. When they found out it was a false alarm, they were mad. But when they learned that Kingsburg now had an international hero like Tulare did, instead of arresting anyone they celebrated.

Now, during my spring break, the town was celebrating again. The Chamber of Commerce decked out the banquet hall in the Veterans Memorial Building and filled it to capacity. City officials, including Mayor Harold Strand, and members of various service organizations, church representatives, and a large contingent of my former classmates were on hand, along with my entire family. When introduced, I received a standing ovation that lasted several minutes. I got choked up, seeing so many of my loved ones around me and the unabashed pride and affection on their faces. I thanked them for their support as best I could; then I shared some memories of my high school days and showed slides from Mexico City.

Sadly, for members of my family, the evening was marred. My father had shored himself up for the occasion by belting down some liquor before he left the house. On the way to the function my brother Jimmy, who was sixteen at the time, saw that Dad was drunk and scolded him. He was quickly told which of them was the father. Jimmy recalls that Dad was loud and disruptive during the event as well, and had to be escorted out of the building. Years later I learned that the incident had had a major impact on my brother. "My whole sense of how things were supposed to be was washed away," he told me. "I was so angry I couldn't acknowledge him as my father for a while. He had lost the right."

Perhaps it's best that I was unaware of all this at the time. It might have spoiled what is still one of my fondest memories. In the years to come I would be honored more times than I can count, by huge crowds and prestigious organizations. Kingsburg would give me parades and the key to the city. But that homecoming holds a special place in my heart. Afterward, as I mingled with the crowd, I felt tremendous gratitude to those fine people who in many ways had shaped me. I wanted to give them something back. Two months later I had that opportunity.

Kingsburg had been selected to host the track and field championships of the AAU's Central California division, along with an invitational decathlon. It had become a tradition for the hometown of a leading decathlete to host an invitational, and Kingsburg, like Tulare three years earlier, proudly took its place.

It had been an amazing spring. I had broken three UCLA freshman records, tied two others, tied the national freshman mark of 14.0 in the high hurdles, and anchored the one-mile relay team that set a new freshman standard of 3:15.4 (although Stan King deserves most of the credit, having run the third leg in a sizzling 47.5). I had broken several meet records, including the 220-yard low hurdles at the Compton Invitational. I had made the NCAA Freshman Honor Roll in eight categories—nine if you count the relay team. I had been voted most valuable athlete by a society of track writers. And the Brubabes had beaten the USC Trobabes for only the second time in history. In the dual meet, I had taken first place in the high and low hurdles and the discus, tied for first in the high jump and broad jump, and grabbed a second in the shotput. By the time the Kingsburg Invitational rolled around, I was exhausted.

Nevertheless, this was my hometown. I had competed in front of over 40,000 people in Mexico, but the idea of performing in my high school stadium with its 3,000-seat capacity, in front of my family and friends, was thrilling. I was determined to rise to the occasion.

As I set foot on the track that Friday night, I felt exceptionally good. I ran the hundred in 10.5, my fastest time ever; then I followed with personal bests in the long jump and shotput. At day's end I had racked up 4,537 points, the highest first-day total in decathlon history.

It did not go without notice that I was now 170 points ahead of Bob Mathias's pace when he set the world record in 1952. I tried not to think about it. Anything that kept me from concentrating on one event at a time could be lethal. But to break the record in Kingsburg, just down the road from Mathias's hometown—with Bob's parents and mine in attendance, no less—well, it was hard to resist thinking about it.

Maybe it was the home cooking, or the rare opportunity to sleep in my own bed, or my high school sweater, which my mother wore for good luck, or maybe the collective hope of the community, but I felt almost invincible when I lined up for the hurdles on the second night. I might have been too wound up, though, for I knocked down the first hurdle and clipped the next two. But I recovered and finished with a 14.5. I followed with a discus toss of 154′ 10.75″. I had done better in both events before, but never during a decathlon. Now came the pole vault, which I considered my weakest skill. Concentrating all my energy on the complex series of moves it takes to launch a 200-pound body into the air, I cleared the bar with ease at 12′ 8.28″. My attempts at thirteen feet failed, but I still had another personal best and 680 more points.

My total was now 7,019, 175 points ahead of Mathias's pace. The record was within reach, and everyone in the stadium knew it.

I fouled on my first javelin throw, then gathered myself and let fly again. The spear soared in a perfect arc and landed 193′ 10.32″ away. It was more than fifteen feet longer than my throw in the thin air of Mexico City.

It was chilly and close to midnight as I prepared for the final event. Craig Dixon told me that to break the world record I would have to run the 1500 in less than 5:10. That was thirteen seconds faster than my previous best, but I could feel the love of everyone in Kingsburg and I wanted to give them the record as a gift.

At the gun, four runners jumped out ahead of me. I stayed close behind, moving at a fast but comfortable clip to preserve my energy. After one lap I heard someone yell, "Step it up, you guys!" Everyone picked up the pace. As we entered the final lap, the leader, Archie Schmitt from Taft Junior College, pulled away. I stayed on the heels of Occidental's Gary Jeffries, who seemed to be deliberately pacing me. "Come on, Rafer, you can do it," he called back to me. He kept prodding me all the way to the tape. I dug deep for every ounce of strength I could muster, fortified by the roaring crowd. I finished in 5:01.5. My total score was 7,983, 96 points better than Mathias. I had broken the world record, way ahead of my most optimistic timetable.

In the pandemonium that followed, I was probably the only person in the stadium who wasn't jumping up and down, or yelling, or running toward the infield. By the time I'd been hugged a hundred times, had my back slapped and my hand shaken a thousand times, and showered and settled down to sleep, it was well past 2:00 A.M. I awoke a few hours later to the sweet, familiar feeling of a Johnson family breakfast. Afterward, to offer credit where credit was due, I went to church with my mother.

4

HIGH JUMP TO FRUSTRATION

And if I should lose, let me stand by the road,
And cheer as the winners go by!
—**Berton Braley,** *Prayer of a Sportsman*

IN EVERY DECATHLON I participated in, I would hope to build a substantial lead in the first three events because I felt I was vulnerable in the fourth, the high jump. Over the years I barely improved on my high school marks in that event, and I never exceeded 6′ 2½″ in competition. Perhaps it's because I wasn't very flexible, but for some reason I never felt that I'd mastered the skill.

Jumpers plot their approach systematically, placing markers on the runway at precise intervals according to the length of their stride and their individual style. The markers define the angle of approach and indicate things like which foot should land on a certain spot and when it's time to speed up or slow down. If your steps are out of synch, you can't plant your take-off foot properly and launch your body over the crossbar. If you approach too slowly, you can't get the momentum you need to achieve height. If you approach too quickly, your momentum will carry you *through* the crossbar instead of up and over. I always prepared extra carefully for the high jump. But on many occasions, no matter how hard I worked and how well I prepared, I was left feeling disappointed and frustrated.

That's also how I ended the next phase of my life. It was as if I had an excellent dash down the runway and took off with great momentum, only to crash into the bar and land with a thud.

After an outstanding performance in one event, a decathlete has only a few minutes to savor it and get some rest before concentrating on the next one. I approached the summer of 1955 much like the time between events. First, I allowed myself a little time to relish the unbelievable feeling of having broken the world's record in my hometown. Press clippings and letters of congratulations arrived from all over the world, although the most satisfying came from down the road in Tulare, from Bob Mathias.

Writers predicted that I would win the 1956 Olympics and become the first decathlete to break the 8,000 mark. That was not unreasonable, since I'd fallen only seventeen points shy in Kingsburg. Some predicted that I'd reach 10,000. Even Craig Dixon believed it. "He is learning to conserve his energy perfectly for a decathlon," he told a Los Angeles newspaper. "If he doesn't hit ten thousand points some day, he may come very close to it." The speculation was flattering, but disconcerting. To this day, no one has come close to 10,000. No one has even hit 9,000. The current record, held by Dan O'Brien, is 8,891 points. I never thought about 10,000, and I wished that no one else would. I just knew I could do better than I had so far.

I badly needed some rest, and what better place to get it than in Kingsburg? The peaceful calm of the valley, the comfort

As an infant in Texas, 1936. (private collection)

With brother Ed (right) in Dallas in the early 1940s. (private collection)

With (left to right) sisters Dolores and Erma, mother and father, 1958. (private collection)

With high school coach Murl Dodson, 1954 (*Kingsburg Recorder*)

Kingsburg High School graduating class, 1954.

With Coach Ducky Drake (left) and Coach John Wooden, circa 1954. (private collection)

After breaking the world decathlon record at the first U.S.–U.S.S.R Dual Track Meet, Moscow, 1958. (Howard Sochurek, *Life* magazine © 1958 Time Inc.)

Cover of *Sports Illustrated*, Sportsman of the Year issue, January 5, 1959. (John G. Zimmerman, *Sports Illustrated* © Time Inc.)

Carrying the American flag at the opening ceremonies of the Rome Olympics, 1960. (Time Inc.)

Running the 100-meter race during the decathlon at the Rome Olympics. (USOC/Allsport)

With C. K. Yang after the grueling 1500-meter race, Rome Olympics. (Hulton Deutsch/Allsport)

With silver medalist C. K. Yang and bronze medalist Vasily Kuznetsov at the medal ceremony following the decathlon, Rome Olympics. (Time Inc.)

of home, and the friendly warmth of people who accepted me for who I was—not what I'd achieved or might become—was just what I needed to recharge my batteries.

To earn some pocket money and keep myself busy, I took my old job at the Shannon Motor Sales company. Among other things, I helped demolish part of the structure and rebuild it. "Johnson said that the heavy work might help him in getting some extra footage in the shot and discus next year," the local paper wrote. That was true: I felt that natural acts of manual labor, like lifting, carrying, and hammering, were excellent for building strength. To keep up my speed and endurance, I ran sprints on the high school cinder and jogged around the track and across the grape fields.

I had lots of time to think that summer and I used that opportunity to make some decisions. One was not to play football or basketball in the coming season. I didn't want to do anything that might interfere with my goal of making the Olympic team. Somehow, this was misunderstood by a local columnist named Ned Cronin. "Red Sanders, the UCLA football tutor, is made of some pretty stern stuff," he wrote. "But catch him in an unguarded moment, and a manly, but salty, tear can be seen trickling down his peaches-and-cream cheek, off his finely chiseled chin and onto his sweat shirt." Why? Because I was never going to play football again. I know Coach Sanders wanted me on his squad but I'm sure he never shed a tear, not over me or any other athlete. Besides, he knew that I hoped to play for him after the Olympics. I'm sure the column gave him a good laugh though.

One day the previous year, two members of Pi Lambda Phi, Bob Liebowitz and Stu Robinson, had knocked on my door at the co-op and introduced themselves. They wanted to invite me to live at their fraternity house. Providing an athlete with a comfortable place to live was a way of performing a service to the university and bringing some added prestige to the frat. A couple of basketball players lived at other fraternities, they told me, and the great running back Jim Brown was in their chapter at Syracuse.

I later learned that Craig Dixon, my freshman coach, had asked his own fraternity, Phi Kappa Psi, to take me in. At the time, UCLA was largely a commuter school. Students who did not live at home lived off campus, at a fraternity or sorority house, or at the co-op. Craig thought a frat house would be more conducive to the needs of a busy athlete. To his dismay, his fraternity brothers rejected the idea. They did not want a black man living at their house.

Meanwhile, Stu Robinson had sold the idea to his Pi Lambda Phi brothers. A track and field nut, Stu had covered the sport for his high school paper in Pasadena and knew all about me. He and Bob seemed like nice guys, and they painted an attractive picture: one roommate instead of two and better meals, with breakfasts made to order. The food aspect was important. As an athlete in training, I wanted more control over when and what I ate. I could have joined an African-American frat, but they were located so far from campus I'd have to spend time on freeways instead of the track or library. So the next semester I moved into Pi Lam's two-story brick house at 741 Gayley Avenue.

Pi Lambda Phi had been established as a nonsectarian fraternity in 1895 at Yale. Its stated purpose was to create a brotherhood based on "a progressive, forward-looking attitude and open-mindedness rather than the religious affiliation of the individual." In practice, "nonsectarian" had come to mean predominantly Jewish, although there was nothing religious about Pi Lam. By 1955, there were thirty-three chapters in the country and over 12,000 members, including some illustrious alumni: Richard Rodgers and Oscar Hammerstein, author Budd

Schulberg, filmmaker Stanley Kramer, singer Tony Martin, a host of business and civic leaders, and baseball players Sandy Koufax and Al Rosen.

During the whirlwind of the Pan Am Games and the freshman track season, I lived at the frat house. I didn't have as much time to hang out as the other guys did—and I never would—but I was accepted easily and was made to feel at home. The friendly atmosphere brought out my extroverted personality. I've always been somewhat slow to open up, but once I get to know people I become very gregarious. That's what happened at Pi Lam.

Years later I learned that Stu Robinson had proposed me for full membership that semester and lost a close vote. Apparently some members were apprehensive about the campus reaction to an integrated fraternity. Also, no one really knew me at the time and they were leery of inviting me to pledge just because I was a well-known athlete. "You would vote for Khrushchev if he could run the hundred in ten flat," they told Stu.

But now, in the fall of 1955, after I had lived in the frat for a full semester, the members voted unanimously to invite me to join. I became the first African American to pledge a national fraternity at UCLA. Some say I was the first one west of the Mississippi. I don't know if that's true, but it might have been since the news was picked up by the wire services. During the time I was pledging, the Interstate Commerce Commission banned racial segregation on interstate buses and trains; the Supreme Court ordered the desegregation of public golf courses, parks, pools, and playgrounds; and Rosa Parks refused to give up her seat to a white man, sparking the bus boycott in Montgomery, Alabama. I was used to breaking new ground. Being the only black in an all-white environment had come to seem pretty normal to me. (Actually, there was one other black man at the frat house: Martin, the cook, who served up delicious food and lots of laughs. He was shocked the first time he saw me, but pretty soon I was just another guy he would chase with a cleaver from time to time.)

Pledging consisted of the usual collegiate lunacy. My pledge brothers and I had to memorize adages, tongue-twisters, and fraternity facts, and recite them whenever we were asked to—which meant anytime, anywhere. We also had to memorize fraternity songs with lyrics like "For all girls who know best, the Pi Lams pass all tests, Pi Lams are a girl's best friend." We had to cater to the whims of the brothers, serving meals, cleaning the house, mowing the lawn, and anything else they thought of. Because I lived at the house I had it harder in some ways, but overall I was lucky: No one wanted to do anything that might interfere with the performance of an All-American athlete.

During Hell Week, the demands of pledging were multiplied by a hundred. Some were ridiculous, some were embarrassing, and some bordered on cruelty. I remember being told to stand in one place for hours and to lean against a wall, supporting my entire weight with one finger. I'll never know how guys who weren't trained athletes were able to do it. But we also had a lot of fun, and I survived with my dignity intact. I was initiated into the fraternity in February 1956, and soon developed a reputation as a reasonably good guitar-strummer and singer of folk songs—and for being, in Stan King's words, a "mischievous rascal." When I run into frat brothers now, they invariably recall some of my practical jokes, like the time I put a big rubber snake in the corner of the shower, or the time I started a fire in a trash can at one in the morning and ran around yelling "Fire!" until everyone was on the street in his underwear or pajamas.

In addition to developing a taste for matzo ball soup, bagels and lox, and other Jewish delicacies, I formed lifelong bonds with many of my Pi Lam brothers. I've attended their weddings and their children's weddings and bar mitzvahs, joined forces with them for charitable causes, and worked with them in their capacities as businessmen, lawyers, agents, and investment advisers.

During those early years at UCLA my commitment to my faith intensified. At first, I attended services at Hollywood Presbyterian Church with fellow students and athletes. Then a new church, Bel Air Presbyterian, opened closer to campus. I was made to feel welcome by the minister, Lou Evans, and some of the members. I attended morning and evening services on Sundays, sang in the choir, and could usually be found at an event or two during the week. At one point I realized that the congregation was not entirely free of prejudice. No one ever said or did anything overtly racist, but I could sense disapproval from certain members and later heard that some, including deacons, had opposed the sale of Bel Air property to people of color.

Needless to say, this troubled me a great deal. Although I would run into bigotry a few times in the coming years—like when a girl I went out with was forced to choose between her sorority membership and dating me—Los Angeles had so far seemed as free of overt racism as Kingsburg. I had to ask myself if I could remain in that church. There were plenty of all-black congregations in the city, but, like the fraternities, they were located a good distance from campus. Besides, I was used to feeling comfortable in all social settings and I intended to keep it that way, because that was how life *should* be. I was not going to let small minds determine where I worshiped God, and I wasn't about to give bigots the satisfaction of driving me away. Why should I be influenced by negativity when religion was such a positive force in my life?

I had a talk with Reverend Evans. Previously I had admired him as a church leader and enjoyed talking sports with him; now I discovered that he was as morally upright as a man of the cloth should be. He acknowledged that the stories I'd heard were true, and he clearly found them unsettling and unacceptable. He did not offer advice, but he said there would always be a place for me in his church. His understanding meant a lot to me.

I stayed, because I could count on Reverend Evans' decency and because I felt that my presence could make a difference. I knew there was a long way to go before we would see genuine equality. Just that summer a black teenager in Mississippi named Emmett Till had been murdered for whistling at a white woman, and the killers had been set free by an all-white jury. Only the year before Jackie Robinson himself had had to fight for the right to buy a house in Connecticut. I thought about men like Jackie and Jesse Owens and Ralph Bunche, and all the hearts and minds they had changed just by being themselves. Maybe, in my own way, I could do the same by simply worshiping where I wanted to.

I remained an active member of Bel Air Presbyterian, eventually becoming a deacon and bringing my wife and children to the church. Over the years I became very close to Lou Evans and his wife, Coke. I often turned to them when I needed someone to talk to. Others must have seen in Lou the same qualities that I did: He went on to become chaplain of the U.S. Senate. As for the deplorable attitudes of some of the parishioners, I did what I learned to do every time a personal incident or news story aroused my indignation: I tried as hard as I could to make my corner of the world better and fairer, and I converted my anger into the energy to run faster, jump higher, and be stronger mentally and physically.

Bel Air Presbyterian was only part of my religious activities. I also found spiritual nourishment in the Campus Crusade for Christ.

In 1951 a former businessman named Bill Bright had created an interdenominational movement whose purpose was to bring the gospel of Jesus to students at every college and university. The Crusade began at UCLA, but by the time I became involved it had spread across the country. Since then, of course, it has become a major influence throughout the world.

Volunteers would hold meetings in various fraternity and sorority houses, and once a week a large gathering would assemble at the home of Henrietta Mears on Stone Canyon Road, just a short walk from campus. By moving some furniture around, we could accommodate as many as 300. We would sing Christian songs, study the Bible, and listen to inspirational speakers. When moved, individuals would give testimony about what Christ meant to them. Some of the most prominent students on campus were active Crusade members, including high-profile athletes like Bob Davenport, an All-American on the Bruin football team that won the national championship.

In Kingsburg church-related activities had been a major source of friendship, support, and community. With the Crusade I was able to recreate that experience, only with a different, and more diverse, group of people. It deepened my faith, taught me important lessons about life, and strengthened my connection to God. Bill Bright and his wife, Vonette, inspired me to give more of myself to others, especially to young people. I've always been grateful to the Brights for giving me the chance to express what was in my heart.

I became chairman of the UCLA group and spoke frequently at college campuses, churches, and high schools. At times the requests to speak cut into my studies and my rest, but I could never say no; I would have felt that I was letting down Jesus. My talks were always along the lines of this essay I wrote for a Crusade publication:

> Ever since I became a Christian in my junior year in high school, I have loved Jesus with all my heart. He is the leader in

my life and without Him I would be lost, for He is all. Without His help, I could not participate in athletics. He gave me an athletic body, good health, and co-ordination, all of which are so necessary in sports.

While participating in sports, I have had the chance to see and meet some of the great athletes from many parts of the world. When I think of the many friends I have made through athletics, I cannot help but thank the Lord; for it is only through athletics I ever would have had the chance to meet and talk with people in other countries about the Lord Jesus Christ.

Being accepted by many athletes as their friend really makes me feel warm inside; but the greatest feeling of all was being accepted by the Lord Jesus Christ. I know He loves us all, for I Corinthians 12:13 declares: *'For by one Spirit are we all baptized into one body, whether we be Jews or Gentiles, whether we be bond or free; and have been all made to drink into one Spirit.'*

In every race I run, I pray before and after the race. I pray not to win, but to do my best. If I win a race, I feel great; if I lose, I do not feel so good, for no one runs to lose. But I know that, win or lose, I am on a winning team, the Christian Team, coached by the greatest Runner of all.

It always gave me pleasure—and quite a kick—to return to my frat house after a Crusade gathering. I relished the idea that I had good friends in both the Christian and Jewish communities. For years I even wore a mezuzah around my neck along with a cross. My frat brothers gave it to me for good luck before the 1956 Olympics, and I continued to wear it, even to church and Crusade gatherings. I was getting used to being a bridge between two worlds, and I would play that role the rest of my life, bridging Jew and Christian, white and black, American and Russian, rich and poor, old and young, disabled and able.

HIGH JUMP TO FRUSTRATION

• • •

In the early months of 1956, Elvis Presley was rocking the nation, scaring parents who thought rock-and-roll would turn their kids into juvenile delinquents. Nikita Khrushchev denounced the policies of his predecessor, Joseph Stalin, yet tightened the Soviet grip on Eastern Europe. During the Montgomery bus boycott, Martin Luther King, Jr., emerged as a powerful new leader, while southern Congressmen pledged to overturn the Supreme Court's desegregation ruling. Candidates were gearing up for the presidential election. I was gearing up for the Olympics.

First, though, came the UCLA track season. It was widely acknowledged that Ducky Drake had assembled the best squad the school had ever seen. Russ Ellis, Bob Seaman, Ron Drummond, and other excellent athletes were returning, and the previous year's outstanding freshmen were now on the varsity. Five of us were considered candidates for the U.S. Olympic team. By season's end we had accomplished the two main goals Ducky had laid out on the day he convinced me to attend UCLA: We won the Pacific Coast Conference (PCC) championship and the NCAA title, each for the first time in school history.

The only blemish was the dual meet with USC at the Coliseum. It was not only expected to be the closest Bruin–Trojan clash in years, but a special one-mile invitational race had been added to the program, featuring the great Australian runner John Landy. The world's record-holder in the 1500 meters (at 3:58), John was one of only five men who had broken the four-minute mark—and he'd done it four times. Forty thousand fans piled into the Coliseum, including Lewis and Alma Johnson of Kingsburg.

With my parents providing extra incentive, I set a new meet record in the long jump (25′ 5³/₄″), then won the one-hundred-yard dash and the 120-yard hurdles. At this point the team was ahead in points and the crowd sensed an upset in the making. Then the tide shifted and USC came back. With the outcome still in doubt, Ducky entered me in the 220. I came in two-tenths of a second behind the winner. In the end I had achieved what was called the "greatest one-man performance ever seen in the Coliseum," scoring eighteen of my team's fifty-seven points, but our opponents had scored seventy-four. In the annual battle for Los Angeles bragging rights, USC had now won twenty-three and UCLA none. Sadly, the Bruins would not beat USC in a dual meet until after Ducky had retired.

Later that spring we made up for the loss by breaking the Trojan's monopoly on the PCC championship (fifteen straight) and the NCAA title (the last seven, and nineteen of the previous twenty-six). For that, Ducky was deservedly named Coach of the Year by *Track and Field News.* In the PCC meet, I grabbed top-scorer honors and we fought off a strong USC comeback to dethrone the Trojans 69.5–67. "The king is dead," wrote the *Los Angeles Times.* "Long live the Bruins."

We were high as kites after that long-awaited victory, but our elation was short-lived. At the airport we learned that the PCC had dealt the UCLA athletic program a heavy blow. It seems that a couple of booster clubs had been helping some Bruin football players financially "in a form not sanctioned by the athletic code of the conference." The school was fined $95,000 and placed on a three-year probation beginning the following year. No UCLA team, *in any sport,* would be eligible for a conference or NCAA championship.

The following month we won the only national title for which we were eligible. At the NCAA meet I ran my fastest high hurdles ever, but lost by a tenth of a second to Lee Calhoun, who broke the meet record. In the long jump I came up five inches shy of Greg Bell. Both Greg and Lee went on to win Olympic gold medals. Losses like that always left me with mixed feelings. I knew how hard it was for a decathlete to compete against world-class specialists who devote themselves to a single set of skills. In that context a close second could be considered a victory. But I hated to lose anything, anytime, to anyone. My total points were the second highest at the meet, though, and they helped us take the national crown in a close, come-from-behind victory over Kansas, the pre-meet favorites.

For me the track season had been doubly satisfying. Not only was it a tremendous thrill to be part of a victorious effort, but because Ducky used me in many different events I had honed most of my decathlon skills in actual competition. Now, like the rest of the track world, I turned my attention to the Olympics.

Being a decathlete is not like being a jack-of-all-trades and master of none; it's more like being a master of ten trades. But few decathletes have excelled in individual events in international competition. I tried to be one of the exceptions by qualifying for the Olympic team in the long jump and hurdles as well as the decathlon.

The Olympic Trials, held at the Los Angeles Coliseum, drew an amazing assemblage of record-holders and medalists. *Track & Field News* called it the greatest track meet in history. Bobby Morrow, Ira Murchison, and Thane Baker all tied the world record for the hundred meters. Lou Jones broke the world record in the 400 meters. Glenn Davis set a new standard in the 400-meter hurdles, earning a huge Cold War cheer because the previous record-holder was a Russian. Parry O'Brien tied his own shotput record. Six men broke the hammer-throw mark. In all, six world records and ten American ones were either broken or tied, and meet records were broken in every event but the long jump.

The most memorable moment came close to midnight on

the first day of competition, when Charley Dumas of Compton Junior College high-jumped seven feet, one-half inch. The seven-foot jump had been one of those seemingly impenetrable barriers, like the four-minute mile and the eighteen-foot pole vault, and now it had been shattered. I was lucky enough to be standing near the high-jump pit and could see Charley's jubilation as the crowd went berserk. It's amazing to think back to that moment in light of what would happen only a few years later. At the time, high-jumpers would go over the bar one leg at a time, clearing the bar either sideways or face down. Then along came a jumper named Dick Fosbury, whose style was so unorthodox that coaches begged him to give it up. He would plant his leg, twist his body, and thrust himself into the air *backward,* clearing the bar headfirst and flopping over it with his arched back facing the ground. Fosbury looked bizarre, but he kept on winning. When he broke the Olympic record in 1968, the floodgates opened. Everyone switched to the Fosbury Flop. Soon, seven feet was commonplace and before long the unthinkable happened: People jumped *eight* feet!

I never got to use the Flop, but I did get to use another innovation. Shotputters used to stand sideways, swing their lead leg toward the throwing area, hop with both feet, and heave the iron ball while making a quarter-turn of the upper body. Parry O'Brien discovered a way to get extra momentum. He would crouch at the back of the throwing circle with his back to the line of flight, then take a gliding step backward and turn 180 degrees while cutting loose. Parry won a gold medal in 1952. By 1956, the O'Brien Technique was the standard.

At the Trials I think I was affected by the excitement of being in such elite company. I was overly aggressive in the hurdles and messed up my timing, grazing two hurdles and hitting another flush with my foot. I finished inches short of qualifying. Fortunately I managed to relax in time for the long jump, where I was up against five men who at one time had leaped more than twenty-six feet. I placed third and made the Olympic team.

Needless to say, I was happy to know I'd made the Olympic squad. But the decathlon was where I stood to make my mark, and the Trials for that were two weeks later, at Wabash College in Crawfordsville, Indiana. I was favored to win over Milt Campbell, the Navy man who had won silver at the 1952 Olympics.

Forty-two decathletes assembled for the two-day meet on a humid Friday the 13th. It was not an unlucky day for Richard Nixon: Despite attempts to boot him off the ticket, he was named President Eisenhower's running mate for the upcoming election. But it was unlucky for me. In the first five events I piled up 4,639 points, the highest first-day total in history and ninety-eight points ahead of my world record pace. But I had reinjured my left knee in the high jump. "He has been kicking his left leg over the high jump bar too hard and strained it," Ducky told the press. In fact, the knee had been giving me trouble on and off all year.

At first I thought it was nothing, since I closed the day with a strong 400 meters and, the next morning, ran the hurdles faster than I had when I broke the world record. Then I aggravated the knee in the discus throw. I was way below par in the last three events but managed to win with 7,755 points to Campbell's 7,559. I figured the knee would heal with a little rest. The possibility that it could ruin my Olympic dreams never occurred to me.

For the first time, the Olympics were to be held in the Southern Hemisphere, in Melbourne, Australia. Because America's summer is Australia's winter, the Games were scheduled for late November—springtime down under. This presented a problem for Americans. With nearly five months between the Trials and the Games, track and field athletes would have to make special preparations to be at their peak. Plus, college students would have to train in the middle of a semester and leave school for a month. For me the extra time seemed to be a blessing in disguise: I thought it would give my knee time to mend.

I spent the rest of the summer in Kingsburg, working the night shift at the cannery. From 6:00 P.M. to 2:00 A.M. I unloaded cartons of cans off the boxcar, then wheeled them on a dolly to the beginning of the assembly line, where I stacked them. It wasn't particularly hard work, but it was tedious. When my shift ended, I'd work until dawn on the cleanup crew, washing everything down for the next shift. I would sleep until midafternoon, and when the temperature cooled down I would do some jogging to stay in shape, as per Ducky's instructions.

To modern fans it must seem strange for a prominent athlete to be working a twelve-hour day. But there was no support for amateur sports in those days. Corporate sponsorship meant having a job. It wasn't hard for me to get a couple of days off to appear on *The Ed Sullivan Show* with other members of the Olympic team, but after an exciting weekend in Manhattan—first-class hotel, VIP tour, fancy restaurants—it was back to hauling cans. I was just another college kid from a working-class family trying to earn a few bucks.

Well, that's not entirely true. Most college kids aren't given the key to the city. Once again the people of Kingsburg chose to honor me. The reception drew two thousand people to the high school field. There were several speakers, including Ducky—who had come up from Los Angeles for the occasion—and my father, who conducted himself well this time. Both men moved me to tears. Ducky said, "Rafer is the finest boy I have ever coached. He is a student and a gentleman. He will win in the Olympics." Dad told the crowd how proud he was and how much he appreciated the community for supporting me.

When school resumed, I registered for the minimum number of credits. My friend Calvin Johnson once told a magazine reporter that "Rafer has always seen his objectives with almost frightening clarity." My objective now was crystal clear: Olympic Gold. I was not going to let anything deter me.

My grades had been okay so far, but they had not come up to the standards I'd set for myself in high school. College was different and much more difficult. Instead of small classes and friendly teachers, I had large lectures by professors who didn't know every student's name. I was also called on to use intellectual skills that hadn't been emphasized in high school. And I missed that group of buddies who had studied together and helped each other excel.

At first I thought I was finding classwork difficult because I wasn't as smart as I had thought I was. But I was spread too thin. Between workouts, games and meets, extracurricular activities, and a part-time job, I hardly had time to study. Not that I hadn't tried. In fact, one Los Angeles sportswriter wrote that he couldn't interview me until after midnight because I'd been in the library all night. Struggling to stay awake in the library was not the best way to study. As a consequence I could not keep up the grades I needed to maintain my academic scholarship. I switched to an athletic scholarship and reduced my class load to make sure I didn't suffer academically while getting ready for Melbourne.

Ducky conjured up a rigorous routine for me. I worked on conditioning every day and individual decathlon events on a rotating basis. The idea was for every skill to become automatic, a habit so deeply ingrained I would not have to think about it.

My left knee throbbed with pain during every workout. Inside the joint is a spongy pad of fat tissue that absorbs fluid and acts as a cushion. The pad had become inflamed. When aggravated it would swell, sometimes so much that it was hard to straighten out the leg. After practice, Ducky would rub the knee, apply heat and ultrasound, and have me sit in the whirlpool. Every week or two, he would insert a long needle and drain the knee of fluid. The treatment was agonizing, but a small price to pay for a gold medal. I could work through the pain. My only fear was that the injury might interfere with my mechanics, making it impossible to move my leg the way it's supposed to move. I figured that if we could keep the swelling to a manageable level I'd be okay.

When the modern Olympic movement began, its stated purpose was "to improve the human race and strengthen friendship and understanding among all people." Individuals, not nations, were to compete against each other. There would not even be an official tally of the medals won by each country. But politics has had a habit of crashing the party, as in 1936 when Hitler tried to use the Berlin Games to demonstrate the superiority of the Aryan race.

Twenty years later, international politics was a loud, vulgar, unwanted guest. The Soviet Union had been pouring a tremendous amount of its resources into sports. Officially, their premier athletes were amateurs in that they were not paid to perform, but they were supported by the state economy and had the full weight of Russian science and technology behind them. Sports was a Cold War propaganda tool, a way of showcasing the Soviet system. At the Helsinki Games in 1952, the Soviet Bloc countries had surprised the world with excellent performances. Since then they had dominated European competitions. Now they sought to topple America's Olympic supremacy.

On November 4, the day after the Olympic torch began its journey from Greece to Australia, sixteen Soviet army divisions invaded Hungary to suppress a popular uprising. In the words of the *New York Times,* Russian tanks were "mowing down youthful Hungarian freedom fighters resisting with sticks and stones." In short order, Budapest and other cities were overrun, leaders were imprisoned, Parliament and military installations were seized, and Hungarian radio was silenced after a last desperate plea for help.

As the United Nations and NATO contemplated what to do, and the world worried about nuclear war, voices rose up insisting that the Olympics be cancelled or that the USSR be banned. Some nations contemplated withdrawing from the Games in protest. Australian officials issued a statement: "The games will go on unless there is a general world war." Avery Brundage, the head of the International Olympic Committee (IOC), declared, "The Games will not be cancelled. We will not let any country use the Olympics for political purposes."

Hungary was not the only hot spot. Egyptian and Israeli forces had been battling on the Sinai Peninsula. As the U.S. Olympic team gathered in Los Angeles for its journey to Australia, Britain and France bombed Egyptian military targets and prepared to land troops to ensure control of the Suez Canal. Now the Soviets threatened to send troops of their own there, and several Mideast nations considered pulling out of the Olympics. Communist China had its own agenda: They demanded that the IOC withhold recognition of Taiwan (then called Formosa or Nationalist China). Meanwhile the American presidential campaign was reaching a climax. Democratic candidate Adlai Stevenson, calling attention to President Eisenhower's poor health, asked if voters really wanted Richard Nixon's finger on the nuclear trigger in such a tense world.

I left Los Angeles with the rest of the track team at 7:00 A.M. on election day, having marked my absentee ballot for Stevenson. We tried not to think about war or the possible cancellation of the Games. In those days, a trip to Australia took thirty-two hours and had to be done in stages. Our chartered Pan Am Clipper stopped first in Hawaii. We stayed on Waikiki Beach for a day and a half, resting, swimming, sightseeing, watching hula dancers, and pigging out at luaus. I began a lifelong love affair with papaya on that trip. In Hawaii, which was not yet a state, we learned that Eisenhower had won in a landslide. I hoped that my first Olympics would turn out better than my first election.

After a pit stop in Fiji we landed in Melbourne to a rousing welcome. Even more rousing was the welcome given to the sixty Hungarian athletes who arrived the same day. A thousand people greeted them at the airport and sang the Hungarian National Anthem. The Hungarians, who had departed before the Russian invasion and were worried about friends and family back home, snubbed the Russian delegation that turned out to greet them. In protest, they wore armbands with Hungary's traditional colors instead of the Soviet hammer and sickle.

When we arrived at the Olympic Village in the suburb of Heidelberg, we learned that Switzerland had pulled its team from the Games. The IOC, whose headquarters were in Switzerland, called the decision a disgrace. There was fear that other European nations would follow suit. Brundage issued an appeal: "In an imperfect world, if participation in sports is to be stopped every time politicians violate the laws of humanity, there will never be any international contests." I didn't always agree with Mr. Brundage—in fact, I often disagreed vehemently—but on this issue I was in complete accord.

The atmosphere at the Village was festive, with athletes from all parts of the world mingling and exchanging souvenirs, but the Eastern Bloc teams were heavily guarded and their athletes were watched carefully when mixing with outsiders. Just four days before the opening ceremonies, Khrushchev issued the most famous boast of the Cold War era: "History is on our side," he told a group of Western ambassadors. "We will bury you."

My teammates and I had other things on our mind, namely getting ready to compete. The weather did not cooperate. It was supposed to be the height of spring in Australia, but it felt like the dead of winter. It was so cold, wet, and blustery that we couldn't strip down to shorts. Some athletes complained that the weather would affect their performance, but head track coach James Kelly hushed them by pointing out that *every* competitor had to deal with the same conditions.

I had bigger problems. While practicing the pole vault one day, I felt a stabbing pain in my injured knee; I hoped it would go away, but it didn't. Luckily, Ducky was head trainer for the U.S. team, so I had my coach, confidant, and medical expert at my side. He wrapped the knee and treated it as best he could. But soon the inflamed pad had swollen to the size of a small orange and got caught in the joint whenever I hyperextended. As long as I was stationary, or walking with my knee bent, I felt no pain. But you can't run without hyperextending, and you certainly can't jump. When I did those things the pain was hard to endure.

Still, as long as the only problem was pain, I knew I'd be okay. Like wounded soldiers who manage to rescue their comrades, or mothers who move cars to save their children, a disciplined athlete can do amazing things when motivated, enduring—and even ignoring—pain that would cripple someone who did not burn with the desire to win. I was favored to win the decathlon; no amount of pain was going to stop me from fulfilling that prediction.

In the end, Spain and the Netherlands joined Switzerland's boycott over the situation in Hungary. Iraq, Egypt, and Lebanon withdrew because of the Sinai battle, and China pulled out when it didn't get its way on Taiwan. Still, a record sixty-seven countries and over 3,000 athletes were represented. The opening ceremonies took place at the Melbourne Cricket Ground before 102,000 people. One of them was my mother. The good folks of Kingsburg had come through again, raising money to send my parents to the Games. It was Mom's first time on a plane. Dad chose not to make the trip; he was one of those people who felt that if God meant for human beings to fly, He would have given us wings.

That day, everyone's wish had been granted: The sun finally broke through. But sometimes you have to be careful about your wishes. It got so hot and muggy that officials feared athletes and spectators might start dropping like flies. Ducky suggested that I sit out the traditional parade of athletes to rest my knee, but I couldn't resist. It was a moment I'd longed for, and I was not disappointed.

There was great pomp and splendor as the Duke of Edinburgh, dressed in the blue uniform and white cap of an admiral, circled the stadium in an open convertible, then walked to the royal box to the tune of "God Save the Queen." In keeping with tradition, the Greek team led the procession, with my UCLA teammate, George Rubanis, carrying their flag. The other countries followed in alphabetical order, except for Australia, whose team entered last. As was our custom, the U.S. flagbearer (wrestler Norman Armitage) broke protocol by not dipping the flag as we passed the head of state. We all removed our hats though. The crowd gave us a huge cheer, but reserved their loudest welcome for the British team and for political statements: Israel, Korea, and Taiwan were roundly applauded, and the Hungarian team was given a tremendous standing ovation. I limped throughout the entire route. But I felt no pain, only joy and gratitude, when the torch arrived and the flame was lit, and John Landy recited the Olympic oath on behalf of the athletes and five thousand pigeons were released into the night sky.

In the week leading up to the decathlon, I worked out diligently while trying to protect my knee. Ducky used every weapon in his arsenal to reduce the swelling. The only breaks I took were to eat and to spend time with my mother. I took her to several events, including a basketball game with the American squad that featured Bill Russell and K. C. Jones, and what turned out to be one of the most memorable moments in Olympic history: the water polo match between the Russians and Hungarians. It was more like a dogfight than a sporting event. Red ribbons of blood spread across the water. To the delight of the rabid crowd, Hungary won 4–0 and later took home the gold.

Meanwhile, my knee kept getting worse. It began to affect my mechanics. The day before the long jump competition, Ducky recommended that I bow out. I wanted the honor of being one of the few Americans to compete in more than one event, but Ducky was right: There was no sense risking the decathlon for an event in which I had only a slim chance of earning a medal. What upset me most about withdrawing was that I hadn't done it sooner. My place could have been taken by Mal Andrews, who had come in fourth at the Trials and was back in California.

Dan O'Brien, who won the gold medal in Atlanta in 1996, once said that the decathlon is "a matter of heart." When I heard him say that, my first thought was of Melbourne. Completing the decathlon took every ounce of courage and faith I could find inside me.

On the first day of competition, the pain was constant and I could not straighten my leg all the way. Still, my time in the hundred meters was only one-tenth of a second behind Milt Campbell's. In the long jump, while trying to protect my knee as I landed, I turned my body in an awkward way and tore my stomach muscle. Ducky gave me smelling salts and taped me around the waist, but each time I breathed deeply a piercing pain ripped through my midsection. Now I was doubly hampered. The shotput was manageable, but the high jump was excruciating because the injured leg was my take-off leg. The

400 meters, which was painful under the best of circumstances, was almost unendurable. My score at the end of the day was a disappointing 4,375. Milt, improving on his silver-medal performance in Helsinki, was 191 points ahead.

I was disappointed, but not dispirited or discouraged. Ducky treated me with ultrasound, hot compresses, analgesic balm and wraps; I also took aspirin to ease the pain. Then, in the great spirit of Olympic sportsmanship, my opponents, Milt Campbell and Bob Richards, joined me for dinner with Ducky and my mother. Sadly, it was a farewell dinner for Mom. Because the only available flight back to the United States was the next morning, she had to miss the conclusion of the decathlon.

I did not sleep well that night, as the torn muscle hurt whenever I changed position. In the morning I found that my injuries had not miraculously healed. Yet I remained optimistic. I felt I could catch Milt if my body cooperated. Before leaving my room, I prayed to be the best I could be, no more, no less.

Unable to lift off properly, I ran one of my slowest hurdles ever while Milt pulled off a fourteen flat. After the discus throw, during which I felt as if someone had torn open my rib cage, I trailed by 612 points. That was an awful lot to make up in three events, but I refused to believe that the gold was out of reach. Sure enough, Milt blew the pole vault. When he failed to clear 11′ 5.75″, he pounded the sawdust in the landing pit over and over with his fists. Then he stormed over to the infield, threw himself on the ground and started banging his head on a blanket as Bob Richards tried to console him. He left the stadium, looking disconsolate. I think he had his eye on my world record and the disappointing vault seemed to put that out of reach. But it renewed my hope. I ignored my pounding knee and burning midsection and literally rose to the occasion; the 12′ 9½″ vault was my highest ever.

Still, for me to win the gold, Milt would have to bottom out while I surpassed anything I'd ever done in the javelin and the

1500. I determined to hold up my end of the bargain, injuries or no injuries. I scored a personal best in the javelin, but Milt recovered from the pole vault disaster with a good throw of his own and I closed the gap by only fifty points. Now I needed a miracle: To make up 443 points, I would have to beat Milt by nearly a full minute in the 1500.

Afterward, people asked why I didn't sit out the race. It never entered my mind. Ordinarily, personal pride would have been enough to force my legs around the track four times no matter how much pain I was in. That day I had extra incentive. Vasily Kuznetsov of Russia could overtake me for second place by beating me by more than twenty-one seconds. I could not let that happen. As dusk settled on the stadium, all that mattered was to put pain aside for a few more minutes and bring home the silver.

It was one of the hardest things I've ever had to do. At times I wasn't sure I could finish. To my astonishment, I clocked my best time ever. Milt Campbell, who had already run his heat, threw a blanket over my shoulders when I crossed the finish line. It was a fine gesture. We walked off the track with our arms around each other.

Standing on the platform with the silver medal on my chest as the National Anthem played, I was filled with mixed emotions: proud on the one hand, bitterly disappointed on the other; happy for Milt, who had settled for second place in 1952 and now had an Olympic record, but frustrated because I should have beaten him.

Once, when Ducky was asked if I hated to lose, he smiled and said, "Any champion hates to lose." I *despised* it. Everyone—Ducky, my teammates, even reporters—tried to console me. They praised my courage. They said I'd have won with ease if I hadn't been injured. They said that coming in second under those circumstances was a great achievement. My response was, "It's not like being first." Their well-intentioned words sounded as hollow as a drum. So did lofty Olympic ideals, like what matters is not winning but taking part.

Losing was the biggest letdown of my life, and what made it worse was the thought that I had let down others—my family, my coaches, my UCLA classmates, the people of Los Angeles and Kingsburg, everyone in the San Joaquin Valley who expected me to pick up where Bob Mathias had left off. I cried inconsolably for three days.

Naturally, time heals emotional wounds just as it heals torn stomach muscles. I was eventually able to look back at my efforts with pride and to soothe the agony of defeat with a treasure chest of Olympic memories: the pageantry of the opening ceremonies; the thrill of going to events with my mother; being with fantastic teammates (Ira Murchison, Tom Courtney, Lee Calhoun, Greg Bell, Bobby Morrow, Charley Dumas, Parry O'Brien, Al Oerter, Glenn Davis, Leamon King) and seeing them at their peak; whipping the Soviet track and field machine (although the Russians won the most medals overall); meeting people from all over the world and learning about their cultures.

I was able to derive some important lessons from defeat. The first is one of the oldest clichés in sports, but it hit home in Melbourne with a vengeance: The past doesn't count. Your records don't count. All the praise that's been heaped on you doesn't count. What matters is how you perform *now.* I was the world record holder. I had beaten Milt Campbell at the Olympic Trials in Indiana. But on those two days in Australia, I did not have what I needed to win and he did, and that's all that counts.

The second lesson relates to my injuries. At the time I felt I was making my very best effort, and in a sense I was. But in retrospect I realized that part of me had held back. Not to ease the pain—there was no way to do that—but because I was afraid I might make things worse and be forced to quit, or perhaps incur permanent damage. The slightest shadow of worry is enough to diminish an athlete's performance. On those two days, the fear of destroying my athletic career might have been the difference between winning and losing. I should have won despite my impairments, and I probably would have if I'd realized that I could go all out without wrecking my future.

In a television documentary about the decathlon, Milt Campbell said that the difference between the two of us in 1956 was "the nervousness [Rafer] displayed and the calmness I displayed." He was alluding to the fact that he'd been through an Olympics before and I had not. I have to set the record straight: Whatever Milt saw in me during our competition was not the jitters. I went into those Games as confident as I'd ever been. I never for a moment thought I could lose, not to Milt or anyone else. What he saw on my face was pain, or perhaps the fear of permanent injury.

Over the years I've been reluctant to speak about my injuries because I didn't want to sound as though I were making excuses. I don't mean to take anything away from Milt. He was a great athlete and a tough competitor, and in Melbourne he was outstanding. But the truth is, I have no doubt that I would have won the gold had I been physically sound.

5

MORE THAN A SPRINT, LESS THAN A MILE

Don't let what you cannot do interfere with what you can do.

—John Wooden

THE 400 METERS is the toughest event in the decathlon. It does not demand as much speed as the 100 meters or as much endurance as the 1500 meters, but it is more difficult than both. It requires the acceleration of a sprinter and the grit of a distance runner. Because you've already competed in four events that day, it always hurts when you run the 400. You're worn out when it's over, and the outcome stays with you into the night, and sometimes even the following day.

When I started competing I hated the 400, even though I knew that my opponents faced the same conditions and that I might have an edge because I was able to perform in pain. Once I developed a style that worked for me, I grew to love it. Ultimately it became one of my strongest events.

The fifth phase of my life also began as an arduous grind, with new challenges to my mind and body. Losing at the Olympics is more heartbreaking than any other defeat, because you can't go back and try again for four long years—an eternity in the life of an athlete. Though it seemed a long way off, I set my sights on the 1960 Games in Rome even before I was back on U.S. soil. I vowed to come back stronger and more focused than ever; nothing short of a devastating injury or an act of God would stop me from winning the gold medal that I had just been denied. I wanted to start with a burst of speed, just as I did when running the 400. But my knee injury forced me to crawl.

My first stop on the road to Rome was the operating room at the UCLA Medical Center. Surgeons removed the inflamed tissue, leaving me with a scar from the top of my kneecap to the bottom. The recovery process was long and tedious. I was on crutches for so long that I wore a pair out. Coach Drake supervised my rehabilitation and watched over my progress daily. It was monotonous, boring, and painful. The doctors' prognosis was as optimistic as could be, but one thought nagged at me: What if I can never run and jump the way I once did?

It was frustrating to be in the training room instead of on the track in the springtime sun. I missed the camaraderie and the sense of immediate accomplishment. But I gave rehab as much time and effort as I would give my usual training regimen. This left as much time for my studies as I'd had before: not enough. Adding to my extracurricular commitments, I had joined the Gold Key, an upper-division honor society; the Cal Club, which promotes intercampus harmony; and the Fellowship of Christian Athletes. Clearly I could not do everything and still keep up academically. I wasn't failing courses or in danger of losing my eligibility, but I was getting B's and C's, and even a couple of D's, when I wanted A's. Something had to give.

Ever since high school I had thought I would become a dentist one day. Maybe it was because I was fond of our family dentist, but for some reason the occupation appealed to me. My plan was to take pre-dentistry courses—basically, a lot of chemistry and biology—and go to dental school after graduation. Meanwhile I would major in political science, having become interested in international relations through my overseas travel and the foreign athletes I'd met. One of my friends even told a newspaper, "Rafer is majoring in becoming Ralph Bunche."

When I finally realized that I couldn't do everything, I opted to major in physical education instead. It was simply easier to manage, given all my other commitments. I ended up minoring in political science and completing my pre-dentistry program as well.

One academic experience is worth noting; it was an early lesson in how something positive can come from failure. I got an F on a paper about François Dominique Toussaint L'Ouverture, who led the campaign to expel the British and Spanish from Haiti. The failing grade shocked me. Evidently, despite my excellent grades in high school, I had a lot to learn about putting together a well-structured thesis. I had to take a remedial course that students called Bonehead English. At first I resented this, but it turned into a tremendous learning experience, giving me a proficiency with the language that I might otherwise never have developed.

It was not until halfway through the track season that I was healthy enough to compete. Even then the team had to do without me in my two best events, the hurdles and the long jump. For the team, the season was disappointing; we placed third in the conference, and, because of the football scandal, we were ineligible for the NCAA meet. For me there was a silver lining: Because I was limited to the weight events—javelin, discus, and shotput—I spent more time working on those than ever before. As a result, I broke the UCLA record for the javelin. But the real payoff was to come later.

First, I had a great adventure. Bob Richards once advised me, "Join a track team and see the world." In the summer of 1957 I saw a big part of it. I had received a letter from Harold E. Howland of the State Department asking if I would be interested in going on a goodwill tour to foreign countries, as Bob Mathias, Mal Whitfield, and other athletes had done. The purpose was essentially to make friends in places where the U.S. government wanted to improve relations.

My eighty-nine-day trip took me to Hong Kong, Israel, the Belgian Congo, East and West Pakistan, Ceylon (now Sri Lanka), the former Yugoslavia, Greece, and Italy. At each stop I would shuttle to cities and villages, meeting with local leaders and U.S. officials, giving demonstrations and speaking to students and educators about sports and the importance of contact between people of different cultures. The school desegregation crisis in Little Rock was in the world's news at the time, so I also had to clarify certain misconceptions and assure people that Arkansas Governor Faubus did not represent all white Americans.

As an African American and a Christian, my strongest emotions were stirred in the Congo and Israel. I was American through and through, but I was aware of my roots and eager to see what Africa was like. The Congolese seemed even more eager to see what *I* was like. Children followed me everywhere. I think it was a source of pride to them that a man who looked like them was some kind of big shot in America. Leopoldville, the capital, was small but more modern than I'd expected. In Stanleyville, a tiny outpost in the middle of the jungle, the tension between natives and colonists was so thick it could have been cut with a machete. A week after I left, a number of whites were massacred. Three years later, the revolution led by Patrice Lumumba and Joseph Kasavubu gave the nation independence.

Leopoldville became Kinshasa and Stanleyville was renamed Kisangani. Later the country would be called Zaire; now it is the Democratic Republic of the Congo.

In the Holy Land, having a mezuzah and a cross around my neck was perfect symbolism. While visiting a kibbutz and staying with a family in Jerusalem, I was struck by the contrast of ancient and modern, secular and sacred. My biggest thrill was walking in the footsteps of Jesus. I visited Bethlehem, where He was born, and Galilee, the center of His ministry. I followed the Stations of the Cross, the path He walked to His crucifixion. I worshiped at the Church of the Holy Sepulcher, which was built on the site of Calvary. It was a tremendously moving experience.

When I returned to UCLA that fall, I resumed physical therapy and got my knee strong enough for basketball. Not only did I miss competing, I also thought it would be a good way to get in shape for track, since the coach, John Wooden, was known for his rigorous conditioning program. Coach Wooden had not yet begun his legendary string of national championships, but he was on his way. In his nine years at UCLA he compiled a 184–66 record and won three conference titles.

A preseason student publication assessed my potential this way: "As a yearling, [Rafer] was strong on the boards and a pretty good shot, averaging 10.2 points a game. But actually he's been away from basketball for three years and so has a lot of work to get ready for varsity play. If Johnson can get his exceptional physical ability under control, he will become a tremendous asset at guard or forward. He isn't a natural shooter but can improve with work."

Considering that I'd been away from the sport for so long, I managed to play well, mostly off the bench but sometimes starting at guard when Coach Wooden needed extra speed. More important, my knee held up to the rigors of basketball, removing any doubt that I would be able to return to the Olympics. An added bonus, and later a cherished memory, was getting to know John Wooden. I experienced first-hand the knowledge and skill that would make him the Wizard of Westwood—and the personal qualities that would earn him the respect and admiration of everyone whose life he touched. Like Ducky Drake, he was an exceptional man who genuinely cared about the young men in his charge.

Coach Wooden felt so strongly about putting the team above individual glory that the first thing he had us do together was learn to lace our shoes the exact same way. It served the purpose of instilling a sense of unity. He also made sure every player was solidly grounded in the fundamentals of the game. I remember endless drills in which I learned how to guard opponents and get into position for rebounds. A firm taskmaster, Coach Wooden made his practice sessions so hard that games were easy by comparison. One reason his fast-break style of play was so successful is that his teams could outhustle opponents when the clock was running down and fatigue set in.

Every season Coach Wooden handed out three pages of rules, suggestions, and advice. In addition to basic health and training information, he included items designed to make us better teammates and better men in general. Here are some examples, which any collegiate athlete would do well to keep in mind:

- Be a gentleman at all times and do nothing that could bring discredit to you or your school.
- Keep basketball *second* in importance to your studies.
- Never criticize, nag, or razz your teammates.
- Place the team above yourself—always.
- Work hard constantly to improve.
- Take your criticism constructively without alibis or sulking.
- Be quick and clever but never get fancy or grandstand.
- Others may be faster than you are, larger than you are, and have

far more ability than you have, but *no one* should ever be your superior in team spirit, fight, determination, ambition, effort, and character.

While working on this book, I asked Coach Wooden what kind of player I was. He said my strengths were aggressiveness, tenacious defense, a good drive to the basket, and quickness. He counted quickness as the most important physical asset a player in any sport could have. I also had speed, he said, but it was straight-line speed. I could not maneuver on the court the way I would have if I'd devoted myself to basketball instead of track. With practice, I might also have improved my mediocre outside shot. Coach Wooden's bottom-line assessment surprised me: He said I could have been an All-American had I concentrated on basketball.

His statement raises an issue that's followed me for over forty years. I've often been asked why I focused on track instead of a sport in which I could have turned professional. The answer I gave a magazine in 1958 says it all: "There is no pro future in track, that's true. But there is a stimulating present, and that's good enough." I loved every sport I played, but I was most passionate about track and field.

Maybe things would have been different if the NFL and NBA were what they are today. In those days, amateurs, not pros, were the most revered athletes. The Olympics were considered the pinnacle of athletic achievement, and belief in the Olympic ideal was strong. A Kingsburg fan told a reporter, "I think he should quit track and try football. He can't eat medals." No, but I could have a gold one placed around my neck, and I *would* have eaten a medal before I'd give up trying.

After the basketball season, I returned to track and field and was named team captain. "We usually have a track captain and a field captain," Coach Drake told the press. "Well, this time Rafer's both of them." With my knee mended, I was eager to get back to top form. Then I pulled my hamstring muscle. I had torn that same muscle in high school, and tears like that never heal completely. Once again I was frustrated because I could not run or jump, and once again there was a silver lining: My skills in the weight events improved dramatically. In a dual meet at Stanford, I scored what was then the best "triple" in history: a 54′ 11½″ shotput, a 170′ 9½″ discus, and a 237′ 10″ javelin.

There was one race I *could* run that spring, even with a bad leg: I ran for student body president. Friends who were active in student affairs urged me to run, saying I could make a valuable contribution. I'd had no intention of getting involved in collegiate politics since my plate was already full and I knew it would be a demanding, time-consuming job. Bill Ackerman, the general manager of the Associated Students of UCLA, confirmed that. But, he added, "It's a great experience, one you couldn't buy anywhere."

I felt I'd be letting myself down if I turned away from the opportunity. As president I would be able to champion issues I believed in, such as ensuring that students of every race and ethnic group were given equal opportunity, starting a program in which UCLA students would tutor youngsters in the community, and doing more to help foreign students adjust to life in America. I also felt that my presidency could have an impact beyond the campus. By then, UCLA had already had two black student body presidents, but neither one had a public profile like mine. If I were elected, the whole country and much of the world would know that an African American was capable of holding the highest student office at one of the nation's premier universities.

Ironically, the only time during the campaign that race became an issue was when a group of black students demanded that my platform support their civil rights agenda. I told them that the student body president represented *all* students and I would not make promises to them that I wouldn't make to anyone else. "If you can't support me because I'm the best candidate," I said, "then you should not support me." Eventually, I believe, I got most of their votes.

The other candidates, Lew Weitzman and Tom Chasin, had such good persuasive skills that they became powerful Hollywood agents. But I had some pretty good supporters, like Stu Robinson, who also became an agent, and Joel Wachs, who became a member of the Los Angeles City Council. The students would have been in good hands with either Lew or Tom, but I guess they liked the idea of having an Olympic medalist represent them.

No sooner did I win than I was cruelly reminded that we still lived in a small-minded world. I received a pile of hate mail—and an even bigger pile the following semester, when I took office and my picture appeared in newspapers with my blond secretary. Most of the letters said things like, "Who do you think you are, black boy?" and "Uppity niggers should know their place." Some were from African Americans who called me an Uncle Tom. It was then that I realized that trying to build bridges between people can bring resentment and heartache as well as respect and satisfaction.

By late spring of 1958 I was able to hurdle and jump for the first time since Melbourne. There was a good chance I would reach full fitness and strength in time for that summer's track events. This was encouragement enough for me to change my summer plans. I had been one of several UCLA students chosen for Project India, an annual Peace Corps–like project that I had looked forward to eagerly. But my future as an athlete took precedence over adventure and diplomacy. As it turned out, I had plenty of both.

When school ended, I competed in a few meets under the banner of the Striders, a Los Angeles track club, and then entered the Kingsburg Invitational Decathlon. I did that mainly because I did not want to disappoint my hometown, but also to test my legs. With my thigh heavily taped, I proceeded gingerly, following doctor's orders by making only one attempt at each of the jumping events. Wisely, Ducky had come along to make sure I didn't push myself. My body responded well. I won the meet with 7,780 points.

A week later I was in Palmyra, New Jersey, for the national AAU decathlon. The meet was notable for two reasons: First, I had clearly returned to full strength; second, my chief opponent was a wiry athlete from Taiwan named Yang Chuan-kwang. Known as C. K. Yang (pronounced Young) in America, he had finished eighth at Melbourne but had improved tremendously since then. Fresh off a first-place finish in the Asian Games, C. K. nearly grabbed the AAU title. I beat him by only 62 points. I had no way of knowing at the time, but C. K. would soon become my close friend, training partner, and costar in the most dramatic decathlon in Olympic history. But first I had to deal with another friendly rival, this time in the glare of an international spotlight fraught with political tension.

I had returned to Kingsburg to start my summer job at the cannery, when I got a call from Ducky. The first-ever dual track meet between the United States and the Soviet Union was coming up in Moscow. Originally, no decathlon had been scheduled. Now it had been added and I was invited to represent the United States. My chief opponent would be Vasily Kuznetsov, a tall, muscular Russian from a village called Kalikino. Since 1953, Kuznetsov had won every competition he'd entered, consistently breaking European records; the only exception was Melbourne, where he'd finished behind Milt Campbell and me. But that May, Kuznetsov had broken my world record, becoming the first decathlete ever to top the 8,000-point mark. Probably because the Soviets wanted to showcase their record-holder, the decathlon was added to the Moscow meet. Kuznetsov and I were to compete face to face in the heart of his homeland.

If I hadn't already withdrawn from Project India, this news would have done the trick. I wanted my record back. I dashed down to Los Angeles to get ready.

It had been twelve years since Winston Churchill coined the term "iron curtain" to describe the Soviet Union's totalitarian control of Eastern Europe. Although the death of Stalin had given rise to the concept of "peaceful coexistence," the Cold War still raged and the possibility of atomic war haunted everyone's dreams. That year, Russia's first Sputnik satellite had sparked a stampede to improve science education in the United States. The explosion of nuclear warheads at high altitudes had launched a frenzied drive to build missiles and fallout shelters. With all the saber-rattling going on, peace-loving citizens hoped that cultural exchanges would improve understanding between Russians and Americans. The dual track meet was a major step in that campaign. It was treated with almost as much gravity as the missile race.

Reading the press, you would think that Moscow was a battlefield where the forces of good and evil were about to face off. And the duel between Kuznetsov and me drew most of the "hype." Our matchup, which was referred to as a "summit meeting," had all the ingredients of a great drama: A product of the Soviet sports machine had taken the record; now an American who had worked his way up from poverty was trying to get it back. It was not just man-on-man for the unofficial title of World's Greatest Athlete, it was Communism vs. the Free World.

Like Jesse Owens at the Berlin Olympics, or Joe Louis stepping into the ring for his rematch with Max Schmeling, I carried the burden of national pride to a sporting event that was supposed to transcend politics. Like them, I was asked to be an ambassador when I just wanted to be an athlete. Like them, I was fully aware of the irony that a black man was an emissary of a nation where discrimination raged and racists still got away with lynchings. I found myself affected by the political overtones despite my efforts to ignore them.

I had not spent much time with Kuznetsov at Melbourne; Soviet officials had kept their athletes under tight rein, for fear that some would seek asylum. But, since opponents have to sit around so much between events, the decathlon encourages brotherhood. I saw enough of Vasily to like and respect him. He seemed to have an endearing personality and an honorable sense of sportsmanship. Evidently, the feeling was mutual. "Rafer Johnson, as an athlete and a man, he made a tremendous impression on me," Vasily told the press. "I think he's a good comrade and a friend who will always help you on the sports field or on the sidelines. I think he is a good American boy."

Good American boys don't like having their records taken away. The politicians and media could fight the Cold War. I just wanted to win.

Looking at the newspapers of that period, I'm struck by how frightening the world situation was. As would be the case for the next thirty years, tension in the Middle East had brought the United States and the Soviet Union to the brink of Armageddon—or so everyone feared. This time it was not just the ongoing Israeli–Palestinian conflict but upheavals in Iraq and Lebanon as well. Each superpower accused the other of warmongering. Diplomats pressured President Eisenhower to take a conciliatory approach, while the Pentagon warned against appeasing the enemy. Ten thousand U.S. troops were poised offshore at Beirut.

I was also struck by a couple of smaller news items, which portended things to come: Fidel Castro's forces were gaining ground against President Batista in the Cuban civil war; and *The Defiant Ones,* with Sidney Poitier and Tony Curtis as escaped convicts bound to each other by chains, had just opened. Sidney's part was called "the most powerful screen role ever written for a Negro."

In keeping with the Cold War atmosphere, the team trained at West Point, preparing for what the *New York Times* called a "peaceful invasion of Moscow." There were rumors that the meet might be cancelled, but our head coach, George Eastment of Manhattan College, assured us that the trip was on and kept us focused on our training.

Our charter flight took us from New York to Helsinki. On board was an all-star track team, including friends of mine from Melbourne like Parry O'Brien, Ira Murchison, Charley Dumas, Al Oerter, and Glenn Davis. It was an overnight flight, and none of us got much sleep—not because it was uncomfortable, but because we were partying. Shotputter Earlene Brown started to sing, others joined her, and before long people were strumming guitars, clapping hands, drumming on anything they could reach, and dancing in the aisles. We landed, fifteen hours later, exhausted.

From Finland we were ferried to Moscow on three small Russian planes with seats as hard as steel. We were greeted by the American ambassador, Russian dignitaries, and about 500 citizens who applauded and handed us flowers. Buses took us into the heart of the city. It was too dark to see much, but one sight sent chills up my spine: the red star atop the Kremlin, brightly lit against the black sky.

Our accommodations at the Hotel Leningrad were decent, but the mattresses were about three inches thick and hard as boards. I was glad we had been told to bring our own soap because there was none in the rooms. The food also left a lot to be desired, and the soft drinks tasted like wine. During our stay we toured the Kremlin grounds, Lenin's tomb, and other historic sites; we also saw the Moscow Circus and visited the enormous department store, Gum, where we did our best to use the spending money—fifteen dollars—we got from the AAU. One of the most amazing sights was the Moscow subway, which was so beautifully designed, and had such exquisite paintings lining the walls, that you would think you were in a museum.

Walking around the center of Moscow, where men and women swept the streets with long brooms that looked like palm fronds, we were struck by how friendly the people were. Everyone was eager for autographs, conversation, and barter. They seemed especially interested in those of us who were black, partly because we were an exotic sight in that part of the world (some of them got a kick out of holding their pale skin next to ours and touching our hair) and partly because they knew all about American racism and wanted to show us how tolerant they were. Some tried to convince us we'd be better off living in Russia. We even met a black man from America, who had moved to Moscow in the 1930s and married a Russian woman. He kept telling us how much more free he was in his adopted country. I'm sure he'd been ordered to speak to us by Soviet propagandists.

Although the people were surprisingly open, their clothing and appearance indicated that they were poorer than most big-city Americans. My general impression was of a drab, depressing country. We could not wander off on our own, but had to stay in groups with Soviet guides. Brown-uniformed police were everywhere. The atmosphere was so paranoid that we were concerned about speaking in our own rooms; Josh Cuthbert, a world-class hurdler, had convinced us that every room was bugged. He even pulled some wires out of the walls. We thought he was crazy, but he turned out to be right.

When we arrived at Lenin Stadium to begin our workouts, we were greeted by the sound of Louis Armstrong over the speaker system. Throughout the meet, the music piped into the stadium consisted largely of what were then called "Negro spirituals." It was probably the Soviets' way of showing their support for America's oppressed. One other thing stood out at the stadium: the track was spectacular. For all their economic shortages, the Soviets managed to find resources for state-of-the-art sports facilities.

They were eager to upgrade their athletes as well. A team of female scientists nipped at our heels constantly, grilling us about our techniques and training methods, while cameramen took thousands of feet of film. We were also besieged by reporters from all over the world. I got a lot of attention, since the decathlon was almost as big as soccer in Europe. In fact, in an article about me, *Sports Illustrated* wrote: "In three big decathlon tests abroad, a quarter million people watched him. In six decathlons at home less than 20,000 Americans have seen him. In the U.S. the decathlon has lacked international flavor, and is, in fact, so poorly understood that it cannot be appreciated."

Once the meet started, the competition was fierce but sportsmanlike. The huge crowds were exuberant in support of the home team but remarkably fair-minded at the same time. They cheered every outstanding performance, regardless of which side the athlete was on. Soviet officials, however, were intent on winning the propaganda battle. Knowing the United States had superior relay teams, they departed from the usual procedure at dual meets and awarded points for second place in relays. Worse, they reneged on their agreement to separate the men's and women's scores. Despite having great female athletes like Earlene Brown and sprinter Lucinda Williams, the American women were at a distinct disadvantage. They received very little support in the United States, whereas the Soviets had invested a tremendous amount in their female athletes—including steroids, if the rumors were true. In the end, the Russian strategy paid off: The U.S. men whipped the Soviet team 126–109, but the Soviet women won 63–44, and the final score that the Soviets trumpeted was: U.S.S.R. 172, U.S. 170.

My face-off with Kuznetsov was the most heavily publicized confrontation at the meet. You would have thought that the other three decathlon competitors didn't exist. I tried to stay focused on my role as athlete, as opposed to ambassador, and to treat this as just another track meet. But it was clearly special, and all the attention made me even more determined to win. *Sports Illustrated* wrote about me: "He went through the week of practice in Moscow with an air of detachment because his concentration was so intense." Coach Eastment was quoted as saying that I'd worked harder than any other athlete.

I missed Ducky's comforting presence and coaching wisdom. But he was with me both in spirit and on paper. Before I left Los Angeles, he had given me a sealed envelope and told me not to open it until I got to Moscow. It read, "You thought 7,000 miles or so could separate us, but they can't. These next couple of days I'll be just as much with you as at Palmyra . . . Remember, you're the champion. You're the one *they* have to beat, so let *them* worry. Go about your work with a quiet confidence that cannot be shaken." Then he addressed each of the ten events with reminders of little things I had to do to perform at my best. Things like, in the shotput, "Don't just play with it, get ready; leg under—good position—quick reaction—and lots of effort." The letter concluded, "No matter what happens, remember if you have faith as a grain of mustard seed, you can move mountains. Remember, victory is sweet. World records come when least expected. Work and think on each event as it comes up. Do your best. No one can ask or expect more." With his words in my hand, it was almost as if my coach were on the sidelines.

It was overcast and humid when we lined up for the hundred meters. I sprinted to a 10.6, two-tenths of a second faster than Kuznetsov. The crowd, which nearly filled the 104,000-seat stadium, seemed to sense that their national hero was in for a tough battle. The rest of the day Vasily and I leapfrogged each other. He won the long jump by about a foot, taking the lead. I got it back in the shotput. The high jump found him ahead once more, but by only ten points. Seldom, if ever, had a major decathlon been that close.

I maintained my intensity throughout the competition. "Between events," *Sports Illustrated* reported, "he lay still on the grass beside the red crushed-brick track, his face immobile and withdrawn, and he answered questions briefly, begrudging the relaxation of concentration necessary for conversation." I was determined to win the 400 and end the day ahead in points, since Kuznetsov was known to be exceptionally strong in the second day's events. Here's how *Sports Illustrated*'s Tex Maule described the race: "Johnson, whose long legs appear odd because the heavily muscled thighs don't match the slim calves and race-horse ankles, flashed away to a quick lead, running very strongly, with a longer stride than the Russian. He built the lead down the backstretch, then, coming through the final turn as rain began to patter gently on the track, he drove himself mercilessly to the tape, 12 yards ahead of Kuznetsov, but not relaxing because he knew he needed all the points he could get in the first day's competition."

I ran a 48.2 to Vasily's 49.6. I had the lead by 104 points, and the psychological edge to sleep on. Before I could rest, I had to climb to the top of the stadium for an NBC *Monitor* broadcast, along with Ira Murchison, who had won the hundred meters and had run the first leg of a winning 400-meter relay. The small broadcasting booth was like a steam bath. The hard chair made it impossible to relax. I answered questions as tersely as possible; all I wanted to do was get to bed. "He walked back down to the waiting bus, moving as carefully and slowly as if he were ill," wrote Tex Maule. I was conserving every ounce of energy for the next day. A reporter asked me how I felt. "I'm gonna win," he quoted me as saying. "I got to."

The next morning the track was soggy from an overnight rain, not the best condition for the hurdles. I won the race, but my time, 14.9, enabled me to pick up only a few points. I'd wanted to build a bigger lead before Kuznetsov's strongest events. I won the discus handily, then surprised myself with a personal best in the pole vault, 12′ 11 7/8″—within two inches of Kuznetsov's height and good enough to keep a decent lead.

Now came the javelin. As the next-to-last event, it carries tremendous weight in a close match because the outcome determines who has to do what in the dreaded 1500. After two throws, my best mark was 205 feet. Kuznetsov had already thrown 214′ 1/2″. With a margin like that, he would only have to beat me by fifteen to twenty seconds in the 1500 to win the decathlon, and he was certainly capable of doing that. Rather than conserve my energy for the distance run, I decided to take one more shot at the javelin, hoping to put my lead out of reach.

I remembered the pointers in Ducky's letter: "Check the wind. Get a good angle of flight. Throw out through the point." Then I prayed that I might throw as hard as I could. I concentrated my energy, sprinted down the runway, and flung the two-pound spear with everything I had. I knew the instant it left my hand that it was an exceptional throw. The javelin was still high in the air when it flew over Kuznetsov's marker. Normally I was oblivious to my surroundings during competition, but this time I could hear a collective gasp from the crowd, followed by cheers. Even though it meant that their hero would surely lose, the Russians expressed their admiration for my effort. The javelin lodged in the earth 238′ 2″ away.

My total was now 8,072 points. I had broken the world record with one event still to go.

There was very little at stake in the 1500; Kuznetsov would have needed a motorcycle to beat me by enough points to win. But decathletes are trained to always do their best, regardless of their prospects of winning or losing. We ran as if the fate of the world depended on it. He beat me, 5:04 to 5:05. My total score was 8,302. I had surpassed the record by nearly 300 points.

With a wide grin on his chiseled face, Vasily grasped my hand with both of his and kissed me on the cheek. All over the world, newspapers and magazines displayed pictures of a black American and a white Russian, emissaries from countries at the brink of war, embracing. I like to think the image served as a balm. At a time when the superpowers were demonizing each other, here was graphic proof of our common humanity and the power of human contact to heal the damage done by politicians and generals.

Even more convincing proof followed my victory. Surrounded by reporters and fellow athletes, I was hustled to the victory stand. Flashbulb bursts lit the night. Someone handed me a bouquet of flowers. Most of the spectators were on their feet, cheering. It was the loudest applause I'd ever heard. I hoisted the flowers overhead, bowed slightly, and spoke the only Russian word I knew, "Spacibo." It meant "Thank you."

After the brief ceremony I stepped down from the pedestal, put on my sweats, and walked off the infield with Kuznetsov. We stopped momentarily to chat with his coach; then I headed for the exit. Suddenly I was surrounded by a horde of screaming Russians. My first reaction was, "This is it!" I thought I was being attacked, like a soldier who had wandered into the enemy's territory and killed their leader—which, in a sense, I had.

Instead I was lifted onto a pair of shoulders and carried around, bouncing up and down like a ball as the people laughed and shook my hand and shouted "Johnson! Johnson!" Except for the Special Olympics, it remains the most amazing display of sportsmanship I have ever seen.

"No sport can cure the world's ills," wrote Coles Phinizy in *Sports Illustrated.* "Moments like Johnson's affirm, nonetheless, that a sport sometimes clears a good path where bigger machines have stalled. A track champion of Johnson's stature serves especially as an agent of good will, because of all the American sports, it is in track that this country mixes most often with others." He noted that the cheering for me was "one of few heartening sounds the world heard in that otherwise grim month."

I once said that international competition breeds understanding because athletes don't beat ideas into each other's heads like politicians. We make friends and leave as friends. My rivalry with Vasily Kuznetsov would continue for another two years, but we had become friends and friends we would remain. We corresponded for years, until time and distance came between us. But we'll always be linked in the annals of sports and the Cold War.

"At 3:30 P.M. yesterday in Kingsburg, Calif., Mrs. Lewis Johnson, a short, hefty woman known to all as Dimples, was briskly ironing a basketful of clothes and listening to music on the radio, when the announcer cut in and said: 'We interrupt this broadcast to bring you an important bulletin from Moscow. Rafer Johnson, star athlete from UCLA, set a new world's record for the decathlon. . . .' " So began the *New York Times* report. Another paper quoted Mom: "I'm tickled pink and jumping for joy. I knew my boy could do it. . . . I was just so happy I couldn't even think clearly for a moment. Then the phone started ringing.''

The calls were from friends and neighbors. KINGSBURG GOES WILD AT RAFER WIN, one headline read. That my hometown would go wild did not surprise me. What *did* surprise me was the response from the rest of the world. I had no idea how much the ''summit meeting'' of track and field had captured the imagination of the public and how much the press and politicians would make of my performance. From Russia, the U.S. team traveled to Poland, Hungary, and Greece for dual meets. The first two countries felt more oppressive than Moscow; opposing athletes could not spend time with us without an official. But word of my record had traveled, and I was gaped at and congratulated constantly. In Athens, where the atmosphere was free, I was treated like a conquering hero.

But that was nothing compared to what happened when I returned home. The press spared no superlatives. My performance was called ''one of the epic single efforts in the history of track'' and ''the greatest athletic performance of modern times.'' I was compared to Jim Thorpe, who had always stood as the greatest all-around athlete ever. I was hailed as ''one of the finest examples of American youth.'' Vice President Nixon sent me a letter of congratulations, calling me ''a one-man track team.'' A congressman read into the *Congressional Record* exactly the kind of rhetoric that sportsmen try to discourage. He said my victory ''demonstrated to the Soviet Union and other critics of our country that we produce the best under a system of incentives and freedom which they would label inefficient and decadent.'' No doubt Soviet propagandists made the most of their overall victory at the meet. But the statement I cherished most came from the Russian newspaper *Trud,* which said of my performance, ''This will dignify the history of world athletic records for a long time to come.''

The team landed in New York, where we were greeted with

an official reception led by Mayor Richard F. Wagner. Then it was on to Los Angeles, where I was flabbergasted by what awaited me. The first person I saw was my mother, beaming like a spotlight with her arms open wide to hug me. Behind her was my father and my brother Jim, along with about 200 cheering people, most of them from UCLA. Over the next two days, with my family at my side, I was whisked from one reception to another. Civic leaders and celebrities shook my hand and sang my praises. At City Hall, Mayor Norris Paulson and the City Council declared it "Rafer Johnson Day" and read a resolution they had passed in my honor. There was only one sad note: Football coach Red Sanders, who had been with the UCLA delegation, passed away the next day. The last picture ever taken of the coach was at the airport with his arm around me.

To everyone else I may have been Jim Thorpe and Dwight Eisenhower rolled into one, but to Mom and Dad I was still little Rafer. Before they returned to Kingsburg, where a huge celebration was scheduled (5,000 people showed up, almost double the town's population), my mother told the *Los Angeles Times,* "If I can get that boy and a stove together all at one time, I'm going to show him his mom can still cook." I couldn't wait. She also said, "Everybody's sure making a fuss over that boy. But it won't spoil him one little bit. I taught all my youngsters to walk straight, talk straight, and take this world just as it comes."

Something else kept me from being spoiled: I had more than a hundred trophies, a pile of medals, and a world record, but no Olympic Gold.

6

CLEARING THE HURDLE

There is no greater glory that can befall a man than what he achieves with the speed of his feet or the strength of his hands.

—Homer

THE HIGH HURDLES RACE begins early on day two of the decathlon. You've had time to rest your weary body, soothe your aches and pains, and reflect on the previous day. Now, regardless of where you are in the standings, you have to focus on the ten 42-inch barriers that stand between you and the finish line 110 meters away. It's a new day, a time to improve your score and set a positive tone for the remaining events.

In the sweep of my life, the phase that began after my triumph in Moscow was a brand-new day. Rome was within sight, the finish line for my Olympic dreams. Between me and the gold medal, though, were obstacles I had to leap over without losing stride. Unlike a race, some of the hurdles were unexpected.

• • •

The afterglow of Moscow persisted through the fall and into winter. The amount of attention I received—the luncheons and dinners, the newspaper and magazine interviews—was astonishing. My room back in Kingsburg filled up with plaques and trophies. Of the myriad awards I received, the one I least deserved was *Mad* magazine's Alfred E. Newman of the Year. I didn't think I exemplified the famous motto, "What, me worry?" Among the others, a few stand out. Each year, the Helms Athletic Foundation presented a World Trophy to the outstanding amateur athlete from each continent. I was chosen for North America. Two other recipients—C. K. Yang for Asia and Vasily Kuznetsov for Europe—would be my chief rivals at the next Olympics. I was also the youngest of the five "outstanding young men" honored by California's Junior Chamber of Commerce (the others were three scientists and a school principal).

But the awards that meant the most to me were ones that were given to other people: Pi Lambda Phi announced that it would give an annual Rafer Johnson Award to an outstanding fraternity member; and, my proudest of all, the *Los Angeles Sentinel* named Mrs. Alma Johnson of Kingsburg its Mother of the Year.

Amidst all the hubbub, two events were particularly memorable. At the NAACP's Freedom Rally in Oakland, which was attended by over 5,000 people, my fellow honoree was Ernest Green. Then a seventeen-year-old freshman at Michigan State, Ernest was one of the nine black students who had integrated Central High in Little Rock. As I listened to him speak about that experience, I thought of my own high school years and felt even more grateful to the people of Kingsburg. I also thought, everyone treats me like a hero for winning a sporting event, but Ernest is a *real* hero. As the NAACP stated, he "daily ran a gauntlet of verbal taunts, threats and abuse, as well as physical assaults and intimidations. In spite of these overwhelming handicaps, Ernest studiously applied himself and successfully completed his senior high school year.''

Remarkably, despite our vastly different experiences, Ernest and I both expressed confidence in the future. ''There would be no problem with integration if it were left up to the students,'' I said. Ernest echoed that idea. ''I enjoyed my senior year at Central High,'' he said. ''I found that most of the seniors were willing to accept me and integration. Many of them came up to me at the end of the year to sign my yearbook. They tried to make up for what had happened earlier.'' There was reason to hope. (Forty years later, chills ran up my spine as I watched Ernest Green speak from the steps of Central High as President Clinton commemorated the anniversary of the integration of Little Rock's schools.)

The other memorable event was the celebrity-filled banquet at the Beverly Hilton Hotel in Los Angeles, when *Sports Illustrated* presented me with its Sportsman of the Year award (I was also *Sport Magazine*'s Man of the Year). I appeared, in jacket and tie, on the magazine's cover, the first of three times I would have that honor (the others were carrying the American flag at the Rome Olympics in 1960 and lighting the Olympic flame in Los Angeles in 1984). The flattering text by *Sports Illustrated*'s Coles Phinizy spent as much time describing my personal life as my athletic achievements. ''It was the impact of the man himself, rather than his victory, that made Johnson the worthiest sportsman,'' he wrote. ''Ray Johnson is a rare concentrate of some old Sunday school virtues: tolerance, humility and godliness, none of which can be said to be gaining too much ground in this go-get-'em age. Johnson's kind of tolerance is not the diluted brand that sells so cheaply around the world these days, good only among people who already think alike. His is the real thing—by Voltaire's definition, the capacity to be tolerant even of intolerance. His godliness is inconspicuous; he never wears it on his sleeve."

I had mixed feelings about receiving such praise. It made me proud, of course, but also self-conscious. I thought that people would know that such statements were too good to be true. Harder to deal with was praise that was unintentionally demeaning. I was called a credit to my race when I wanted to be a credit to my entire community, or to humanity as a whole. One article called me "one of the most remarkable Negroes in history." Writers praised me so much for being articulate and intelligent that it was as if they were surprised to find those qualities in a black man. I was even called "the tall Tarzan from UCLA," as if the writer couldn't resist a jungle reference even though Tarzan was white. Still, society had progressed a great deal from the days when Joe Louis and Jesse Owens were in the news; and as time went by, white reporters learned to handle the race issue in a more agreeable way.

I tried to go about my business without paying too much attention to the fuss. I stayed realistic by remembering the influences that made me what I was: family, community, and God. No matter how busy I was, I set aside half an hour every day for Bible reading and prayer. In one religious publication, I summed up my feelings this way: "All the trophies and championships received from men will pass away. I would rather strive to be the greatest Christian in the world than the greatest athlete because when the lights go out it will be the Christian team, coached by Christ the Saviour, that will finally win."

I had hoped that by the time classes began in September, 1958, my life would return to normal. I looked forward to playing basketball, serving as president of the student body, and completing my final year of studies. But my usual whirlwind was twice as wild that semester because being student body president took up at least twenty hours a week. Coles Phinizy's profile for *Sports Illustrated* described a day in my life. As soon as I entered my office, he wrote, two secretaries presented me with a list of phone calls and an armful of mail and memos. The State Department wanted to know if I could make another goodwill tour. Another letter inquired about a blood drive. A television station wanted me to speak. Someone else wanted me to give a speech at a dinner. There were letters from the Toluca Lake B'nai B'rith, a Chicago YMCA, the Culver City Rotary Club, the Youth for Christ in Muskegon, and a nurse who says she cared for me when I ripped open my foot in the conveyor belt in Kingsburg. The president of the university system wanted me to serve on a committee. Australia invited me to compete down under. Someone in Sweden wanted my autograph. The Olympic committee asked me to appear in a movie. ''He progresses through the work load,'' wrote Phinizy, ''but not without interruption. Secretaries and officials from other offices come and go, bringing contracts, letters and checks for Johnson to sign. . . . A secretary from somewhere asks if he will pose with a Hula-hoop.''

All of which had little to do with my actual duties as president: presiding over Student Council meetings and various committees, dealing with budget and policy issues, and speaking at special events like the inauguration of President Kerr or the appearance of gubernatorial candidate Edmund ''Pat'' Brown. While I was treated like a king by some people on campus, to those in the student government I was just the guy with a title and a gavel. They didn't hesitate to argue with me just because my picture was in the newspapers. It took a while to get the hang of it all, but I enjoyed the feeling of being an executive. Bill Ackerman, the general manager of the Associated Students, told a reporter that I started out slow in the job but learned quickly and became ''one of the best student body presidents we've ever had.''

Needless to say, all this took away from my study time. On the day Coles Phinizy spent with me, I went to basketball practice at three o'clock, squeezed in an hour of study, spoke to the American Legion about the Olympics at seven o'clock, then studied in the student union building until after midnight because I was sure to be disturbed if I tried to read in my room. It was a nose-to-the-grindstone existence, but training for the decathlon had taught me how to shift attention from one set of demands to another without losing concentration or intensity. Like the decathlon, daily life was a series of constant transition.

Friends who were concerned about my health and my grades advised me to turn down some invitations. But, as an African American, I felt compelled to speak in public whenever I could, to help clear up misconceptions and open doors. "I am not a crusader in the true sense of the word," I told *Sepia,* a magazine for the black community. "And I can't cure all the ills of the world. Nevertheless, I have a feeling I can be of service if I make even one small contribution to better understanding and goodwill."

I also knew I was learning things I could never have learned in a classroom. The best example was the evening I spent with my two biggest heroes. There was a bookstore in Westwood owned by UCLA supporters Bob and Blanche Campbell. I had worked there at one time and continued to stop in to browse. Among the Campbells' friends were UCLA alumni Ralph Bunche and Jackie Robinson. When they heard that I was going to New York for a function, the Campbells arranged for me to meet Mr. Bunche at his office at the United Nations, where he was Undersecretary General for Special Political Affairs. He invited me to dinner at his home. Also present were Mrs. Bunche and Jackie and Rachel Robinson. Jackie had been out of baseball for three years and was a vice-president with Chock full o' Nuts.

I wish I could live that evening all over again. I was so

awestruck that I forgot to ask most of the questions I had in mind. As I remember it, the conversation was not particularly deep or profound. It was simple, pleasant, and relaxed. We talked about our experiences at UCLA and what each of us was doing at the present time. They were curious about me, the youngster, and asked a lot of questions about my life. I'd like to say that one of these great men said something that changed my life forever. But they had already changed my life. That night they stepped down from the pedestals I had built for them in my mind and became real human beings. What I found remarkable about them—and their wives, who were as smart and gracious as they were—was their ability to just be ordinary, and to make me feel perfectly at ease. That, in itself, was a valuable lesson.

My schedule was so packed I had to ask Coach Wooden to excuse me from the early stages of basketball practice. I actually missed a game when I went to New York to receive *Sports Illustrated*'s Sportsman of the Year award on *The Ed Sullivan Show*. The team was on a road trip to the Northwest. After the second game, in Pullman, Washington, I took an all-night flight to New York. I was so wiped out that I fell asleep before we took off and didn't wake up until we landed. Groggy, I got off the plane, jumped into a cab, and said, "Take me to the Roosevelt Hotel." As we drove I kept dozing off. The driver woke me up in front of a hotel entrance. I looked out the window. I had been to the Roosevelt Hotel before, and this was not the same place. I told the driver he'd made a mistake. He looked at me like I was crazy and pointed to a sign. We were at the Roosevelt Hotel all right, only we were in Philadelphia! The plane had made a stopover en route to New York. Luckily we were able to rush back to the airport before the plane took off again.

That night I appeared on the Sullivan show. The orchestra

played "God Bless America" as I was handed the beautiful Grecian urn that *Sports Illustrated* gives to its annual award-winner. A replica of a vase from 510 B.C., the urn symbolizes the concept of *areta,* the unity of virtues of body and mind that the Greeks felt a complete man should have. My flight to Seattle, where I was to meet the basketball team for the next game, was cancelled because of bad weather. I never got there.

For the rest of the season, though, starting at forward, I played solid defense, crashed the boards hard, and hustled for enough layups to lead the team in field goal percentage. It was my last experience in team sports, and it was memorable because of Coach Wooden and a great group of teammates, two of whom stand out in memory: Denny Crum, who went on to national fame coaching the University of Louisville; and Walt Torrence, who averaged 21.5 points a game and would have had an NBA career if he had not been tragically killed in a car accident.

When the season ended in March, I traded in my sneakers for spikes. I was no longer eligible for collegiate track, so I worked out on my own and with C. K. Yang. After the AAU decathlon in 1958, C.K. had stayed in the United States to attend college and get the best track and field training possible. He had been all set to go to USC when he was invited to visit UCLA. The opportunity to train under Ducky, and alongside me, appealed to him. So did being closer to the ocean. "When I went to UCLA my eyes were better," he recalled. "Not so much smog."

This was the beginning of a unique friendship and one of the most unusual competitive relationships in the history of sports. With support from a benefactor in Taiwan, C.K. settled into an apartment in Westwood with his official interpreter, Wei Chen-wu, a coach from Taipei. He started learning English, taking courses to qualify for UCLA admission the following year, and working out with me under the guidance of Ducky Drake and Craig Dixon. Despite the language barrier, we formed a fast friendship. Having seen other foreign students struggle with their new environment (C.K. had been charged about fifty dollars for a taxi ride from the airport that should have cost ten), I tried to help him adjust to American life. I helped him with the language, introduced him to my friends, took him bowling, and invited him to parties, double dates, and other things I did.

When he first arrived, C.K.'s English was so limited he always ordered the same thing in restaurants; "beefsteak" was one of the only words he knew. He learned quickly, just as he did on the track. I've never met a more knowledgeable decathlete. His technical understanding of each event was so solid it was like having a second coach. That and hard work had enabled him to grow from an unknown in Melbourne to a world-class competitor and a threat to my world record. C.K. taught me a lot, especially about the pole vault, which he was so good at that he later broke the world record. I helped him too, especially with the weight events—javelin, discus, and shotput. We worked side by side, pushing each other like teammates with a common purpose, spotting each other's weaknesses and helping to correct them. Each of us understood a basic truth: If I help him be the best he can be, he'll help me be the best I can be. We never faltered in this belief, even at the height of our competition.

The weight events were C.K.'s weak points largely because he was, in his words, "a skinny kid." In Melbourne he had packed less than 170 pounds on his six foot one frame. He said that when he saw me and Milt Campbell, with our bulky upper bodies, he was in awe. To build up his strength, he began lifting weights. That strategy was to have a big impact on *me* as well as C.K.

At the time, the only athletes who lifted weights were body builders, wrestlers, and shotput specialists. For track men, weights were discouraged. The conventional wisdom was that weights would make you slow and inflexible. Some coaches would throw guys off their teams if they were caught lifting. They weren't sophisticated enough to know that weights could build strength in specific muscle groups without sacrificing speed or agility. But some of the younger coaches understood this. One of them was Craig Dixon, who arranged for C.K. to train at an off-campus gym under the guidance of a weight expert named Bruce Conners. In turn, C.K. recommended it to me. It turned out to be one of the most important things I did as an athlete. It made me stronger and enabled me to get more out of my body. Now, of course, every athlete uses some form of weight training.

In the spring of 1959, C.K. and I worked out every day, attracting the attention of writers who called us a "two-man United Nations." Ducky's system was to have us work on general conditioning each day and cover the ten decathlon events on a rotating basis. Ducky spent as many hours at the track as we did. He was there when we arrived and he was still there when we left. To keep a competitive edge, I entered every "all comers" meet I could, either as an independent or a member of the Striders. I was gearing up for a busy summer. That June the National AAU Decathlon was to be held in Kingsburg, the smallest town ever to be given that honor. In July the second U.S.–U.S.S.R. meet was scheduled for Franklin Field in Philadelphia. And the 1959 Pan Am Games were to be held in Chicago in August. I eagerly anticipated all three, but especially the rematch with Vasily Kuznetsov in Philadelphia. On May 17, in Moscow, he had once again broken my world record, this time with 8,367 points.

Then fate intervened once more. My brother Jim had spent a year at Santa Monica Community College, thinking that a year of varsity football at that level would be good preparation for playing at UCLA. Now he was a receiver and defensive back for the Bruins, and my housemate at Pi Lam. It was great to be near Jimmy again. He had grown from a skinny kid to a slim athletic machine who starred in football, basketball, and track, and from a sweet kid to a good friend.

Now Jimmy and I were riding to Kingsburg for our sister Erma's high school graduation. It was early in the morning. Jimmy was driving while I lounged in the back, strumming my guitar and singing, with my legs draped over the front seat. As we descended a long hill on the approach to Bakersfield, a car passed on the left and started to pass the truck in front of us as well. When the driver saw a car coming at him from the other direction, he cut in front of us, forcing Jimmy to swerve. Our car fishtailed. We smashed into a concrete barrier. The impact propelled my body forward, ramming my lower back into the base of the front seat.

Fortunately Jimmy was not hurt and the car was in good enough shape to get us to Kingsburg. My back was stiff and sore the entire weekend; I could not sit without pain. When I returned to Los Angeles, Ducky took me to the UCLA Medical Center for X-rays. Nothing was broken, but the muscles of my lower back were in spasm and the bottom portion of my spinal cord was badly bruised. Some of the bone was crushed, and the tailbone was slightly bent. I stayed in the hospital a short while and then went home with a regimen of physical therapy that Ducky administered in the training room.

During this time I received a letter from Kuznetsov in Russia. "I am very sorry to hear about your injury," he wrote. "I hope you will be able to compete in Philadelphia." I fully expected to be there. I did not think it would take that long to heal, but I was sorely mistaken. I was in so much pain that I did not attend my graduation exercises and had to skip the speech I was supposed to give as student body president. Weeks later, despite whirlpools, massages, ultrasound treatments, and daily wraps, I still could not bend low enough to touch my knees. I had to walk gingerly to avoid pain, and it hurt so much when I sat down that I had to carry a pillow around with me. I could not perform before my loved ones in Kingsburg (happily, my friend C.K. won that meet, becoming the first foreign athlete to win an AAU decathlon). Nor could I defend my Pan Am crown or face Kuznetsov in Philadelphia.

Missing those events was agony. It would be a full year before the next opportunity to take back the world record, assuming I'd be well enough to compete even then. Several times I woke up in the night, soaked in sweat. In one dream a doctor said I would not heal in time for the Olympics. In another, someone hung a second silver medal from my neck.

Injury or no injury, it was time to get on with life after college. My original plan had been to go to dental school. Because I wanted to stay in Los Angeles to train for the Olympics with Ducky, I applied only to UCLA and USC. But the opening of UCLA's new college of dentistry was postponed and, to my surprise, I was not accepted by USC. Many years later, I learned why. A former UCLA classmate, who was then on the USC faculty, had seen my file. He said that I had done well enough on the entrance exam to get into the school, and that students who had not done as well had been admitted. He asked around and discovered that USC had rejected me because I had rejected them when I enrolled at UCLA instead.

I was forced to put dental school on the back burner. Instead I worked part-time for Ducky as an assistant coach and enrolled in graduate courses in education. In addition to classwork, my twelve units toward a master's degree required student teaching at a junior high school. To pay my bills I also worked at a place in Culver City called Hamburger Handout, which served nineteen-cent burgers at a take-out window. (My employer, Jim Collins, went on to found the Sizzler's chain of restaurants.)

It must sound strange that a well-publicized athlete who was expected to represent his country in the next Olympics would be flipping hamburgers. Nowadays, anyone in that position would have enough sponsorship to devote all of his time to training. At the very least, he would be able to get paid for speaking engagements and other public appearances. But back then, corporate sponsorship was forbidden and cashing in on your stature as an athlete in any way would jeopardize your amateur status. In fact, those in charge of amateur athletics were such sticklers for purity that I had to turn down an offer from Hollywood. I was offered a role in *Spartacus,* which starred Kirk Douglas and Laurence Olivier and was directed by Stanley Kubrick. The position of Dan Ferris, head of the AAU, was that I was offered the role only because I was a famous athlete, and therefore I would be considered a professional if I got paid.

On some days, my back would feel okay. But just when I thought I'd turned a corner, I'd move a certain way and the pain would be so bad I could hardly walk. I spent time in the training room, did weight exercises to keep my legs strong, and hung around the track learning whatever I could from the coaches and C.K. And I prayed. Every morning when I started the day, every night when I went to bed, and sometimes in between, I'd ask to be made whole again.

It was not until February 1960, seven months after the accident, that I was able to jog. Gradually I stepped up my regimen, introducing slightly more strenuous work while taking care not to reinjure my back. One afternoon in April, Ducky suggested that I try to sprint. I burst from the blocks and ran about ten yards as C.K. and Ducky watched nervously. No pain! With the Olympics less than three months away, this was an encouraging sign.

Ducky once said, "When an athlete goes in for the decathlon seriously, it's not just a matter of physical conditioning and training, it's a whole way of life." What with teaching, coaching, taking classes, holding a job, giving speeches, and attending church functions, that way of life had to be well-organized if I was going to be on the track three or four hours a day. I could run now, and work on certain decathlon techniques, but jumping was still out of the question. We had to proceed with caution as we fought the clock. If I waited too long to challenge myself, I might not be in shape for the Olympic Trials in July; if I did too much too soon I could destroy all my dreams.

The Trials were less than a month away by the time Ducky felt I was ready to risk a modified long jump. Until that point, I had only run down the runway without jumping. The big fear was that landing in the sand pit might be too jarring for my back. Now I was ready to explode off the board, but instead of pushing for altitude, as I would normally do, I would basically take a long stride forward. Ducky was as tense as an explosive expert defusing a bomb. When I hit the sand, I waited a moment and then slowly stood up. I felt completely normal. We breathed a huge sigh of relief.

With my hopes of gold renewed, I stepped up the intensity of my workouts. But I still did not dare an all-out long jump, and in the high jump and pole vault I practiced only my approach to the bar. I still could not risk landing from such heights. Going into the AAU Decathlon in Eugene, Oregon (which served as the Olympic Trials), I felt confident that Ducky had handled my rehabilitation wisely and I'd had enough time to get ready. But, in the back of my mind, doubts and fears kept cropping up. I had not performed certain events in over a year, and I had not competed in a decathlon for two. Would my back hold up? If it did, was I in good enough shape to perform well?

• • •

To make the Olympic team, all I had to do was place third. I knew I could probably accomplish that without going all out and risking further injury. I went all out anyway. It was just not in my nature to give anything less than my best. Besides, after so much down time, I wanted to see what I was capable of. There is also something about competition that makes an athlete push himself further than he would in practice. The muscles and nerves know that something is different. This is especially true at the Olympic Trials. Everyone thinks the Olympics themselves carry the most pressure. But, if you've been dreaming Olympic dreams, the Trials represent your one chance to get there; if you fail you can't try again for four long years, and in some cases, *never* again.

Even the best athletes know that making the team is not automatic. I'll never forget watching Dan O'Brien, the best decathlete in the world at the time, fail to make the 1992 team when he could not clear a single height in the pole vault. When Dan left the field he looked devastated and bewildered, like a man who had just gotten the biggest shock of his life. It seemed as if all the blood had been drained from his body. He was humiliated. He knew that people would think he had choked. I don't think he choked, but he may have succumbed to pressure on his third vault, when he faltered on the way up. I had been trained to set the bar for the high jump and pole vault fairly low on the first attempt. The idea was to use the first jump to warm up and work out the wrinkles. Starting low also guaranteed that I'd at least post a score. That takes some of the pressure off. But Dan didn't do that, and by his third attempt he may have been spooked, knowing that everything was riding on that final vault. In 1996 he seemed to know that the Trials were different from other meets, and he was able to come back and win the gold.

I entered the Trials thinking that Rome was my last

chance. I would be pushing thirty by the time of the next Olympics, my injuries were a big question mark, and without financial support it would be difficult to train adequately for four more years.

I ran the hundred meters in 10.6. Then came the first big test—my first all-out long jump since my back injury. I landed in the sand with a jolt and held my breath. My back was fine. I felt confident enough to take another jump. Again, no pain. I was so exhilarated that I heaved the shotput fifty-two feet, my best throw ever in a decathlon. Then came another big test: my first high jump. Apprehensive about landing, I cleared only 5′ 10″. But I had no pain! In the 400, I got off to a slow start but finished strong for a 48.5. What mattered most at the end of the day was that my body was sound. The scoreboard told another interesting story: I'd scored 4,750 points, the highest first-day total in history.

I had come to Eugene hoping to get through the meet in one piece and qualify for the Olympics. Now I had a shot at once again breaking the record that Kuznetsov had taken from me. I ran the hurdles in 14.5, then hurled the discus 170′ 6″, an excellent throw that inspired me even further. Now I faced my first pole vault since Moscow, and once again thoughts of reinjuring my back on the landing came to mind. I not only walked away pain-free, but scored a personal best of 13′ 1/4″.

As I moved to the javelin runway, I knew the record was within reach. I was determined to put everything I had into my first throw. I let loose and watched the silver missile soar farther than ever before. It came down 233′ 3″ away. The crowd roared, knowing that something special had happened: I'd broken the world record with one event still to go. Normally, I was self-contained during competition. But this was the culmination of a year of painful, tedious rehabilitation and the result was far more satisfying than anything I could have expected going in. I ran toward the javelin and then, overcome by emotion, kneeled down and offered thanks. One reporter wrote that my "normally stoic face was twisted in an unsuccessful fight against tears."

Of course I still had to run the 1500. I pulled myself together and ran a 5:09.9, fast enough to bring my total to 8,683 points, surpassing Kuznetsov by more than 300. That night, I sent a telegram to my family in Kingsburg: "I did it with God's help. New world's record."

Amidst all the extravagant praise that was heaped on me after the Trials, one thing surprised me: the attention given to something I did during C.K.'s heat in the 1500. I was on the sideline as he approached the final stretch. He seemed to be fading. I thought he was tired, but I later learned he had a cramp in his thigh. I found myself shouting, "Keep going, keep going!" When he crossed the finish line, I threw my arm around him and walked around the track at his side. Since C.K. was my closest competitor, the press viewed this as some kind of amazing act of sportsmanship. To me it was a perfectly natural, automatic response. Growing up in Kingsburg, I had been taught to do my best and to encourage my friends and teammates (and C.K. was both) to do their best. C.K. must have learned the same lesson; during the meet, knowing how apprehensive I was about my injuries, he'd been a constant source of help and encouragement.

Sports Illustrated called my performance "one of the most remarkable athletic achievements of history." Lost in the shuffle was just how remarkable C.K. was. He too had broken Kuznetsov's mark, but he did not get to own the record for even a moment. C.K. seemed destined to walk in my shadow.

For the next month and a half, he and I devoted every minute we could spare to getting ready for Rome. With Ducky, we formed a trio unprecedented in history: the two top contenders for Olympic gold, representing two different countries (C.K. was on the Taiwan team), training together on the same track with the same coach. It was an odd situation: The man I counted on to help me win was helping my opponent beat me. To make the story even more interesting, Ducky was named to the Taiwan coaching staff; he would be in Rome to work with both of us. Only an exceptional human being could have handled such a delicate balancing act. Not for an instant did he display any sign of favoritism. Never did he slight either one of us. If he cared who came out on top, or had an opinion about who would win, he never gave it away. "They are both ready," he told the press before we left for Rome. "I don't know who it will be, but despite their close friendship, both Rafer and Yang want that title. The Russian will have to be a miracle man to whip this pair."

Kuznetsov was no miracle man, but he was a great champion who had already broken my records twice before. His presence added Cold War overtones to an already dramatic story. Relations between the United States and Russia were as tense as ever. Just before the Olympics, Premier Khrushchev vowed to defend Cuba from U.S. intervention, warning that Soviet missiles were now capable of reaching American targets. President Eisenhower replied that the United States would not tolerate a Communist regime in the Western Hemisphere. At the same time, American pilot Francis Gary Powers was on trial in Moscow, having been shot down while on a spy mission over Soviet territory. A scheduled summit conference and Eisenhower's visit to the U.S.S.R. had been called off. (After a three-day trial, Powers was sentenced to ten years in prison.)

At home the Cold War hovered over the presidential campaign, with both John F. Kennedy and Richard M. Nixon flexing their muscles and promising to protect the Free World from the Communist menace. I did not know who would handle foreign affairs better, and I certainly had no idea that I was destined to become linked to the Kennedy family, but JFK won my vote when he said, "The next president must exert the great moral and educational force of his office to help bring equal access to public facilities, from churches to lunch counters, and to support the right of every American to stand up for his rights, even if on occasion he must sit down for them."

Like athletes, the superpowers vied for supremacy in outer space. In *Time* magazine's Olympic preview edition, with me on the cover throwing the javelin, sports metaphors were used to describe Russia's latest advance—sending two dogs into orbit. Russia had won "that week's lap in the space race," said *Time,* and a "scorecard" compared U.S. and Soviet progress. On earth, each country tried to use sports to prove that its system was superior. Angry debates raged over whether the Soviet system of subsidizing athletes violated the Olympic's amateur spirit. On top of all that, Russia's ally, Red China, had fought to get C.K.'s country ousted from the Olympics. In the end it had settled for a compromise: Taiwan could be represented, but it had to be called Formosa—the island's original name—not the Republic of China or Nationalist China. The Communists wanted C.K. to win the gold even less than they wanted me to.

For C.K. and me, what mattered was being the best that we could be on those two crucial days in Rome. We knew that we stood the best chance of doing that if we helped each other. I was already a better athlete because of him, and he was better because of me. Ours was the purest of rivalries: We each wanted the other guy to do well, but we wanted even more to win. So, when a reporter asked me how I thought C.K. would do in Rome, I did not hesitate to reply, "He'll be second."

In truth, I was nowhere near as cocky as that statement suggests. The press had virtually handed me the gold medal. *Sports Illustrated* went so far as to say that the only competition would be for second place. But I knew exactly how good C.K. was, having seen him improve every day for two years. I knew that he might have beaten me at the Trials if he had done well in the high jump instead of coming up short of his personal best by over a foot. And although I feared C.K. more, Kuznetsov was a tremendous athlete who had no doubt worked every bit as hard as I had. Bob Mathias hit the nail on the head when he said, "Let any one of the three have one bad event and school's out."

Before I left for Rome, I was asked to speak at my church. "I'm proud of the honor and mindful of the responsibility of being a member of the U.S. Olympic team," I said. "I feel that my trip to Rome has a double purpose. First, with God's help, I want to do my best to win a gold medal for my country. But equally important, I want to bring a feeling of friendship to the athletes of the eighty-five nations I will meet at the Olympic Village. I ask you to pray with me that in this small way the Olympic Games can contribute to the furtherance of world peace."

The spirit of this ideal was immediately evident when 7,000 athletes gathered in Rome amidst a blend of ancient ruins and modern accommodations. In a sense, the 1960 Games inaugurated a new Olympic era. Not only were more countries and more athletes present than ever before, but new training methods had elevated the level of competition. It was a rare day that at least one record wasn't broken. World War II had been over for a decade and a half, and the animosities of that period had faded considerably. A new generation had come of age and looked forward to a bright and peaceful future. Perhaps the biggest change, though, was television. For the first time, viewers in the United States could see Olympic highlights on the same day the events took place.

In the Olympic Village, men and women of every race and nationality mixed eagerly, exchanging souvenirs, snapping photos, singing, dancing, struggling with language differences to make small talk and discuss big issues. Most encouraging was the open mingling of Russians and Americans, a big change from the restrictions of the past. No one could explain what had caused the Soviets to lighten up, but everyone welcomed it. At one point my friend and nemesis, Kuznetsov, popped up at a patio party for the U.S. and Soviet teams. When a reporter asked him how he felt, he took out a piece of paper and wrote down a list of figures. They were the scores he predicted he'd achieve in each of the ten decathlon events. Smiling, he added up the total: 8,176 points. Then, said the reporter, "he wrote down Johnson's total—8,683—and stopped smiling."

I don't know if Vasily was being honest or trying to make me overconfident, but there was no doubting his friendship when he smiled broadly and asked me to pose for a picture with him. I said, "Sure, but I'd like to include a friend," and pulled C.K. over to join us. Kuznetsov immediately drew back and looked around to see who was watching. He did not know how Soviet officials would take to him posing with a Nationalist Chinese. I managed to coax him into it. He pretended to scowl at C.K., and said to him, "Okay, but I don't know you."

The photo, with the three of us smiling and our arms around each other, appeared in newspapers around the world. So did countless other pictures of friendly athletes of different races and nationalities, some of whom were supposed to be mortal enemies. The impact of the pictures on the conscience of humanity was incalculable. So were the verbal messages we sent out. "In sports we do not carry on a cold war," Kuznetsov told *Newsweek.* "We have heated contests, but they are athletic ones. If everyone in the world were an athlete, we would have a much better chance for peace. We would break records—not each other's heads." I could not have agreed more.

Moments like that were vivid proof that I had done the right thing when I was confronted with a decision prior to the

Games. Activists had tried to organize an Olympic boycott by black athletes to protest racial conditions in America. I was well aware of the tragic irony of black athletes bringing glory to the nation while others were fighting for the right to eat at a lunch counter. Earlier that year, a demonstration at a Woolworth's in North Carolina had sparked a series of sit-ins that spread to a hundred cities in twenty states and led to over 3,000 arrests. But I felt strongly that politics had no place in the Olympic movement. I also felt that black athletes could contribute more to the cause of equality by showing up, doing their best, and conducting themselves with dignity.

My decision was validated when I was named captain of the American team. The title carried with it the honor of marching with the nation's flag in the opening ceremonies. Normally that distinction is given to a previous gold medalist or a veteran participating in his last Olympics. Our team had nine members competing for the fourth time. That the honor was given to me instead was extraordinary.

Because it was the first time a person of color had been named captain, the choice generated a tremendous amount of attention. I was the most interviewed and photographed American in Rome. "The selection of Johnson would seem to be a reaffirmation before the world of tolerance and rationality in these embarrassing days of racial controversy," wrote Melvin Durslag. Another columnist said, "He was chosen simply because he's our finest athlete, a typical leader and a man of whom we all can be proud. The Olympic committee has been criticized over the years for the way it has bungled many issues, but in this case it scored a 10-strike." A British journalist called my selection "an example of true democracy at its best." The picture of me in a blue blazer, white pants, white straw hat and red striped tie, walking at the head of our delegation with the stars and stripes, appeared on the cover of *Sports Illustrated* and in countless newspapers. All of which probably did more good than a boycott would have.

It was 90 degrees and humid when we marched into the magnificent Stadio Olympico for the opening ceremonies. A hundred thousand spectators gave our delegation a deafening ovation, second in volume only to the roar for the Italian team. The thrill was so intense it was all I could do to walk straight and keep from dropping Old Glory. When we passed the box in which Italy's President Giovanni Gronchi sat, I kept my eyes straight ahead and held the colors high and proud, continuing the American custom of not dipping the flag to the host country's ruler. Then we joined the rainbow of other countries in formation.

As the Olympic flag was raised and cannons thundered and hundreds of doves were released, as the Olympic flame was lit and the oath was recited and the games were declared open, I contemplated the words spelled out in lights on the huge scoreboard. They had been spoken half a century earlier by Baron Pierre de Coubertin, the founder of the modern Olympics: "The most important thing in the Olympic Games is not to win but to take part, just as the most important thing in life is not to have conquered but to have fought well." It is a noble ideal, I thought, and I would try to live up to it. But I'd fought well in Melbourne and lost; this time I was determined to conquer.

Every day, the American quarters at the Olympic Village seemed to buzz with amazement—either over some great victory or a stunning defeat. Ours was called the best team the United States had ever assembled. To many Olympic historians it still is. In track and field, we broke two world and nine Olympic records. The basketball team was led by two legends, Oscar Robertson and Jerry West (the Magic Johnson and Michael Jordan of their time), and also included future NBA stars Jerry Lucas and Walt Bellamy. The team went undefeated in Rome, averaging over one hundred points a game.

Then there was the amazing Wilma Rudolph. One of twenty-two children in an impoverished family in Tennessee, Wilma was stricken early on with polio. She wore a brace on her leg until she was ten. In Rome, at twenty, she won gold medals in the 100 and the 200 meters, setting new Olympic standards in both, then anchored the women's 400-meter relay team as it broke the world record. More than a magnificent achievement, this was a turning point in women's sports, not to mention racial equality: Her homecoming ceremony in Clarksville, Tennessee, was the first integrated event in the town's history.

Most legendary of all was a brash eighteen-year-old boxer named Cassius Clay. Even then, the lightning fists and dazzling tongue that would make him, as Muhammad Ali, the most famous person in the world were very much in evidence. I loved him then, and I love him now, even though his personality was the exact opposite of mine—or maybe *because* of it. I spoke to the press only when asked; he couldn't shut up. I never predicted victory unless I was pushed into it; he shouted it from the rooftops in verse. He was so clever and likable that his antics never seemed arrogant to me, just part of some master plan. It was obvious even then that he was meant to make a mark in the world. I got to know him well when we lectured at colleges after the Games. At times I thought it would be great to be like him.

Rumor had it that Cassius and sprinter Ray Norton were competing for Wilma's affections. Many believe that the rivalry was the cause of Ray's disappointing performance. He had entered the Games as the overwhelming favorite in both the 100 and the 200 meters, but ran out of contention in both. It was the first time since 1928 that an American had not won those events. Then, in the 4 × 100 relay, the United States was disqualified because Ray received the baton outside the exchange zone. Norton wasn't the only American disappointment. Charley Dumas and John Thomas were beaten in the high jump by Russians; Harold Connolly failed to get a medal in the hammer throw; Parry O'Brien had to settle for silver in the shotput. But Ray received most of the press, probably because so much had been expected of him, and because of his romantic connection to Wilma.

Even with all that talent and all those great stories, the decathlon received an amazing amount of attention. Trying to ignore the buildup, C.K. and I worked out with our respective teams and also together, with Coach Drake. Like King Solomon, Ducky dispensed wisdom to both of us with impeccable fairness.

I awoke on the morning of the competition at six o'clock. The butterflies that had fluttered in my belly the night before were gone, driven away by adrenaline. I felt loose, strong, and focused, prepared to win at any cost. I knew very well that C.K. and Kuznetsov were as determined and confident as I was. Either one was capable of emerging two days later as "the world's greatest athlete." I could not afford a single lapse. I prayed that I might perform at my best.

The overcast, muggy morning reminded me of summers in the San Joaquin Valley when my brothers and I would fish in the river, glancing up at the gray sky in hopes of keeping the rain away. Only instead of torn-up sneakers, I had track shoes, and instead of a fishing pole, I had a javelin and a steel pole for vaulting. Instead of sitting around waiting for fish to bite, I was about to push myself to the limit, physically and emotionally—"to be fierce ten times," as George Eastment, our coach at the Moscow meet, had put it.

It's a good thing I didn't believe in omens. Four consecutive times, an opponent jumped the gun to start the hundred meters. One false start is frustrating; four can be exhausting.

Once, I ran a full forty meters before I heard the recall gun. I was so bothered by the distraction that I lacked sharpness when we finally ran the race. I finished with a 10.9, three-tenths of a second slower than at the Trials. That may not seem like much, but it represented a 132-point difference in decathlon scoring. I tried not to think about it, or the fact that C.K. and Kuznetsov had run in different heats without expending energy on false starts.

My first long jump was only 23′ 7³/₄″. My second was almost a foot less. Dissatisfied with those efforts, I dug a little deeper and managed to exceed twenty-four feet on my last try. Still, I was not happy with myself when we broke for lunch. I was ahead of Kuznetsov, but behind C.K. by 130 points.

When we resumed at three o'clock, I was determined to make up lost ground. The shotput was one of my strengths and one of C.K.'s weaknesses. On my second throw I exploded with a toss of nearly fifty-two feet. C.K.'s best was under forty-four. I was now ahead by 143 points. The sky above the stadium grew ominously dark.

Just before six o'clock, as the high jump competition began, the clouds burst open. Some ran for cover, but many spectators sat in their seats covered by whatever they could find, determined to see the drama unfold. I sat in a training room inside the stadium, keeping to myself and trying to maintain my physical and mental edge. When the downpour continued I decided I'd be better off resting, so I went to sleep. Finally, more than two hours after the rain started, we were back on the field. It was dark and chilly, and we had to warm up all over again. Only a fraction of the 40,000 spectators had stuck it out through the deluge. One of them, I learned a few years later, was Betsy Thorsen, my future wife.

I high-jumped 6′ ³/₄″. C.K. topped that by two inches, narrowing my lead to seventy-five points. I went to the training room and got a rubdown to loosen my muscles for the 400-

meter race. It was nearly 11:00 P.M. when we lined up in the starting blocks, which were partly submerged in a puddle. This time C.K. and I were in the same heat. I got off to a fast start, but C.K. passed me on the last curve and burst ahead by five yards. I fought back, but did not have the juice to close the gap completely. I finished at 48.3 to C.K.'s 48.1.

Nearly fifteen hours after taking the field that morning, I collapsed into a seat on the bus and returned to the Olympic Village. I went straight to the cafeteria for the first real food I'd had since breakfast. Because of the rain, our normal routine had been thrown completely out of whack. I was not pleased with my performance. I led by fifty-five points, but that was nothing. In Eugene I'd led C.K. by almost 200 at the end of day one and he still nearly beat me. Kuznetsov was basically out of contention. Perhaps not fully recovered from an ankle injury he'd incurred two months earlier, he had not even reached the 4,000-point mark.

By the time I got to sleep it was after 1:00 A.M. Five hours later, I awakened tired and sore. After a light breakfast, I boarded a bus to the stadium. The pressure inside me was intense. I was the favorite, the world-record holder, the captain of my team, trying to complete the quest I had begun nearly ten years earlier. But I faced a competitor whose skill and staying power I was all too familiar with. I had always used pressure to spur me on and rev me up. That morning, I tried once again to turn it into a positive force.

I may have tried too hard. The key to the hurdles is to spend as much time on the ground as possible. You want to take off as close to each barrier as you can, clear it by as little as you can, and come back down as quickly as you can. If you watch a hurdler, you'll see that he or she seems to be running before the trailing leg hits the ground. Normally hurdling was my best event. Rome was a major, and almost disastrous, exception.

It was hot and humid. I had not gotten much sleep. I decided to conserve energy by shortening my warmup ritual. This was one of the biggest mistakes I made in my athletic career. My body was simply not stretched and ready for action. When the starting gun went off, I felt completely out of rhythm. I smashed into the second barrier and nearly toppled over. Fortunately I regained my stride and finished the race, but the 15.3 was my worst time since my very first decathlon six years earlier. To make things tougher, C.K. had run a good 14.6, taking the lead by 138 points. At the Trials I had been *ahead* by 62 after the hurdles.

It was shaping up as the closest decathlon in Olympic history, and I faced an uphill battle. I put on my sweats and walked over to Ducky. He told me what I needed to hear: Don't get down, it's far from over, and your best events are coming up.

In my entire career, I had never felt as much pressure as I did before the discus throw. If C.K. were to keep his lead now, I'd really be in hot water. My first two attempts were disappointing. I put every ounce of strength into the third throw. It soared to 159′ 1″.

Looking back, I would call that throw the single most competitive moment in my career, and my single best effort. When I see myself on film, whirling in the ring and letting loose the discus, I can almost feel the incredible energy and intensity I felt that day. I picked up 272 points on C.K. I was ahead by 134.

It was two-thirty when we began the pole vault, and the heat and humidity had become more oppressive. Now it was C.K.'s turn to have his strongest event. A superb vaulter, he sailed over the bar at 14′ 1¼″. But I came through with my best decathlon vault ever: 13.5¼″. I still had the lead, but it was only twenty-two points.

I had hoped to wrap up a victory after the javelin, as I had at the Trials. I hated the thought of having everything ride on that onerous 1500, especially against a guy who was a better distance-runner than I was. I approached the javelin with the intention of padding my lead and, if possible, putting myself out of C.K.'s reach. My best throw came down at just under 230 feet. That was about six feet better than C.K.'s throw, but it didn't add much to my lead. I felt I'd let myself down. On film I seem to lack energy and quickness. My approach was too slow and my body too upright when I threw. This meant that less body weight was behind the release. I attribute the mistake to a lapse in concentration. I may have been thinking too much.

It came down to the final event, the 1500 meters. This had not happened in the Olympics since 1920, when Brutus Hamilton—my friend and the athletic director at Berkeley—led Helge Lovland of Norway after nine events only to lose the 1500 by nine seconds and the gold by thirty-two points. It was ten o'clock, thirteen hours after the day's work had begun. The moon was full. The tension was as thick as the humidity. Between me and my goal were 1500 brutal meters. I was ahead by a precarious sixty-seven points. I didn't have to win the race, but I could not let C.K. win by more than ten seconds. It wasn't going to be easy. C.K.'s personal best was fifteen seconds better than mine, and he had beaten me by twenty-three seconds at Palmyra.

As if it had been scripted for dramatic purposes, we were running in the same heat. We warmed up and stretched, trying not to look at each other. This was no time for our usual camaraderie. I walked over to the stands to speak to Ducky. His advice was to stay on C.K.'s heels, not let him pull away, and be prepared for a hellish sprint at the end. I looked my coach in the eye, shook his hand and walked away, thinking, "This is my last race. No matter how much it hurts, I'm going to stay with C.K.''

As I ambled toward the starting line, I saw C.K. walk over to Ducky. Afterward, I learned what the coach had told him: Build up a big lead and go all out in the final quarter-mile. With perfect impartiality he had told each of us what we had to do to win.

Now came what one writer called ''the most dramatic head-and-head competition in the history of track and field.'' There were others in the race, including a Swiss athlete named Fritz Vogelsang who set a lightning pace, but none of them mattered. All that mattered to me was to not let C.K. open up a lead.

I stuck to him like a shadow, dogging his footsteps stride for stride. About midway through the race, C.K. picked up the pace. I stayed with him, on his inside shoulder, a couple of strides behind. Then I moved to his right side. Runners are trained to turn only to their right if they have to look behind them, and I wanted to be in C.K.'s face. I thought that knowing I was still with him might deflate his will. But he was too gutsy for that. On the third lap, he caught me by surprise and took off in an all-out, desperate sprint. By now my strength was almost gone, but I could not let him get away. Dipping into my last dregs of energy, I sprinted after him and stayed on his heels all the way to the finish line.

I finished two strides and 1.2 seconds behind him. I knew I had won the decathlon. What I didn't know was that I had run the fastest 1500 meters of my life. Anything less and I'd have gone home with another silver medal, because C.K. had run *his* fastest as well. I also didn't know that my 8,392 points had broken the Olympic decathlon record. So had C.K.'s 8,334. Once again that gallant warrior had to settle for second best.

I had cleared my final hurdle.

When I crossed the finish line, I caught up to C.K. and leaned my head on his shoulder. I just wanted to be next to him at that moment, so great was my respect and admiration for him. We walked together for a while, trying to keep our legs from buckling, leaning on each other physically the way we had leaned on each other emotionally for the past two years. We were too exhausted to utter a sound, but each of us could feel what the other was thinking. As good as I felt about winning, I felt equally bad that my friend had lost; as bad as he felt about losing, he felt equally glad that his friend had won.

When we returned to the finish line to put on our sweats and get ready to leave the track, Ducky and Mr. Wei were waiting. The four of us embraced. Not a word was said, but we knew we had all accomplished something great together. On the way to the exit tunnel, another old friend came over. Vasily Kuznetsov, who had finished a distant third, kissed me on the cheek.

In the locker room I was mobbed by reporters and photographers. I don't remember much of what happened in that room, it was such a blur. But the quotes attributed to me ring true:

- I never thought at any time that I would lose. I didn't know how I was going to win, but I knew I must and I would.
- Winning this compensates for every ounce of energy and every hour of time I put into it. There is satisfaction in putting your body and mind to a great test and coming through.
- I don't know what I'll do next or where my athletic ambitions—if any—will lead. It's too soon to make up my mind. But no more decathlon. I never want to go through that again—never. This is my last one, and you can print that.
- Tonight I'm going to shower and then just walk for about four hours and look at the moon. I don't know where—just walk, walk, walk. I've got to unwind. I'm through, man, I'm through.

And that's what I did. I had slept only five hours the night before and had spent nearly thirty hours on the track in two days. I had never been so exhausted in my life. But I couldn't sleep. I was too wound up, too happy, and it hurt too much to lie down. I showered, ate, and wandered the streets of Rome, looking at the moon and thinking about what I had just done.

I hadn't slept a wink when, the next morning, I climbed the platform, flanked by C.K. and Kuznetsov, and bent forward for Avery Brundage to place the gold medal around my neck. I cried like a baby when they played our National Anthem.

7

SPINNING INTO REAL LIFE

To every thing there is a season, and a time to every purpose under the heaven.

—ECCLESIASTES, 3:1

DECEPTIVELY COMPLEX, the discus throw calls upon a unique set of skills. You have to turn your body about one-and-a-half rotations and move forward at the same time, remaining within a concrete circle that's slightly more than eight feet in diameter. While spinning, you have to pay attention to various technical details—for example, dipping your shoulder just the right amount—so you get the most leverage when you release the 4.5-pound discus. Coordination and flexibility are as important as strength and foot speed. If you don't move in a straight line and complete your spin in perfect alignment, your throw will not achieve maximum distance.

In the period after Rome, my life was like a discus throw. While whirling from the thrill of victory, I had to keep my feet on the ground, maintain my balance, and make sure I was pointed in the right direction as I hurled myself out of athletics and into real life. This would have been challenging at any time, but the social and political upheavals of that period made it all the more demanding. Between 1961 and 1967, America witnessed the Cuban missile crisis, the erection of the Berlin Wall, and the escalation of the war in Vietnam; President Kennedy's assassination (which affected me deeply, not only as an American and a black man but as a friend of Robert Kennedy and his family); the growth of the civil rights movement despite murders, lynchings, riots, and stubborn opposition; the antiwar movement, "flower power", sexual freedom, and other expressions of the counterculture. In the midst of this whirlwind, I was trying to find my place in the world.

Once again, one award after another was bestowed upon me: Associated Press Athlete of the Year; California Athlete of the Year (for the second time); track and field honors at the Tops in Sports banquet; the coveted Sullivan Award, given to "the amateur athlete who by performance, example, and good influence did the most to advance the cause of good sportsmanship during the year" (in 1956 I had come in second in the balloting to Olympic diver Pat McCormick, and in 1958 I had finished second to Army halfback Glenn Davis in what was then the closest vote ever). I was also honored by civic organizations like the Junior Chamber of Commerce, B'nai B'rith, the National Conference of Christians and Jews, and the George Washington Carver Memorial Institute. Receiving that last organization's Merit Award was one of my proudest moments, since the only previous athlete to win it was Jackie Robinson.

As always, the most moving tributes came from my hometown. The *Kingsburg Recorder*'s Olympic coverage included this report:

> The community should be proud of Rafer Johnson, not only as an athlete but as an individual. Tobacco chewing, beer drinking, loud talking athletes receive the plaudits of the crowd so long as they can hit a baseball or run with a football. There are communities proud of being their home towns. But how proud can they be of the individual as an individual, not just as an athlete?
>
> Quantities of character are at least as important as physical ability, even in this day when standards seem to be no higher than the gutter. When character and ability are combined, you have an unusual individual. They are combined in Rafer Johnson. Writers have come to Kingsburg to try and discover what makes him as he is. They seem baffled. Why it should be unusual to have a young American with high moral standards and outstanding athletic ability is a question. Perhaps fame does something to the head, and to the heart; makes one bigger and the other smaller.

I have included this to show how proud Kingsburg made me feel, and also to point out that the character of athletes was an issue forty years ago, before Dennis Rodman was born or end-zone dances were invented.

Everyone in my jubilant family shared in the glory, even Ed, who was in the Army and stationed in Germany. "When my platoon sergeant found out who my brother was, life in the Army got pretty good," he wrote. My mother told the *Recorder,* "This is the proudest moment of my life. I've had thrills before, even when he was a little boy in elementary school and won some ribbons, but this year has been the biggest. . . . I can hardly wait now until he gets home." Neither could I, and this time the homecoming celebration topped all previous receptions.

The awards and accolades kept coming, well into the next year. My life story was the subject of a documentary produced by David L. Wolper and narrated by Mike Wallace. I was also honored on the television program *This Is Your Life.* But at the end of the day I was still a twenty-five-year-old facing decisions about his life. If a gold medalist today were to receive as much attention as I had for six straight years, he would already be a wealthy man. In this age of professionalism, he would be getting paid for speaking engagements, commercials, and endorsements. He would also have the incentive and means to continue in sports. But in those days there was no monetary payoff for track and field stars. The thought of torturing my battered body for another four years of training while trying to hold down some kind of job to make ends meet was more than I was willing to do—especially since it would mean postponing until I was thirty any real progress on a postathletic career.

Actually, I did have an opportunity in professional sports. To my amazement, the Los Angeles Rams drafted me. I considered signing with them, but I did not think my knee and other injuries could hold up to the daily pummeling of pro football. Plus, the only gridiron experience I'd had in five years was tossing a ball on the frat house lawn. Although I might have had enough size, speed, and raw talent, my football education had stopped at the high school level. I felt that my lack of experience made me a longshot at best. Evidently the Rams' general manager, Pete Rozelle (who went on to great fame as the NFL commissioner), felt the same way, or else he would have drafted me earlier than the twenty-eighth round!

I also had offers from the Harlem Globetrotters and the Los Angeles franchise of the American Basketball Association. I turned down the ABA because the money was inadequate and I wasn't sure I had the desire or the skills to excel at basketball on the professional level. As for the Trotters, much as I loved watching them, I simply did not want to live my life on the road. Mainly, however, my whole life until then had revolved around sports, and I'd had enough of the physical ordeal, the pain, and the constant pressure. It was time to call "time out" and use other skills and meet other challenges.

A generation earlier, Jesse Owens had tried to make a living off his Olympic glory. He ended up tap dancing on tour with Eddie Cantor and racing against horses and trains in exhibitions. I had better opportunities than Jesse had, but nowhere near what would await Bruce Jenner in 1976; and Bruce did not have what Carl Lewis or Florence Griffith Joyner or Dan O'Brien would have in later years. The changes in the life of a track star have been enormous, thanks to television and the loosening of restrictions on amateurism. Still, even in 1960, my fame opened doors that were not open to every recent college graduate, and certainly not every African American.

I might have gone ahead with my original plan to become a dentist, but UCLA still had not opened its dental school and would not do so for another four or five years. By then I was earning a living in other ways and enjoying it. I suppose my desire to be a dentist never really burned strongly enough.

The first opportunity to present itself came from Hollywood, when Twentieth Century-Fox offered me an acting contract. I'm sure my name recognition appealed to the studio more than my talent, but I wasn't a complete novice. Acting had been an interest of mine ever since I performed in school plays and community theater in Kingsburg. Other athletes had turned to acting, notably John Wayne, Chuck Conners, and Jim Brown. Athletes bring to acting such qualities as body control, concentration, and discipline, which can help make up for a lack of formal training. They are also used to performing under pressure and know how to turn nervousness into energy. Responding to the starting gun on the track is not unlike responding to "Action!" on a movie set. Preparing for a meet or a game is not unlike rehearsing. Working with a coach is not unlike working with a director. It seemed a natural transition and a new, exciting challenge.

At the press conference announcing my signing, Robert Goldstein, head of production, predicted that at Fox I would become "a big star." The legendary Hollywood reporter Hedda Hopper wrote in her column, "Rafer has the poise and dignity of a king. There is a gentleness and honesty about him along with his competitive spirit which lifts your heart." Well, I never became a big star, and the closest I got to playing a king was a role as an African tribal leader. But I put whatever "poise and dignity" I had to use in a number of minor roles in minor movies, and I had a lot of fun along the way.

In many respects, being in Fox's stable of young actors was like being in college. We studied drama, worked on our speech and acting techniques, and learned skills such as fencing and fighting for use in action scenes. Some of my classmates—James Brolin, Sam Elliott, Katharine Ross—went on to become stars. Over the next few years I appeared in a number of films for Fox and other studios. The ones I remember best are:

Sergeant Rutledge. Directed by the legendary John Ford, this was about a sergeant in an all-black cavalry unit who is court-martialed for a rape and murder he didn't commit. Ford's social conscience, so evident in films like *The Grapes of Wrath,* was very much at work in this picture. The newspaper ad contained this headline: SEE HOW MUCH THE COLOR OF THE SKIN WEIGHS ON THE SCALES OF JUSTICE!! The title role was played by Woody Strode, a fine actor who had played football at UCLA with Jackie Robinson. I played one of the Buffalo Soldiers, as the black cavalrymen were called, and can be seen riding in formation and battling Indians; many of the soldiers were played by black athletes, including my brother Jim. Part of the time we were on location in Monument Valley, where

Ford had shot so many magnificent scenes in his early Westerns.

The Sins of Rachel Cade. Set in the Congo but actually shot in Burbank, this featured Angie Dickinson as a missionary nurse who gets involved in a love triangle with Peter Finch and Roger Moore. As Kosongo, a native who works in Angie's clinic, I'm on-screen a lot but I don't say much. Angie was one of the most likeable people I met in Hollywood. We stayed in touch for years and would run into each other at political and charity functions.

The Fiercest Heart. Another movie set in Africa and shot at a studio, this one stars Stuart Whitman, Juliet Prowse, Raymond Massey, and Geraldine Fitzgerald. I play Nzobo, one of the natives who guides a wagon train of Boer settlers through hostile territory. I don't have much dialogue, but I do get to show off my javelin technique, throwing spears at the Zulus who attack the caravan.

Wild in the Country. This featured an unusual combination: Elvis Presley and a script by Clifford Odets, the dramatist known for intense social-protest plays like *Waiting For Lefty* and *Awake and Sing*. Elvis plays a backwoods delinquent who aspires to a literary career. I'm in a couple of scenes, playing a lawyer named Davis who has no impact on the story. Unfortunately, I was with Elvis only long enough to shake his hand.

None but the Brave. This is best remembered as Frank Sinatra's directing debut. I play a member of the crew of an American troop plane that crashes on a remote Pacific island only to encounter Japanese soldiers who don't know the war is over. In my best scene, I'm attacked by an enemy soldier while trying to capture a boat so my comrades and I can escape. We fight it out in the water. I knock him out and swim back to the boat, only to meet my doom when another Japanese soldier tosses a grenade into the boat. The entire shoot, on the spectacular Hawaiian island of Kauai, was a blast. Sinatra, who also starred in the film, could not have been more gracious; the other players could not have been better company, and the accommodations—a lush resort next to the set—could not have been more idyllic.

The Pirates of Tortuga. This swashbuckling film about buccaneers in the Caribbean was shot entirely on the Fox lot, largely in a huge water tank that was used for a television series called *Adventures in Paradise.* As John Gammel, a pirate on the side of the good guys, I have to steer my ship through gun battles on rough seas, which were created by rocking the "boat" in the tank. It was a lot of fun, as were the scenes with fencing and hand-to-hand combat.

A Global Affair. In this Bob Hope comedy, a baby is found at the United Nations and women from various nations try to convince Bob to give them the child. I was in one scene, as a delegate from Nigeria. In later years I appeared on Bob's television show a couple of times. He and I exchange Christmas cards to this day.

Tarzan and the Great River and **Tarzan and the Jungle Boy.** By the time these films were shot, Hollywood had already made thirty-two Tarzan movies, many of which featured Olympic medalists like Johnny Weismuller and Buster Crabbe in the title role. The two I was in starred Mike Henry, an ex-linebacker for the Rams. Neither film was a candidate for an Academy Award but I still enjoy watching them, and being on location in Brazil was quite an adventure. They were shot back-to-back, along with one episode of the Tarzan television series; this kept me in South America for over a year.

While shooting the first Tarzan film, Mike Henry got bitten by a chimp and could not come to the set for quite a while. The director, Robert Day, worked around the star's absence, expanding my part as Chief Barcuna. (I suggested that I play

Tarzan instead, but he didn't go for it.) I played the bad guy, the leader of a cult called the Leopard Men who pillage villages and enslave their inhabitants. Tarzan kills me in a spectacular fight that starts on a bamboo bridge and ends in the river.

The second Tarzan film was especially memorable to me because my brother Ed played my twin brother. Our father, the chief of the tribe, is dying. To determine which son will inherit his rule, he has them compete in a series of athletic contests. As the evil twin Nagambi, I try to kill my brother during the competition. I actually had to swim, hurdle, jump, and pole-vault. I had kept in shape with regular workouts, and actually weighed less than I had at the Olympics, but doing take after take seemed more grueling than a decathlon. There was even a distance run through jungle terrain, where Nagambi tries all sorts of nasty things to do away with his brother. The brother manages to survive, and later kills Nagambi in a duel with spears. All of which is just a subplot while Tarzan searches for a lost boy.

It was enormous fun to play someone so unlike myself, to pretend to be evil and put on war paint and speak in the Hollywood version of a tribal accent. It was also a great opportunity to bond again with my real-life brother. Whereas Jimmy had lived in Los Angeles for a few years, Eddie had been away in the Army and we'd missed each other. We lived through some wild times during that shoot: torrential rains, terrible floods, an invasion of snakes, an expensive set destroyed by fire, a shootout between drunks at a samba party. At one point the producer hired a local shaman to try and stop the disasters. But it wasn't all bad; we spent a lot of "down time" on Copacabana beach in Rio and got to enjoy the world-renowned Carnival.

I also appeared in several television shows during that period. If you watch old reruns you might catch me rescuing Lassie, or appearing on *Dragnet* (with O. J. Simpson), *The Six Million Dollar Man,* or *Alfred Hitchcock Presents.*

• • •

These acting credits took several years to earn, since the work came sporadically. There were very few substantive roles for black actors then, and those that did come up went to guys like Sidney Poitier and Harry Belafonte, who had certain advantages such as professional experience and exceptional talent. Looking back on it, I think I made a mistake by not getting help from an agent or a lawyer. Naively, I had Bill Ackerman, who administered the Associated Students of UCLA, negotiate my deal with Fox. Bill was well-intentioned and a very good friend, but he did not know the intricacies of Hollywood. An agent might have obtained better terms and, more important, guided my career so I might have had better opportunities.

Another obstacle to my success as an actor was my mixed feelings about Hollywood. I didn't know if I wanted to spend the rest of my life in such an uncertain world. The money was great when you worked, and the life was often exciting. But it wasn't like sports, where the goals were clear and I was willing to make any sacrifice to attain them. In movies there did not seem to be a direct correlation between hard work and success. It seemed whimsical and arbitrary, with people becoming stars for reasons that had little to do with their dedication or skill. Nothing you could do would guarantee that you would find work, and I was uncomfortable with that.

I also wasn't sure I wanted to run in Hollywood circles to the extent it was necessary for advancement. I attended dozens of Hollywood functions, usually in support of a charity or political cause that mattered to me, and was often surrounded by celebrities. I was also active in both the Screen Actors Guild and the American Federation of Television and Radio Artists, sitting on both boards and getting involved in equal opportunity efforts. These activities and the film work itself enabled me to meet some wonderfully creative, decent people, like John Ford, whose home near UCLA I would often visit to talk about sports and movies. But I also met my share of superficial, self-centered people, and I had no interest in the glamorous "Tinseltown" night life, no matter how much it might advance my career.

Most of all, I wanted to work at something that had a real impact on people's lives. If I thought I could do what Sidney Poitier was doing—play major roles in high-quality films that changed the way the public viewed important issues—I might have found the motivation to pursue acting more vigorously. But playing a native in Tarzan movies was not my idea of meaningful work.

For all these reasons, I was wide open when another opportunity presented itself.

People to People International had been started in 1956 by President Eisenhower. Its purpose was to promote international goodwill by creating opportunities for ordinary Americans to get to know the citizens of other countries. The Sister City program was part of that effort, along with exchanges of letters, literature, and personal visits. By the early 1960s, People to People was in need of a booster shot. Two young men from the Midwest who were active in the organization, Bill Dawson and Rick Barnes, went to Bill's uncle—J. C. Hall, the founder of Hallmark Greeting Cards—and asked for his help. Mr. Hall provided office space in Kansas City and a substantial infusion of cash, and the program was reestablished as a nonprofit, nongovernmental organization. Former president Eisenhower was Chairman of the Board of Trustees, which consisted of such eminent people as Walt Disney, Eddie Rickenbacker, Norman Rockwell, David Sarnoff, Lowell Thomas, Jesse Owens, and Ralph Bunche.

I had met Bill and Rick when they were at the University of Kansas and I was student body president at UCLA. Knowing of my interest in international exchanges and helping foreign students adapt to America, they asked me to help develop the university aspect of the program. Because I did not want to live in the Midwest permanently, I kept my apartment in Los Angeles and took a room in the home of a black family in Kansas City.

Bill, Rick, and I traveled constantly, setting up programs on campuses around the country. That first year we spoke at 400 colleges in twenty-four states. In some places it was unusual to see a black man and two white men traveling together. We were gaped at, and in some cases ostracized. I remember being turned away from a motel in Oklahoma City. The fact that we were to meet with the governor of Oklahoma the next day meant nothing. We stayed instead at a motel in the black section of town. The next day we told the governor of our experience, and he promised to phone the motel and make sure it never happened again. From then on we planned more carefully and made reservations in advance.

Eventually, People to People set up a West Coast office in downtown Los Angeles and I was put in charge. I enjoyed my work, believed very strongly in the organization's goals, and found the results of our work thrilling. Making the job even more ideal, I was given a great deal of flexibility to make movies, give speeches, and volunteer time to worthy organizations. Many of the films described above were made while I was on leave from People to People. I guess I was never cut out for a normal routine, or for specialization. As with the decathlon, I have always thrived on variety and the excitement of going from one challenge to another.

Thanks to the great support I had from the People to People staff, I was able to pursue those other interests without compromising my responsibilities. I served on the California State Recreation Commission, for example, traveling around the state to help set up local youth programs. I made a trip to Israel for the Maccabee Games, serving as a special coach along with high-jumper John Thomas. I made the Tarzan movies in Brazil, serving People to People at the same time by speaking to student groups when I wasn't needed on the set. I also did some work for the Peace Corps, helping to recruit volunteers for the newly created program and traveling to South America to speak on its behalf to citizens and officials. This came about because I had met Robert F. Kennedy at an awards dinner, and Robert introduced me to Peace Corps director Sargent Shriver. Both men would become close friends of mine and have a powerful impact on my life.

During that period I broke into broadcasting, working with experienced sportscasters like Jim McKay to cover major track events. That led to an invitation to join NBC's broadcast team for the 1964 Olympics in Tokyo. For the first time, Americans received two full weeks of live television coverage via satellite. The main anchors were Bud Palmer and Jim Simpson. I covered track, weight-lifting, and wrestling.

There had been serious doubts whether Tokyo, the world's largest city, could handle Olympic-size crowds. But the Japanese, with their national pride at stake, came through. The result was a marvel of modern technology and efficient planning. The Japanese tried hard to counter their image as a hostile, insulated people, and made the thousands of visitors feel at home. I was treated as something of a celebrity by fans and athletes who remembered me from Rome, and I got to renew some cherished acquaintances.

The Games themselves were memorable for several outstanding performances: Al Oerter winning his third consecutive gold in the discus; Peter Snell of New Zealand breaking the Olympic record in the 800 meters; Billy Mills, an unheralded Marine with a Sioux Indian heritage, becoming the first American to win the 10,000-meter run; Ethiopia's Abebe Bikila running the fastest marathon ever for his second consecutive gold (he had run barefoot in Rome); the high-jump standoff between John Thomas and Valeriy Brumel of the Soviet Union; and Bob Hayes tying the world record in the hundred meters, then running the anchor leg of the 4 × 100-meter relay with such blinding speed that he went from fifth place to first.

Naturally, my chief interest at the Games was the decathlon. Since Rome, my friend C. K. Yang had come into his own, literally vaulting out of my shadow. Having mastered the new fiberglass pole, whose powerful recoil altered the course of vaulting forever, he'd soared to a height that the decathlon tables didn't even have a score for. Under the guidance of Ducky Drake and Mr. Wei—and to some extent myself, since I assisted Ducky in my spare time—C.K. also improved in other events. In 1963 he broke my world record, becoming the first to exceed 9,000 points.

Prompted in part by C.K.'s performance and the advent of the fiberglass pole, the International Amateur Athletic Foundation later changed the scoring tables. Previously, certain events had been valued more than others. The new, more balanced tables worked to the advantage of good all-around athletes as opposed to those with exceptional talent in a few events. C.K.'s world-record 9,121 would have been reduced by over a thousand points under the new system.

Despite the changes, which worked to his disadvantage, C.K. was favored to win in Tokyo. Three days before the decathlon, he came down with what seemed to be a stomach virus or flu. When I visited his room, I found him too weak to get out of bed. His muscles ached so much he could barely straighten his legs. Gamely, he competed anyway, but he was way below par and finished in fifth place. (The gold went to Willi Holdorf of Germany; it was the first time since 1928 that an American had not won the Olympic decathlon.)

Needless to say, C.K. was gravely disheartened. He wanted to win not only for himself but his country. He once told a reporter, "All of the Chinese Republic—those of us who had not been crushed by the Communists after World War II—was looking for me to become the first champion we have in the Olympics." In Rome he had received a message from President Chiang Kai-shek himself, saying that he must win for the sake of his nation's pride. At thirty-one, C.K. was too old to think of trying again four years later. I did my best to comfort him, knowing full well how his future would be affected by the loss. I was personal proof that a gold medal leads to opportunities. Influential people in Los Angeles's Asian community had big plans for C.K., but when he failed to win, nothing materialized. He worked in sales for a big alcohol distributor, then in his wife's family's food business, before returning to Taiwan; there he was a national hero, became a leader in amateur athletics, and was elected to the national assembly. Had he won gold, his life would have been much easier and far more prosperous.

In the 1970s, C.K. had dinner with a man from Taiwan's counterpart to our FBI. They were talking about the 1964 Olympics when the man dropped a bombshell: C.K. had been poisoned, he said. Because of the tension with mainland China, Taiwan had assigned two bodyguards to C.K. at the Games. Despite that precaution, this man told him, a teammate had spiked C.K.'s orange juice at one of their meals. Shortly afterward, that athlete and two Taiwanese journalists defected to Red China. C.K. had always considered himself unlucky for having gotten ill at the wrong time. Instead, he may have been a victim of political warfare. "I was so angry I thought I would cry," he told me.

After Tokyo I was offered broadcasting jobs at several television stations. None of them were in California, though, and I did not want to relocate. By now I had done something

I'd been hoping to do for years: reunite my family. I bought a roomy two-story house in the more affordable section of Baldwin Hills—a racially mixed neighborhood lined with eucalyptus trees—and moved my mother and sisters down from Kingsburg.

When I went away to college, it had fallen upon Ed and Jim to look after Mom and the girls, and to keep our father's drinking from destroying the family. When Jimmy left for college, the burden became Ed's. Before long, having grown tired of Dad's binges and tracking him down every time he disappeared, Ed joined the Army. That left Erma and Dolores, who would phone Mr. Fishel (our parents' employer and landlord) for help when Dad got belligerent. Sometimes Mom and the girls would check into a motel or stay with friends in Fresno. Finally my parents separated. Dad moved to Oakland. Mom and the girls stayed in Kingsburg for a while, then moved to Los Angeles when I bought the house on West Boulevard. This became our new family home, and a great source of pride after all those years in cramped quarters. Eddie lived with us for a while when he returned from Germany with his wife and child. Dolores stayed until she got married. My mother lived in the house until her death in 1990. Erma and her son, Brian, who has always been like a son to me, still live there.

Jimmy, who bought into the house with me, played football for the San Francisco Forty-Niners and lived with us in the off-season. He had been drafted as a wide receiver because they felt that a wiry 175-pound cornerback could not stand up to pulling guards and lumbering fullbacks who were built like tanks. But Jimmy made up for his stature with a sturdy heart and impeccable technique, earning his ticket to the Hall of Fame as a defensive back. I flew up for most of his home games. However, my pride in watching my brother play pro ball was offset by my father, who would make a drunken spectacle of himself. He would shout things like, "That's my boy, number thirty-seven, and he can kick anyone's butt!" He'd try to enter off-limit areas, and when he was stopped he'd scream at the security guards, "My son's a Forty-Niner and I can go wherever I want!" Those were some of the most embarrassing moments of my life. Eventually, Jimmy had to tell Dad he could no longer come to games.

Even as an adult I had powerfully mixed emotions about my father. I loved him deeply and respected the decent, responsible man that he was at heart. But I resented the destructive Mr. Hyde he turned into when he drank, and the way he treated my mother at those times. I think *his* feelings were mixed too. He was as proud of me as a father could be, but he may have been somewhat envious. Held back by poverty and racism, denied the opportunities that his children would have—thanks in large part to his efforts—his life had been hard. I think he saw in me what he might have been himself, and felt cheated. As angry as I was at times, I felt that I owed him. Until he died in 1987, I tried to treat him with respect and help him financially as best I could. No matter what else passed between us, I was always the son and he was always the father. It broke my heart that he and my mother couldn't stay together. Not long after we moved into the house in Baldwin Hills, I tried to create a new beginning for them by having Dad come live with us. The attempt at reconciliation did not work.

In 1966, Los Angeles's NBC affiliate offered me a position as a sports reporter. KNBC had openings because it was expanding its newscasts and its regular sports anchor, Chick Hearn, was leaving to do play-by-play for the Lakers. (As I write this, Chick has just broadcast his three-thousandth consecutive game.)

I started out doing reports during the week and sometimes filling in for the regular anchor. Then I became the weekend anchor, and finally moved up to the nightly report at eleven

Cover of *Time* magazine, August 29, 1960. (©1960 Time Inc.)

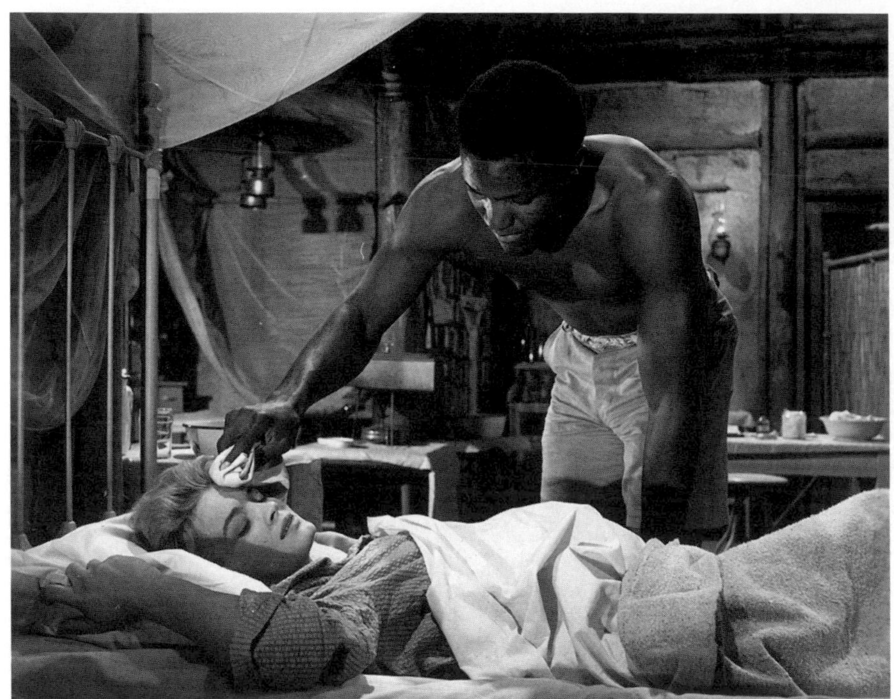

With Angie Dickinson in the movie *The Sins of Rachel Cade*, 1961. (private collection)

With Marlon Brando and Anthony Franciosa at a civil rights demonstration, 1966. (private collection)

With Robert F. Kennedy, 1968. (private collection)

On the campaign trail with Bobby Kennedy. (private collection)

At wedding reception with Elizabeth and her parents, Paul and Margaret Thorsen, 1971. (private collection)

With brothers Jim (left) and Ed (center) and nephew Brian, 1973. (private collection)

With wife Betsy, son Joshua, and daughter Jennifer, circa 1977. (private collection)

With (left to right) son-in-law Kevin Jordan, daughter Jenny, son Josh, wife Betsy, 1997. (Rob Shanahan)

Carrying the Olympic torch on the final leg of its journey from Greece at the opening ceremonies of the Los Angeles Olympics, 1984. (private collection)

At the opening ceremonies of the 1984 Olympics at the Los Angeles Coliseum. (private collection)

Lighting the Olympic flame at the opening ceremonies of the Los Angeles Olympics. (private collection)

With Special Olympians at the California Summer Games, 1986. (Southern California Special Olympics)

At Hershey's National Track and Field Program, 1994.
(Lancaster Newspapers, Inc.)

With Muhammad Ali at the 1996 Olympics in Atlanta.
(Howard Bingham)

o'clock. I found the work exciting, challenging, and more difficult than anything I'd done before.

My first glimpse of the stress I was in for came when I noticed that the man who did the weather report was shaking. I thought the air conditioner was turned up too high. The same thing happened night after night. Finally I asked him about it. He said, "Rafer, I'm a nervous wreck." Doing the weather is not as easy as it looks, but this guy had been a fixture in Los Angeles for years. If *he*'s shaking, I thought, then the tension I feel may be more than just rookie jitters. This may be a real nerve-wracking job.

It was. From day one, I had to write my own scripts and edit them to fit the time allotted for the sports report—and that was subject to change up to the last second. There were no teleprompters in those days. I would memorize my scripts and carry a typed copy in my hand—often with lines crossed out and words penciled in—to refer to on air. In the nervous atmosphere of the studio, looking at the right camera, having the right facial expression, remembering the script, filling my time slot without going over or coming up short—none of it was easy. The field reports I had to do were also a departure from anything I'd done before, but at least they weren't live.

I had performed before hundreds of thousands of people under tremendous pressure, and yet now every night I was as nervous as a kid on his first date. I worried about everything from my posture to my pronunciation. I was terrified that I would mangle a word or a name. In truth, the only time I remember doing that was when I called the daredevil motorcyclist Evil Knievel "Evill Kanevill." (I'm told that Jess Marlow, a longtime Los Angeles newsman, remarked, "Rafer's such a decent guy, he can't call anyone evil.") In any event, the pressure was so nerve-wracking that I sometimes had to take a Valium before going on the air.

Part of the problem was that I had absolutely no training.

In sports I'd had years of coaching and had practiced every decathlon move countless times before doing it in competition. In the movies I'd had acting classes and rehearsals, plus the opportunity to do additional takes if I got something wrong. But in live television I had only my instincts and a hastily edited script to rely on, while crew members counted down the seconds with their fingers or ran their hands across their throats to tell me to cut my segment short.

I also had a problem with some of the things that were asked of me. For example, I wanted to chat on-screen with the anchor once in a while, but the head of the news division, Bill Brown, was strictly opposed to this. He didn't even want me to say "Thank you" when I was introduced, just look directly at the camera and begin my report. It seemed terribly artificial. I was hired because I was Rafer Johnson and I wasn't allowed to be Rafer Johnson. Instead, I was supposed to fit the mold of a generic newsman. Today, of course, individuality is encouraged and broadcast banter is so commonplace that it sometimes seems artificial.

On a couple of occasions I actually refused to comply with assignments I was given. Once, a couple of intoxicated Rams players were involved in a serious car wreck, resulting in one of them losing a finger. The dispatcher ordered me to the accident scene with a live camera crew. I refused to go; that seemed to me tasteless and intrusive. I felt it was appropriate to report the story, but not to show sensational footage. The other occasion was when Sandy Koufax and Don Drysdale joined forces to demand better contracts from the Dodgers. As one of the earliest challenges to the power of baseball's owners, that was a legitimate story. But I was asked to knock on Drysdale's door and stick a microphone in his face, or to camp outside his house until he came out. That was a line I couldn't cross.

Incidents such as those created conflict between me and Bill Brown. A strict, impatient man, Bill thought he had the answer to everything and did not have time for other opinions. Once I had to interview Pelé, the great Brazilian soccer player. I thought it would be gracious, and add some color to the interview, to say a few words in Spanish, and I did so. Bill ordered me never to do that again, even though the spot elicited a great response from viewers. I wondered if Bill looked down on me because I was not a professional journalist. I later realized that he treated everyone the same way. Well, maybe not quite the same; I was told that Bill had a powerful disdain for sports.

All of this made me wonder if I could make a career in broadcasting. As with acting, there was a lot I liked about the profession, and I did pretty well for an upstart with no training. But I felt uncomfortable. Perhaps that would have changed in time, or under other conditions, but once I left KNBC (for reasons I'll discuss in the next chapter) I never gave it another chance. Still, I remember the years at the station fondly because of the great sports figures and broadcasters I got to know and work with.

One colleague deserves special mention. Tom Brokaw was about twenty-seven at the time, and not far removed from the South Dakota town in which he'd grown up, but he was a skilled journalist on the fast track to national prominence. Everyone knew he was gifted and destined for bigger things. He and I hit it off from the day I arrived. He claims he was star struck when we met because I had been one of his sports heroes. But I never sensed anything in Tom but genuine warmth. I thought his personality was as impressive as his talent. I spent many lovely evenings with him and his wife, Meredith, in restaurants or at their home with their daughter, Jenny, who is now a physician. Tom says he wouldn't let me take off my shirt when we sat around the pool because his physique suffered by comparison to mine. Frankly, I don't remember that, but it would have been consistent with Tom's sense of humor.

Tom and others taught me some tricks of the trade, but it

was no substitute for real training. Years later Tom concurred with my assessment: "Rafer had a terrific work ethic, but unfortunately they threw people into the pool and hoped they'd swim. No one stopped and said, 'We have this great resource in Rafer, how do we get the best out of him?' Under the circumstances he did very well, but he did not get enough help."

During my years at UCLA I dated quite a bit, but did not develop any lasting romantic relationships. For the most part I channeled my energies into the decathlon. After Rome, my social life became more complicated and less innocent. I was young and "eligible," living and working in an environment that grew more and more permissive as the 1960s progressed. I dated many women, both black and white. To me, race was not an issue. If I liked someone, it was for qualities far deeper than skin color. I was not about to let anyone else's standards affect my decisions, whether white people who disdained interracial love or black people who were afraid of "losing" desirable men to the majority population.

Mixed couples were not very common in those days, even on the west side of Los Angeles. I never encountered outright hostility when I was with a white woman, but I was stared at relentlessly. I learned to make light of it, telling my date that people were looking at us because she was so beautiful and I was familiar from sports and movies. In many instances that was surely true, as I was also stared at when I was alone or with a black woman. But there was a clear difference between looks that read "That's Rafer Johnson" and those that read "Look at that nigger with a white girl." It bothered me a lot, but I wasn't going to let anyone else's ignorance stop me from being with whomever I pleased.

Reactions to my dating white women ran the gamut of attitudes toward race at the time. During my senior year at

UCLA, and for a short while after graduation, I went out with someone who worked for the university and attended Bel Air Presbyterian Church. Instead of picking her up at home, I would meet her in public places. Her parents would have had heart attacks if they had known we were dating. When they found out, it caused a big rift in her family. What disturbed me even more was learning that certain members of the church had made noises about it. I had a long talk with Reverend Evans, whose advice was, essentially, to follow my conscience.

In the summer of 1963, I began dating a young woman who was participating in one of the People to People programs. Joan Andersson's family heartily endorsed our relationship; as liberal activists, they were pleased to know that their daughter was not prejudiced. My family took to Joan as well. She and Erma became exceptionally close; in fact, they recently renewed their friendship after many years.

Race reared its ugly head a few times when I was with Joan. Most harrowing was the night we were parked on a hilltop above UCLA, where young couples went to be alone. Suddenly we were blinded by a flashlight. It was a policeman. From the way he looked at me, and the hostile tone of his voice, I knew he would like nothing better than an excuse to use his nightstick on my head. It was terrifying. However, the minute the cop saw the name on my driver's license, his whole demeanor changed. "Oh, Mr. Johnson, so sorry," he said. If I hadn't been *that* Mr. Johnson, I'd have just been a colored guy with a white girl—fair game for the nightstick or a trumped-up arrest.

A few years later I dated an actress named Patricia Morrow, who was a regular on the television series *Peyton Place.* We met during the 1968 presidential campaign, while working for Robert Kennedy and, after Robert's death, for Hubert Humphrey. In those days, when everything was treated as a political statement, our liaison was applauded by liberals. In fact, Pat and I had the same agent and he considered it great publicity. We were the subject of many a gossip column, with constant speculation about whether we would marry. (This was not the only time: I was once said to be engaged to Carol Lynley, whom I had met only once at a charity event.) Pat and I never even considered marriage, but a lot of people fed the rumor mill to show how progressive they were.

That none of these relationships stood the test of time had nothing to do with race. They ended because of the usual changes and incompatibilities—the same kind that came between me and the black women I dated. I had thoughts of marrying two of my African-American girlfriends, but one had children from a previous marriage and I did not want to take on that responsibility, while the other drank a lot, and I knew all too well what alcohol can do to a family.

With Joan, the most serious of my relationships in those years, the end came in part because she went away to law school, but also because of the turbulence of the mid-sixties. In the time we were together, Martin Luther King, Jr., delivered his "I have a dream" speech; the National Guard escorted black students past George Wallace into the University of Alabama; four black children were killed in a Birmingham church bombing, civil rights workers were murdered in Mississippi; the voting rights bill was passed; the Free Speech Movement erupted in Berkeley; the Vietnam war escalated and Congress authorized the Tonkin Gulf Resolution. It might seem odd, since Joan was the white one, but her views on the state of American society were more radical than mine. I thought her ideology was too extreme and she thought I wasn't militant enough; confrontation was simply not my style.

Some people assumed that I didn't settle down because I was living a wild and carefree bachelor existence. Not so. I enjoyed my life but I was as earnest as ever, working hard and devoting time to church and various causes. I just wasn't ready for marriage. I was always, by nature, a family man; I wanted a wife and children, but I was afraid of making the wrong choice or jumping into marriage prematurely.

And without a job I could depend on, my future seemed too uncertain. I wasn't even sure what kind of work I would end up doing or where I would live. I was also helping to take care of my mother and, at various times, my father or one of my siblings. I was painfully aware that the doors that had opened to me as a public figure would not necessarily open to the others. With the exception of Jimmy, my loved ones were affected by discrimination and limited choice as much as any blacks in the 1960s. I could not fulfill my responsibilities to them and also assume new ones. If I'd been able to see clearly, though, I would have realized that a woman I began to date in 1966, Elizabeth Thorsen, was perfect for me, and we might have been married sooner.

When a discus thrower releases the discus, he's often slightly dizzy from the rapid spin. It takes a moment to get his bearings. In the 1960s the whole world was spinning wildly. I felt somewhat disoriented. And just as I was starting to get my bearings, fate dealt me, and all of us, a cruel blow.

8

VAULTING HIGH, FALLING FAR

Some men see things as they are and ask, "Why?" I dream of things that never were and ask, "Why not?"
—Robert F. Kennedy

IN THE YEARS that I competed in the decathlon, pole-vault poles were made of bamboo, and later of steel. Because they did not have the recoil of today's fiberglass poles, the technique for using them was different from what it now is. You ran down the runway with the pole at your side, planted it in the take-off box, and pushed your hands out in front of you. Lifted off the ground by the speed of your run, you swung your feet up over your head and pulled on the pole to force your legs still higher. Then you pushed off, letting your momentum carry you over the bar.

At that time, before there were huge air bags to land on, you also had to be concerned about your landing. Your vaulting technique had to include a balancing system so that when you cleared the bar you were in a position to land feet-first in the sand-and-sawdust pit. If you landed awkwardly you could injure yourself, perhaps severely.

The higher you soar, the harder you fall, if you're not prepared. In 1968 my life attained heights I had never dreamed possible. I was at the side of a close friend who seemed about to become president of the United States. Then, with the speed of a pistol shot, the world around me exploded in turmoil, and I plummeted and crashed.

In January 1961 I was in New York to accept the People to People award as Athlete of the Year. The featured speaker was the new attorney general of the United States, Robert F. Kennedy. I don't recall his exact words, but these lines from a later speech of his capture the spirit of what impressed me on that occasion: "Each time a man stands up for an ideal or acts to improve the lot of others or strikes out against injustice, he sends forth a tiny ripple of hope, and crossing each other from a million different centers of energy and daring, those ripples build a current which can sweep down the mightiest walls of oppression and resistance."

In accepting that award I mentioned that I was interested in international relations and foreign exchange programs. Afterward, Mr. Kennedy said to me, "If you're really serious about that, come down to Washington with me." I ended up spending a week at his Virginia home with him, his wife Ethel, and their children, which at the time numbered seven. I met the president and First Lady at a White House party, I met other prominent and powerful people at Robert's office at the Justice Department, and I was introduced to Sargent and Eunice Shriver, who became lifelong friends of mine. Because of the Shrivers I did some work for the Peace Corps, which was just getting off the ground under Sargent's leadership; later I became deeply involved with Eunice's passion, the Special Olympics.

From that first visit on, I was privileged to call myself a family friend. I would visit the Kennedys virtually every time I was on the East Coast, whether for a speaking engagement, People to People business, or meetings of volunteer organizations such as the President's Council on Physical Fitness. I would always try to go a little early or leave a little late so I could spend time with the Kennedys. And just about every summer I would accept their standing invitation to visit them at the family compound in Hyannis Port, on Cape Cod.

During President Kennedy's administration, Robert and Ethel's home, Hickory Hill, was said to be the most famous residence in the country other than the White House. Only twenty minutes from Washington, D.C., the white, gabled house was set on a hilltop in the rolling countryside of McLean, Virginia, surrounded by oak, maple, and hickory trees. The first time I drove through the gate on Chain Bridge Road, the estate seemed imposing. The house itself could have held at least a dozen of the boxcar-sized houses I knew in Kingsburg. I expected the atmosphere to be formal and reserved. I should have known better when I saw the sign on the lawn: "Trespassers will be eaten."

As informal as my frat house, and more unpredictable, Hickory Hill was a constant hubbub of energetic activity, with cooks, governesses, secretaries, and maids scurrying about; ferocious tennis matches and endless touch football games, with children, women, and out-of-shape men playing alongside the likes of Roosevelt Grier and members of the Washington Redskins; people swimming and diving while music blasted from the jukebox by the pool; kids climbing rope ladders, riding ponies, and frolicking with dogs; Bobby Junior showing off his collection of reptiles, rodents, and birds; clamorous meals with down-home American food.

Inside, the house was a veritable museum of Kennedy family history. The walls and shelves in every room were festooned with photographs, paintings, awards, and mementos. On my first visit I spent hours enthralled by the memorabilia. I also nearly froze to death. It was the height of winter and every window in the house was open. Maybe because they were from New England, the Kennedys enjoyed the cold. I was used to California weather. When I awoke that first morning, my forehead was like an ice cube. On subsequent visits I came prepared for the cold. I also came prepared to keep from getting thrown into the pool with my clothes on, something that seemed to happen at least once to every guest.

Speaking of getting wet, one of my most vivid Kennedy memories occurred while sailing on Ted Kennedy's yacht. We were anchored off Nantucket, and I decided to try my hand at scuba diving. I put on the gear, jumped into the sea, and quickly found myself under the boat, sinking fast in the dull, murky water. When I realized that too much weight had been strapped to me, I removed the belt and let it sink. Afterward, it dawned on me how reckless it was to dive into the ocean with no lessons and no instructions from the experienced divers on board. The Kennedy spirit must have been contagious. Around them, life was one big decathlon. They were always creating contests, finding new challenges, pushing themselves to the edge, taking risks.

I loved the seven Kennedy children I met on my first visit, and felt as happy as an uncle when each of the other four was born. The entire bunch—from Kathleen, the oldest, to Rory, the youngest—had their mother's boundless energy and love of life and their father's empathy and intense curiosity. Over the years I became quite close to some of the kids, especially Max. From the minute he was born, in 1965, he and I had a natural affinity for one another. I loved his imagination and sense of wonder. I also spent a good deal of time with the Shriver children, whom I saw often as they grew up because of their involvement in Special Olympics. Now the Kennedy and Shriver kids are politicians, lawyers, activists, business executives, and, in Maria Shriver's case, a well-known journalist with a superstar husband named Arnold. I remember them as skinny bundles of energy riding on my shoulders and tumbling around on the lawn.

I used to get a kick out of doing ordinary things with the Kennedy children. For instance, instead of eating at home, I would pile some of them in a car and drive into McLean to get hamburgers at a fast food place. Or I'd take them to an ice cream stand, even though the freezers at home were stacked high with containers of it. On some occasions we would wander around a department store or a mall. They got a big boot out of such commonplace adventures, and their parents seemed to like the idea too.

On one occasion, in Hyannis Port, I proposed to Chris, Max, and Douglas that we build a go-cart, like the ones my brothers and I used to make when we were their age. I told them it would look something like a wagon, but could be used as a one-person car to zoom down hills in. We picked up some wood at a lumber yard and nuts and bolts at a hardware store, and built a wagon with a seat and foothold. The boys sailed gleefully down the long hill from the golf course. I think it was special to them because they had built the cart themselves. To me it was special because I had done it with them.

One of the many things I admired about Bobby Kennedy was his insatiable curiosity. He was always learning, and not just from experts. He wanted to hear about everyone's background, how people felt about different issues and how they were affected by what was going on in the world. During the 1960s, with civil rights and racial tension in the forefront of everyone's concerns, he would often solicit my feelings and those of other people of color.

Ethel, too, appeared to thrive on having people around. A strong, vivacious woman, she had an inexhaustible imagination when it came to thinking up things to do and interesting combinations of personalities to bring together. Her parties were exuberant affairs, with fascinating people from all walks of life. She and Bobby seemed to get a special charge out of high achievers. They loved having athletes around, because they saw sports as a shaper of character and a training ground for achievement in other areas of life. Maybe that's why there was always some competitive event going on at Hickory Hill and Hyannis Port.

In addition to athletes, politicians, and scholars, regular visitors included journalists like Rowland Evans and Art Buchwald; entertainers like the Smothers Brothers and Andy Williams; and adventurers like John Glenn, who had orbited the earth, and Jim Whittaker, who had climbed Mount Everest. Bobby and Ethel would throw questions at their guests because they loved success stories and wanted their children to hear them. "Rafer, what was it like growing up in Texas?" they might ask, or, "Tell us about your relationship with Coach Drake," or, "Tell the kids how you and C. K. Yang fought it out at Rome."

Perhaps because all Kennedys were groomed for public service ("From those to whom much is given, much is expected" was almost a family motto), Robert and Ethel made sure important issues were discussed around the children. These were far from idle conversations. Often their dinner companions were Washington insiders who had been making history during the day. The Justice Department was at the center of monumental events in those years, like Bobby's assault on organized crime, and federal intervention on behalf of civil rights in the South. I can remember one meal at Hickory Hill with Bobby and two high-ranking Justice officials (Nicholas Katzenbach was one). At the time, Bobby was trying to decide how to deal with Governor George Wallace, who was blocking the integration of the University of Alabama. I'm certain that more delicate strategy sessions were held in private, but this conversation was remarkably substantive. I went to sleep that night amazed that they had actually asked my opinion on matters of such great importance.

As attorney general and later as a U.S. senator, Robert Kennedy was often criticized for not being militant enough on social issues. I took heart in that because I found myself in a similar position. Like him, I thought I was having an impact for good in the world, yet I was sometimes told I wasn't doing enough, or not going about it the right way.

I was sickened by the injustices that proliferated in response to the civil rights movement. Televised images of Southern sheriffs unleashing police dogs and fire hoses on protesters; and the church bombings, the murders of Freedom Riders, the cross-burnings—all of it filled me with rage. Activist friends and well-intentioned strangers urged me to march, demonstrate, join radical organizations and lend my name to various causes. As the atmosphere grew more and more charged, militancy became a badge of honor and, in some circles, a measure of status. But my politics remained moderate. I believed very strongly in Martin Luther King's vision of a color-blind, integrated world where people are judged by the content of their character, and I supported his strategies. The militant tactics of Stokely Carmichael, H. Rap Brown, Angela Davis, and Malcolm X seemed divisive and sometimes destructive. Still, I was glad they were around. They dared to utter truths that others could not, and their fervor accelerated the process of social change. The larger society might never have awakened if those fierce, threatening voices had not been raised.

But I had to be true to myself and my nature. Confrontation was simply not my style. For this I was often accused of not being black enough, a charge that not only made no sense to me but was deeply repulsive.

There were reasons for my moderation. Responsibilities to loved ones who depended on me were my primary concern. For their sake if not my own, it would have been foolish to do anything that could jeopardize my ability to earn a living. Second, I *was* angry, but my anger was directed at ignorance, bigotry, and selfishness wherever I saw it, not at American society or white people as a whole. I understood how everyday frustration could lead to a generalized rage, and I might have felt that rage myself had my family remained in Texas. But after my experiences in Kingsburg and at UCLA, how could I possibly hate all white people or believe that they were out to bring me down?

Nor could I hate "the system." In my travels I had met enough people from other countries to know that, despite everything, America was still the best place to live, even for people of color. I don't think any of the black Americans I competed with in Russia, Hungary, Poland, Mexico, Pakistan, or Africa wanted to live in any of those places. None of this made me any less angry about what was going on in our country, but it mitigated my rage and tempered my sense of what strategies for change were appropriate and effective.

I felt that, as a public figure, I could do the most good by maintaining a positive image. For change to be lasting and meaningful it had to take root in individual hearts and minds. I seemed to be in a position to accelerate that process, since I was frequently the first or only black person in various situations. By doing whatever I did well, and doing it with integrity, I felt I could help break down stereotypes, chip away at ignorance, and shed light on our common humanity. For me it made tactical sense to stress cooperation between the races, not separatism. I had read that when the Brooklyn Dodgers arrived at a hotel dining room, Jackie Robinson would tell his black teammates,

"Spread out." He meant, Go and mingle with the white players. Like Jackie, I felt I could do more good by spreading out.

It was for similar reasons that I did not support the proposed boycott of the 1968 Olympics. Led by sociologist Harry Edwards, a number of black athletes had voted to stay away from the Mexico City Games as a form of protest. I was among those who were asked for a reaction. I said, "What you have to ask yourself is, 'What good is it going to do? Is it going to help housing? Is it going to help education? Is it going to help job opportunities?' I don't see where a boycott of the Olympics is relevant at all to these problems." I pointed out that the Olympics was one of the rare institutions in which blacks and whites were treated exactly the same. The Games ought to be embraced as an opportunity to build bridges and educate people. At the same time, I noted that there were no black members on the United States Olympic Committee (USOC) despite their prominence as athletes. I advocated that Jesse Owens be appointed. He never was.

Of course, the threatened boycott never took place. The enduring image of the 1968 Games is of Tommie Smith and John Carlos on the medal stand raising their fists in the Black Power salute. While it would not have been my style, I felt they were on solid ground in making the gesture, and I criticized the USOC for expelling them from the Olympic Village. Punishing two medalists made the United States look worse than anything the athletes did.

For the most part, my activism centered on issues that were close to home, and to causes that were worthy even if they were not hot-button items. As a union representative I pushed for equal opportunity in the entertainment industry. I gave time and energy to the Fair Housing Congress and to projects organized by the NAACP and the Urban League, especially in the aftermath of the 1965 Watts riot. I worked for Tom Bradley the first time he campaigned for mayor of Los Angeles, and for John Tunney and Alan Cranston when they ran for the Senate. In addition to my job with People to People, I volunteered for causes I believed in, such as the Fellowship of Christian Athletes, the Campus Crusade, the Peace Corps, various youth groups and other organizations that helped people in need regardless of ethnicity—for example, the Committee on Mental Retardation of the Department of Health, Education, and Welfare.

The one time I attended a national demonstration was in June 1966, when James Meredith organized a twenty-one-day march to mobilize black voters in Mississippi. For one reason or another, I had been unable to be in Washington in 1963 when Martin Luther King, Jr., delivered his "I Have a Dream" speech, or at the march in Selma, Alabama, in 1965. But in 1966 a labor strike freed me from my job at KNBC, and I signed on for a chartered flight to Mississippi with a contingent from Hollywood. That plan was dropped when the Ku Klux Klan threatened to blow up the plane. Since James Meredith had already been wounded by a sniper earlier in the march, the threat was taken seriously and the charter was cancelled.

Some of us still wanted to go, however, and Frank Sinatra offered to lend us his private plane. I flew down with Sammy Davis, Jr., Marlon Brando, and Anthony Franciosa. We joined about 10,000 people at a rally at Tougaloo College. Sammy, James Brown, and Dick Gregory performed, and Marlon gave a moving speech in which he called civil rights workers "the real heroes of America." Afterward we drove to a small airport in the middle of a sugar cane field; we were inspired by the rally but concerned that we might be marked men, driving in a conspicuous limousine in the dark Mississippi night. We took off safely, feeling good that we had lent support to those who had bravely stood up for justice.

• • •

My friendship with the Kennedys had a strong influence on my political views. Knowing that powerful people were willing to put themselves on the line for equality made me confident that working within the system was not a lost cause.

At the time, it was fashionable for commentators and political opponents to call Bobby "ruthless." That quality might have been evident in his earlier years, or behind closed doors in the corridors of power, but I never saw any sign of it. Aggressive, yes; ambitious, yes; combative, yes. But those are traits we like our leaders to have, as long as they stand for what is right, decent, and equitable. Bobby had a quality that great athletes have: He knew how to win. In a small way, I had an early taste of what he could do when he put his power and can-do attitude to work. When People to People was having difficulty moving students into and out of the country due to governmental red tape, I called the attorney general's office. Within hours, the problem was solved. I had no doubt that Bobby could make bigger things happen as well.

Many observers have noted that Bobby changed a great deal during the course of his public career. In fact, one thing that always impressed me was his consistency. His compassion for the less fortunate and his dedication to improving their lot were part of his makeup. Many historians believe that he was the real force behind the civil rights agenda in his brother's administration. Under Bobby's leadership the justice department finally exercised its power on behalf of minorities—enforcing desegregation laws, investigating voting rights violations, and recommending qualified blacks for positions as federal judges and U.S. marshals.

I never doubted Bobby's sincerity and basic decency. Unlike most politicians, he did not pander to his audience. At times he would even say things that made his supporters uncomfortable. I saw him with rich people and poor, young and old, whites and blacks, liberals and conservatives; he always spoke his mind, and he treated everyone, from servants to cabinet members, with respect.

In some ways he did change, though. He grew wiser, better informed, and more decisive about the issues facing the country. I saw him respond to a tour of Brooklyn's Bedford-Stuyvesant with a major restoration plan that transformed that blighted neighborhood. I saw him fight for Native American rights after observing conditions on reservations. I saw him befriend Cesar Chavez and lend his support to the United Farm Workers after visiting the migrant labor camps in California. I also saw him come out against the Vietnam War, even though he himself had supported military intervention during his brother's administration.

If I needed any further convincing about Bobby's integrity, I got it the night I had dinner with him and Stokely Carmichael. After courageously leading the Student Nonviolent Coordinating Committee's voting rights campaign, Stokely had grown increasingly inflammatory, using "Black Power" as a rallying cry for radical change. The fact that Bobby would invite to his home a man who compared black membership in the Democratic Party to Jews becoming Nazis was a statement in itself. Bobby listened to Stokely's views with interest. Then the subject shifted to an event in the news: A black man had hijacked an American plane and forced it to fly to Cuba. Stokely's position was that the United States was not a true homeland to blacks, and that violent acts like hijacking were justifiable reactions to oppression. Acknowledging the nation's shameful legacy of racism, Bobby spoke the plain and simple truth: The hijacker was a criminal who just happened to be black, and he was endangering the lives of innocent people.

This is a solid man, I said to myself. He has a strong sense of justice, and he tells it like it is without altering his message or manner to suit the occasion. I vowed that if he ever ran for national office, I would do everything I could to help him get elected.

When Bobby declared himself a candidate for president in 1968, I was overjoyed. Like many others, I had come to see him as the one person who could keep the country from tearing itself apart. The Democratic Party and the nation needed a peace candidate, and Bobby was the logical choice. He had hesitated to enter the race, though, and Senator Eugene McCarthy had filled the void, demonstrating that President Lyndon B. Johnson was vulnerable by scoring big in the New Hampshire primary. Then Bobby joined the fray and President Johnson announced that he would not seek re-election. It was a three-way race for the Democratic nomination between Senator Kennedy, Senator McCarthy, and Vice President Hubert Humphrey.

I immediately geared up to help my friend win the all-important California primary. Each step of his campaign strengthened my conviction that he was the right man at the right time. His speeches were not only galvanizing, they were unlike politics as usual: He spoke his heart, telling audiences what he felt they needed to hear, not what would win him votes. Then came his defining moment as a candidate—the devastating night that Martin Luther King, Jr., was assassinated. Bobby was on his way to a campaign stop in Indianapolis when he heard the news. Instead of cancelling his speech, as his handlers and police advised, he stood before a mostly black crowd of about a thousand and told them what had taken place. With his voice cracking, he kept the shaken audience calm and urged them to "make an effort, as Martin Luther King did, to understand and to comprehend, and to replace that violence, that stain of bloodshed that has spread across our land, with an effort to understand with compassion and love.'' In the following days, riots erupted in 167 American cities. Indianapolis was not one of them.

Named an official delegate for the Kennedy ticket, I immediately began to devote all my spare time to the campaign. Shirley MacLaine, Andy Williams, and I organized a ''Hollywood for Kennedy'' fund-raising gala at the L.A. Sports Arena. I flew to wherever in the state I was needed, addressing rallies, speaking at press conferences, trying to convince voters that Senator Kennedy was someone who could bring the fractured nation together and deliver on his promises.

All of which made my employer, KNBC, nervous. Management feared that if a member of the station's news division was too closely identified with a candidate for office, other candidates would demand equal time and the station might be penalized by the Federal Communications Commission. They told me I would have to stop making public appearances. I refused. Their position seemed absurd to me. I never uttered a word about politics on the air, and I wasn't about to wear RFK buttons on my blazer or insert campaign slogans into the football scores. Nevertheless, I was taken off the air. I remained on the payroll and was given writing assignments, but I was not allowed on camera.

My lawyer, Donald Dell, filed a complaint. The FCC ruled in my favor; my political activities did not violate the equal time regulations. But then my relationship with management—which had not been ideal in the first place—had chilled. In addition, the primary was only weeks away and the race was close. At that crucial time I wanted to contribute as much as I could. I had to choose between staying on my job or working full-time for the campaign: a salaried position with a future versus volunteer work for a cause that would either end in defeat or launch the nation—and probably my life—on a new path.

In my heart, the choice was easy. To reassure my mind I

asked the advice of friends and colleagues. Tom Brokaw remembers it this way: "I said, 'Gosh, Rafer, you're just starting to get your career going. I'd think long and hard about it if I were you.' The next day, Bobby Kennedy came into the studio to be interviewed. The bond between him and Rafer was so deep, so meaningful, so rich, there was so much love and respect between them, that I said to Rafer afterward, 'You've got to follow your heart on this one.' "

The next few weeks were a sleepless frenzy. From one end of California to the other we campaigned nonstop. Rosey Grier and I stayed so close to Bobby that people thought we were bodyguards. We weren't. Officially, that job belonged to an experienced security man named Bill Barry. But big, athletic guys like Rosey and me came in handy. Bobby's charisma and ability to connect with people inspired fervent responses from the mobs that flocked to his rallies. We tried to keep the senator and Ethel from being overwhelmed by admirers.

At times the atmosphere was so delirious that supporters would fight for position just to be able to touch the candidate's hand or tousle his hair. Some tried to steal his cuff links or tear off pieces of his shirt or jacket. On one occasion I had to chase down a man who ripped Bobby's shoes off his feet and ran away with them. Another time, in Riverside, Bobby took off his jacket to work the crowd in rolled-up shirt-sleeves. Someone tore the jacket from his hands. I had to run through the crowd like a defensive back to catch him.

Oddly enough, even with JFK's assassination fresh in memory, I never gave much thought to the possibility of violence. The immediate danger was of Bobby or Ethel getting knocked down or crushed, or that the candidate would fall from a moving convertible while trying to shake hands. Often, we'd ride in open cars with me holding onto Bobby and somebody else holding onto me.

At times the mobs were more hostile than adoring. One

evening in Oakland stands out. The packed auditorium was dominated by Black Panthers. Bobby was sincere and forthright in asking for their support. Justifiably suspicious of all white politicians, the people in the audience asked tough, sometimes belligerent questions, which boiled down to: "Why should we trust you?" Bobby answered patiently. At one point he asked me to speak. I told the crowd, essentially, that RFK would serve them well, that I had been with him in every kind of community and the words he'd spoken that night he'd also spoken in Beverly Hills and Brentwood. I was booed. Cries of "Uncle Tom!" rang out.

When the meeting ended I tried to reason informally with people. Some listened, some argued, some stood defiantly silent, some made threatening remarks. I responded cautiously, knowing that any careless statement could ignite a violent outburst. At one point I realized, to my horror, that the entire campaign staff had left without me. This was more than an inconvenience; the atmosphere was so tense that anything could happen. Fortunately, Bobby discovered my absence while crossing the Bay Bridge and sent a car back to get me. I was never so relieved in my life.

The next day, against the advice of his handlers, the senator returned to Oakland for a ride-through. To my surprise, I saw some of the same people who had been antagonistic the night before run up to the motorcade and reach for Bobby's hand. Either they had been posturing at the rally or they had reconsidered their attitudes overnight.

My fondest memory of the campaign trail is of the final swing through the San Joaquin Valley. There was magic in the air, not just because it was my home territory, but because it was where Cesar Chavez had mobilized migrant farm workers into a force to be reckoned with—and into Kennedy supporters. Tens of thousands, including many of my Kingsburg friends, turned out to hear Bobby speak about his vision for the nation. They lined the train tracks between Fresno and Sacramento to greet the campaign on its whistle-stop tour through the valley. It was just the emotional high we needed after losing to McCarthy in Oregon. Then it was on to Los Angeles for the final days before the primary.

On the night of June 5, the campaign staff assembled in the senator's suite at the Ambassador Hotel to watch the primary election returns on television. Shortly before midnight it became clear that he had won. Euphorically, we piled into elevators to join the celebration downstairs. Outside the Embassy Room, where about two thousand jubilant supporters were partying, I found myself, for one quiet moment, alone with the candidate and his wife. I wish I could remember exactly what was said; it was the last conversation I ever had with my friend Bobby.

A moment later we were inside the ballroom, where bedlam reigned. I stood on the small stage, about ten feet from the senator. The space between us was packed shoulder-to-shoulder with politicians and staffers. In his victory speech, Bobby thanked by name everyone who had made a significant contribution: press secretary Frank Mankiewicz, campaign manager Fred Dutton, speech-writer Jeff Greenfield, Rosey Grier, Cesar Chavez, Ethel and the family and so on, even Don Drysdale who had pitched his sixth straight shutout that night. He referred to me as "my old friend, Rafer Johnson." His last public words were, "My thanks to all of you, and now it's on to Chicago, and let's win there." As cheers filled the room, he flashed the thumbs-up sign, then the "V" for victory (or, perhaps, peace). These ordinary words and gestures are frozen into memory now, like the image of JFK in his motorcade, waving to the crowd in Dallas.

From the minute I quit my job to join the campaign, I had

not given a thought to myself or my future. Now that we had accomplished our goal, it seemed that nothing could stop the Kennedy tide. Robert F. Kennedy was likely to become the Democratic nominee for president and go on to vanquish Richard Nixon in November, as his brother had done in 1960. I saw myself in Washington, working for the new Kennedy Administration in some capacity, doing whatever I could to bring people together and fulfill Bobby's vision of a peaceful nation where everyone is treated with compassion and dignity. I felt as if I had vaulted to some extraordinary height and was flying, weightless as a feather, over the bar.

The fall was sudden, swift, and devastating.

The senator turned to step down off the back of the platform. This was a surprise. He was supposed to walk through the crowd on his way to the press conference in another room. Why he decided instead to take the shortcut through the kitchen we'll never know. I assumed it was because he was too exhausted to work his way through the pandemonium. The campaign had been so grueling it made a decathlon seem like a stroll through a garden. Bobby was visibly drained.

Throughout the campaign the Kennedys had turned down offers from local police to provide protection. They did not want a uniformed presence, preferring to leave security matters in the hands of Bill Barry and their friends. I had taken it upon myself to look after Ethel, who was pregnant and often ignored in the commotion surrounding the senator. When Bobby changed his route that night, I pushed my way through the crowd and reached Ethel as she followed him through the curtain to the pantry.

That's when I heard the shots. At first I thought they were balloons bursting, or firecrackers, like the ones that had gone off a few days earlier in San Francisco's Chinatown, scaring the wits out of everyone in the motorcade. I turned in the direction of the sound. I saw smoke. Then I saw a gun. It was about a foot from the senator's head. More shots were fired. Holding the gun was the small, dark, wiry man the world would know as Sirhan Sirhan. I pushed Ethel out of harm's way and ran, lunging, toward the gun.

Everything seemed both starkly real and dreamlike. Time unfolded in both lightning speed and slow motion. Bodies darted about in quick, decisive movements. Screams and shrieks filled the air where exuberant cheers had just been heard. When I reached the gunman, others were trying to wrestle him down and grab the gun. Cries of "Oh, my God!" repeated over and over like a chorus, punctuated by "Grab the gun! Grab the gun, Rafer!" My hand clamped down on the weapon. Rosey's hand came down on mine. With a dozen others pushing and shoving, we forced Sirhan onto a steam table, then to the floor. He squirmed and jerked, but couldn't go anywhere. I told Rosey to let go, that I had the gun. He did. I twisted Sirhan's fingers to free up the weapon. I would have broken them if he had resisted. I stuck the gun in my pocket.

In the chaos, vengeful hands and feet tried to get at Sirhan. People yelled "Kill him!" and no doubt some in the frenzied mob would have gladly done so. He tried to shield himself from the blows. Rosey and I fended off the attackers. We did not want another Jack Ruby on our hands. Soon a cluster of men lifted the assassin and carried him through the swinging doors to be arrested.

Through all this, Bill Barry and others had attended to the senator. They emptied the room as best they could and cleared a path for the medical help. I saw Bobby being laid gently on a stretcher and quickly wheeled away. Ethel, protected by staffers, was at his side. In the space they had vacated was a sickening pool of blood.

The room was suddenly hushed. I leaned against the steam table, in a state of shock, trying to comprehend what had just taken place. I have no idea how long it took, or whom I was with, but I remember riding in a car to Good Samaritan Hospital. It was a tense, somber vigil, as we waited for news and braced ourselves for the worst. I was so dazed that I totally forgot about the gun in my pocket. Hours later, when I realized that the police would be looking for it, I turned it in and gave my statement.

With declining hope, the vigil continued for more than twenty-four hours. When the official word came that Bobby was dead, I landed, shattered and broken, in a sawdust pit of despair. It was a long time before I could crawl my way out.

9

OUT OF THE PIT, ONTO SOLID GROUND

What lies before us or behind us are small matters compared to what lies inside us.

—Ralph Waldo Emerson

THE DECATHLON'S ninth event, the javelin, comes late on the second day. At that point, you're battling fatigue and all the accumulated aches and pains from the previous events. This makes throwing the two-pound metal spear a far greater physical challenge in the decathlon than it is by itself. Its place in the schedule also makes it a psychological and strategic challenge. If you're out of contention, you have to swallow your disappointment and muster the pride and sportsmanship to give it your all anyway. If you're *in* contention, the pressure is on to increase your lead or, if you're behind, close the gap. You know that your throw will determine how much you have to accomplish in the final event, the arduous 1500 meters.

I entered the next phase of my life as if I'd been crushed by the pole vault landing and had to find the energy and strength to sprint down the runway, position the eight-foot javelin perfectly, and hurl it with power into an imagined hole in the sky. The assassination of Robert Kennedy, and my proximity to it, had left me traumatized and depressed. I despaired for myself and for my country. Yet I had to pull myself together and fling myself into an uncertain future.

Still in a daze, and virtually sleepless, I flew to New York for Senator Kennedy's funeral at St. Patrick's Cathedral. In six-man shifts, we maintained an all-night vigil with the purple-draped coffin. The next morning I attended a private Mass for Robert's close friends and relatives at the quiet, elegant Holy Family Church on East 47th Street. I remember Ethel walking to the chapel with some of her children. She had chosen to bravely face the throng of reporters and photographers rather than hide in a limousine. That same implacable courage and dignity was also on display after the service. At a luncheon at the home of Douglas Dillon, a close friend of the Kennedys and a former secretary of the treasury, Ethel kept trying to coax me into eating caviar, which I hated, and teasing me for being so stubborn.

More than two thousand mourners, including President and Lady Bird Johnson, Richard Nixon, Coretta Scott King, and Jacqueline Kennedy Onassis, packed the cathedral for the funeral. Many more crowded Fifth Avenue to hear the service over loudspeakers. I was in one of the pews reserved for close friends, just behind the family and dignitaries. The Mass was both sorrowful and uplifting. Leonard Bernstein conducted a thirty-piece orchestra in a somber movement from Mahler. Bobby's friend Andy Williams sang "Battle Hymn of the Republic." Archbishop Cooke, Cardinal of New York, conducted the Mass; Cardinal Cushing of Boston delivered the Absolution. The most moving moment was Ted Kennedy's eulogy, in which he said, with cracking voice, "My brother need not be idealized or enlarged in death beyond what he was in life, [but] to be remembered simply as a good and decent man who saw wrong and tried to right it, saw suffering and tried to heal it, saw war and tried to stop it. Those of us who loved him and who take him to his rest today pray that what he was to us and what he wished for others will someday come to pass for all the world."

As one of the pallbearers, I helped carry the coffin up the cathedral's long aisle and into Fifth Avenue, where it was placed in a hearse and taken to Pennsylvania Station for the final journey to Washington, D.C. The train, filled with Bobby's family, friends, and associates, passed by a virtually unbroken line of mourners. Men and women of all ages, all colors, and all strata of society lined the tracks, weeping openly, waving American flags, holding up signs that read "We'll miss you" and "Goodbye, Bobby." At one point during the ride, Ethel walked the length of the train to thank people and lift their spirits.

Five hours behind schedule, the train pulled into Union Station. As a band played the "U.S. Navy Theme," we carried the casket to a hearse. The motorcade stopped briefly at the Lincoln Memorial, where a chorus sang "Battle Hymn of the Republic," then proceeded past thousands of grieving people to Arlington National Cemetery. It was close to midnight, four full days after the shooting, that we lowered Bobby to his final resting place on a grassy hillside, close to his brother Jack. Then, despite the hour, Ethel had a few dozen friends to Hickory Hill for dinner.

Back in Los Angeles, I holed up in the house on West Boulevard. I saw only my family and close friends. I became slightly paranoid. No one knew whether the assassin had acted alone or was part of a conspiracy. No one knew what might come next, or who among Bobby's associates might also be targeted. I even resorted to subterfuge at times: When I wanted to see someone I went to a phone booth, called person-to-person for a fictitious name, and said I'd call back in an hour, meaning I'd be there at that time. It sounds irrational now, but I was concerned for my safety.

My main concern was for my privacy. I did not want people staring at me, offering me condolences, or asking me questions. Some people deal with trauma by talking about it. I understand the need for such a catharsis, but that has never been my way. I find solitude more healing. I could not bear to speak about the assassination, and spent time only with people who would understand that. I testified at Sirhan's trial, of course, but I spokc to the press about the night of June 5 only when I felt it was absolutely necessary. I still get calls from authors, conspiracy theorists, and news reporters, especially when Sirhan comes up for parole. I turn down virtually every request. To this day it's difficult for me to speak about the tragedy. In fact, one reason I did not write this autobiography years ago was that I knew I would have to relive the events in detail.

Over the years I've been approached by people who are convinced that Sirhan was not the only gunman, or that he was just a fall guy for the Mafia, the CIA, or some other powerful groups. They are amazed that I have no interest in their theories or evidence. For the sake of this book, I looked at some of their material. I read about the missing police data, the mysterious woman in the polka dot dress who allegedly shouted "We killed him!" as she ran from the murder scene, the possibility that more bullets were fired than Sirhan's gun could hold, and so forth. It's all very provocative, but the counter evidence is also convincing and I've never been inclined to look into it deeply enough to form an opinion. I'd prefer to leave the investigating to others and the final conclusion to history. All I know is, I literally saw a smoking gun in the hand of the man who's in jail. I only wish I had seen it before it was fired.

In the dark days following my friend's death, I found solace in contemplation, the tenderness of loved ones, and the spiritual truths I held sacred. Throughout the 1960s I had remained active in my church. Unless I was out of town, I was at Bel Air Presbyterian for services every Sunday morning, and often on a weekday night as well. I sang in the choir. I helped in the Sunday School nursery. I gave speeches periodically as part of the church's outreach program. I became a deacon. Now, in my grief, I turned to my faith for strength. It had always been my rock. In good times it taught me to be humble and thankful. In bad times it anchored me, soothed me, and helped me make sense of what seemed unfathomable.

Thanks to my religious grounding, I knew, deep in my heart, that no matter how bad things were, there was reason to go on and reason to believe that the dark cloud that covered me would one day lift. I read the scriptures at home, attended services, and allowed myself the company of members of the congregation who understood my suffering and did not have to talk about it or make a display of compassion. A pat on the back or a firm hand on my arm was sufficient, and every such gesture gave me strength.

I also found refuge in physical labor. Building or repairing objects had always been a way for me to relax and take my mind off things. If you're hammering a nail you have to focus on what you're doing with your hands; you can't let your mind buzz around like a bumblebee or get obsessed by some problem. Construction is clean and pure. Like a good story it has a beginning, a middle, and an end, and it's not satisfying unless you see it through to completion. So I built a fence around my property. It served my need for physical activity and, unlike a cabinet or a porch, it fed my desire for isolation.

I knew I could not stay secluded forever. But I could not summon up the motivation to do anything. No project or job seemed worth the bother. Fittingly, it was a Kennedy who got me up and moving again.

Eunice Shriver, Bobby's sister, had been working for years on behalf of children with mental retardation. Under the auspices of the Joseph P. Kennedy Foundation, which was named for her father, she had been instrumental in the creation of the President's Committee on Mental Retardation and the passage of the Mental Retardation Facilities Act of 1963. Each summer she turned her estate in Maryland into a day camp for individuals with mental disabilities. Seeing that athletics could help these neglected citizens realize their potential and gain self-confidence, she spearheaded the development of sports programs for them. Now Eunice had organized an international track and field meet, to be held in Chicago that July. It was to be called Special Olympics.

I had helped Eunice with some of her efforts in the past and had come to have enormous respect for her. Of all the Kennedy's, she just might have made the best president. She was a strong leader, a well-organized administrator, and an inspiring speaker. Watching her convince congressmen to support programs for people with mental retardation made me think she could persuade anyone to do anything.

It had not taken much persuading for Eunice to get me to promise to participate in the Chicago event, but after the assassination I thought it might be cancelled. I had forgotten that the Kennedy way to deal with tragedy was to gather one's strength and get to work again, doing some good in the world. That's what Bobby himself had done after his brother Jack was murdered. When Eunice called to ensure that I'd be in Chicago, I could not say no, regardless of how much I wanted to be alone.

A few weeks later I was in Soldier Field as Mayor Richard Daley welcomed the parade of a thousand special athletes. A torch-lighting ceremony modeled after the modern Olympic

Games opened the competition. The weekend was a tonic for my grief; no doctor could have prescribed a better therapy. I had always appreciated the healing power of sports, but this was a demonstration of a higher order. Here were children and young adults who all their lives had been made to feel unworthy and incompetent. Many had been shunted into lifeless institutions. Now they had a chance to know the thrill of accomplishment. Tapping into courage and strength they never had a chance to display, their bodies straightened, their eyes brightened, and their faces lit up with joy. They competed with one another, but every participant was made to feel like a winner. It was impossible to come away from that without feeling better about the world. I made a commitment to help Special Olympics, and I've been doing so ever since.

One month later, in August, I was once again in Chicago, this time for an entirely different experience: the tumultuous 1968 Democratic National Convention. Delegates pledged to Robert Kennedy were free to throw their votes to the candidate of their choice. We tried to use that leverage to influence the party platform and extract promises from the remaining candidates—Hubert Humphrey, Eugene McCarthy, and George McGovern—to honor Senator Kennedy's position on Vietnam and other issues. Some of us also staged a battle to have a film about Bobby shown on the convention floor.

The big story was the terrifying riots that took place in Lincoln Park, directly across the street from my hotel. Mayor Daley, who had been so gracious in helping us stage the Special Olympics, unleashed the full force of the police on the young people who had come to Chicago to demonstrate and have their voices heard. Normally, witnessing such bloody brutality would have enraged me. Coming on the heels of assassinations and urban riots, it merely sickened me. When will the violence end? I wondered. Where is the country headed?

I could not help but wonder how different Chicago would have been if the senator and Martin Luther King had been present. With leaders like them to rally around, the angry young people who took to the streets might have been inspired instead of alienated. In all likelihood, RFK would have been nominated and gone on to be president. If that had happened, the war in Vietnam would have ended in 1969, not 1972, and thousands of lives would have been spared. We would also have been spared the humiliation of Watergate and the loss of faith in government that has followed. Over time, Americans with disparate backgrounds and interests might have found common ground instead of being pitted against each other.

Eventually I decided to cast my delegate's ballot for Humphrey. I liked him and respected his long-standing commitment to civil rights. I was disappointed that he had not come out against the Vietnam War, but I knew that as Vice President his hands had been tied. I hoped that when elected he would take a strong stand for peace. Unfortunately, the madness in the streets of Chicago and the divisions within the Democratic Party helped to elect Richard Nixon instead.

My two trips to Chicago that summer made me feel the loss of Bobby even more deeply. Yet at the same time they helped me stay close to him. I've remained close over the years, through my friendship with his children and with Ethel—who has always been as much my friend as Bobby was—and the Shrivers. I have seen many of the Kennedys at Special Olympics events; I have visited Hickory Hill whenever possible, and I spend part of many summers at Hyannis Port. I continue to participate in tennis and golf tournaments that Ethel holds in Bobby's memory to raise money for humanitarian causes.

Of my many fond memories of Ethel in the years following Bobby's death, several stand out. One was the evening in December 1968 when she gave birth to her last child. Few people had known that Ethel was pregnant during the campaign. A week before she was due to give birth, her doctor advised a cesarean section. Along with Ted Kennedy and a few friends, I accompanied Ethel to Georgetown Hospital. We had hoped to keep her arrival private, but were greeted by a cadre of reporters. Ethel named her daughter Rory.

The second memory is what the media termed Ethel's "coming out after a year of mourning." She always felt more comfortable having close friends around when she had to appear in public, so she asked me to accompany her to a party in Southampton, New York. It was a benefit for Cesar Chavez's United Farm Workers, a cause that Bobby had championed.

Another memory was the sail across the choppy waters of San Francisco Bay when Ethel visited a group of Native Americans who had occupied Alcatraz Island. On that same trip we went to Salinas to visit Cesar Chavez, who had been jailed for refusing to call off a lettuce boycott. To avoid the hostile demonstrators yelling "Ethel go home!" police hustled us through the back door of the jailhouse.

I remember the unveiling at the National Gallery of the official White House portrait of JFK; the canoe trip on the Chattahoochee River with Ethel, football star Fran Tarkenton, and mountaineer Jim Whittaker; and the trips to Paris, Hawaii, and other places on behalf of Special Olympics. One of those occasions, in July 1969, is especially memorable. I had escorted Ethel to the Connecticut Special Olympics. She seemed to be her usual congenial self. It was only later that I realized how remarkable this was: That morning, a car registered to Senator Edward Kennedy had been found submerged in the water off Chappaquidick Island.

One of my most cherished possessions is the Christmas

present Ethel gave me in 1968, a plaque inscribed "With so much love from Ethel." On it is a passage from Bobby's speech in Indianapolis right after Martin Luther King was killed. It reads, in part, "What we need in the United States . . . is love and wisdom and compassion toward one another, and a feeling of justice toward those who still suffer within our own country, whether they be white or black. Let us dedicate ourselves to what the Greeks wrote so many years ago: to tame the savageness of man and make gentle the life of this world. Let us dedicate ourselves to that, and say a prayer for our country and for our people."

Over the years, I've tried as best I could to live up to those words and honor the memory of my friend.

Once again, I had to find a way to earn a living. After the assassination, KNBC had asked me to come back to my broadcasting job, but I was not ready to do *anything* at that time, let alone face a camera and deadline pressure every day. Besides, I had left the station with a bad taste in my mouth. I didn't think I was treated well even before the controversy over my campaigning, and I felt I'd been pulled off the air for political reasons, not concern about FCC regulations. If another offer had come along I might have continued in broadcasting, but the only opportunities at the time required moving to a location far from my Los Angeles home.

In 1969 an agent approached me about going back to acting. At first I said no, but the more I thought about it the more it made sense. Making films was fun, and it paid well as long as you could find work. It would also enable me to maintain some privacy, not only between films but during a shoot as well, since locations are guarded environments. Every reporter who interviewed me—whether the ostensible subject was the Mexico City Olympics, a film I was working on, or the charitable organizations with which I was involved—had questions about the assassination. I simply did not want to talk about it.

I signed with the agent, an aggressive dynamo who swore he was going to make me a star. I enrolled in a top-notch acting class and began working on my craft. I wanted to be taken seriously as an actor, not just cash in on my athletic fame. Soon I was offered a role in a movie titled *The Last Grenade.* Set in the Far East and shot in southern Spain, it's about a group of British mercenaries, led by a character played by Stanley Baker, who track down a renegade who has fled to the jungle after turning against his comrades. The subplot involves Baker in a love triangle with Richard Attenborough and Honor Blackman. I play one of Baker's troops. Physically, I hadn't worked that hard since my decathlon days. At age thirty-four, I was in pretty good shape, but I was not prepared for running a hundred yards at full speed with a pack on my back, or falling backward into an icy river and holding my breath while the scene played out, or carrying a 180-pound man up a hill—and repeating these ordeals take after take after take. For all that effort, my character gets killed early in the film.

I loved every minute of it. It felt good to be productive again, and the cast and crew could not have been better company. Even though we were shooting for sixteen hours a day, six days a week, on the seventh day we played—golf mostly, with Richard Attenborough and Stanley Baker, and Stanley's buddy, Sean Connery, who owned a house nearby. Being far away from reminders of the assassination helped me to regain the emotional strength that the tragedy had sapped from me.

Shortly afterward I was in Rome to shoot *The Games.* This was a strange sort of *déjà vu,* as the film takes place during the Rome Olympics of 1960. This time around I got to see some of the Eternal City in the daylight. The movie tracks four runners as they prepare for the marathon, and follows them during the race. I play myself as a sportscaster who covers the event, following the runners through the streets of Rome in a mobile unit. The race ends up in Olympic Stadium, where I had won the gold medal a decade earlier. I was in good company: Michael Crawford, Sam Elliott, Stanley Baker, Charles Aznavour, and Ryan O'Neal were all in the cast. When the film was released, I organized and emceed a premiere to benefit Special Olympics.

Then came what I consider my most worthwhile role. The film actually started out as a PBS documentary produced by the University of Nebraska about a neglected piece of American history: the hundreds of African Americans who helped settle and develop the Great Plains. Called *The Black Frontier,* the film was originally a four-part series covering black pioneers and traders, cowherders, the all-black 9th- and 10th-Cavalry regiments (the "Buffalo Soldiers"), and the freed slaves who migrated westward after the Civil War. In the film, I portray an ex-slave and cattleman named Ned Huddleston.

While shooting the documentary, the film-makers realized they had the makings of a feature film about the Buffalo Soldiers. A black businessman and a white lawyer from Kansas City raised the funds, and the cast and crew descended on Texas. We shot in and around Fort Davis, which had been the headquarters of the actual 10th Cavalry. The resulting film was not bad, considering the budget was less than a million dollars. It depicts the Buffalo Soldiers in all their complex reality, as both heroic warriors and human beings with flaws and inner conflicts. It also highlights a great irony: The soldiers were hated by the Texans because they were black; hated by the Mexicans because they were American; hated by the Indians because they were U.S. soldiers; and neglected by the U.S. government, which issued them inferior supplies.

I play Private Armstrong, a good man who is torn between his sworn duty and his friendship with an Indian chief who is supposed to be his enemy. It was my best role by far, and the one I am proudest of. It was also the easiest part to play, since the most difficult thing for me was to be in a scene where I had nothing to do. I'd had plenty of roles like that, but this time my character was pivotal to the story and affected the lives of other key characters. The most enjoyable scene for me was one in which I ride into the fort reeling drunk, singing at the top of my lungs and insulting my superiors. I had never even been tipsy in my life, so I researched the scene by watching other actors play drunks on television.

Called *The Red, White and Black,* the movie had a brief release in 1970. Two years later, Fanfare Films bought the rights and recut the film, adding a new score and correcting some technical flaws. It was re-released as *Soul Soldier* with a lot of publicity. At the time, films with predominantly black casts were doing big business. Most were what came to be called "blaxploitation" films, like the *Shaft* series with Richard Roundtree. But there were more serious pictures as well, and I'm proud to say that *Soul Soldier* was one of them. I only wish more people had seen it.

During those years I also appeared on several television shows, as a bad guy on *Mission: Impossible,* for example, and a runaway slave who steals furs to earn passage to Africa on *Daniel Boone.* I also played *The Dating Game,* shot a pilot for a sports series that never aired, and even hosted a talk show called *Monday Through Friday.* This was an early version of the Regis and Kathie Lee format, hosted by a different male–female team each night of the week. It lasted less than a season.

By 1971, I craved a more settled life. Acting was creative and exciting, but my future in the film business felt uncertain. I was not sure I would ever get beyond minor roles in mediocre movies, and I was tired of wondering when my next job was going to come. I was past my thirty-fifth birthday and had never had a steady income or anything resembling job security. If I was ever going to have a family of my own, I would have to change that, but I didn't know how. I wanted work I could count on every day, something with a future I could actually see. Strange as it may seem, what I wanted more than anything was to have a small business of my own, where I made a product or provided a service, where my days would be simple, orderly, and productive. I have never found that.

I did find the next best thing, however: a good job. On a trip to Washington for a meeting of the National Advisory Committee on Physical Education and Recreation for Handicapped Children, I met a man named George Valos. George had been a school superintendent in Bakersfield, California, and was then working for Continental Telephone. An independent company providing telephone service to small communities in forty-two states, Con Tel had recently started an affirmative action program. George knew that the company wanted a person of color to be involved. He set up a meeting for me with George Atmore, the personnel director, and Jack Maguire, the president of the company. I was hired as a part-time consultant for affirmative action.

I began commuting to Bakersfield a few days a week, driving about 120 miles each way. The area felt like home to me, Bakersfield being at the southern end of the San Joaquin Valley, but the corporate world was entirely new. To my surprise, I found it fascinating. I took to the new challenge like a fish to water. Con Tel was a big-time, first-class company in a small town; the people who ran it were terrific and I was doing something worthwhile—providing opportunities to minorities. Before long, I was asked to head up the affirmative action program full-time. Suddenly I had a company car, stock options, good health insurance, country club memberships, and a huge office.

Within two years I was made vice-president of personnel. Each division of the company had its own personnel department; I was in charge of the whole system. On my first morning as vice-president, my assistant placed a memo on my desk. I never got to it. Before long it was at the bottom of a huge pile of memos and messages, the reading of which got interrupted by a barrage of phone calls and meetings. That's how the job was to be: a constant challenge in problem solving. There was a lot of pressure, but I was used to that. I also had to deal with the unexpressed resentment of employees who felt I'd been promoted because the company wanted to display a black executive, or because the president liked playing golf with a celebrity. I focused on getting the job done to the best of my abilities. As far as I can tell I eventually earned the respect of every key person in the company.

I'd had no training and no administrative experience other than People to People and student government, both of which were smaller and vastly different. But I used the assets I did have to advantage. I knew how to work with a team; I knew how to treat people with respect and motivate them to perform well; I knew how to get help from those with expertise. I was also an eager student. Ducky Drake used to say that my greatest asset as an athlete was my ability to take instruction and make adjustments. Because everything was new to me, I had no preconceptions, no biases, and no axes to grind. I could look at every issue with fresh, wide-open eyes. When push came to shove, I turned to common sense and my personal code of ethics.

Jack Maguire, the company president, was smart enough to know that my fame was more of an asset than my lack of experience was a liability. I was able to get to people—politicians, legislators, government bureaucrats—whom other executives could not. I gave speeches at events to which others would not have been invited. I gave motivational talks at company conventions, using my athletic experiences to inspire the audience. I used the connections I'd made to do some important lobbying on behalf of the company and the telephone industry. My reputation and access also enabled me to play an instrumental role in Con Tel's acquisition of other companies.

When I started working full-time, I considered moving to Bakersfield. I even began looking for an apartment near the office. But the manager of one complex told me to my face that they did not rent to Negroes. That soured me on living in Bakersfield. I grew to love the city and its small-town sense of community, and especially the people I worked with. However, in those days, part of Bakersfield's population had emigrated from areas of the country where racial bigotry was a way of life. I did not personally encounter much of it, but I knew it existed. It was not the right place for me to raise a family.

It was, however, the right time. Now that I finally had a steady income, not to mention benefits and generous perks, I could think seriously about settling down.

One of the few pleasant things that happened to me at the 1968 Democratic Convention in Chicago was meeting Gloria Steinem. She too had been a Kennedy supporter who was trying to move the party in the direction RFK would have taken it. I believe we met on a bus going to or from one of the convention events.

Sometime the following year I looked up Gloria in New York, where she lived. That was the beginning of a friendship and romance that continued on and off for a couple of years. Our lives were not exactly conducive to steady intimacy. We would see each other when I had to be in New York or Gloria had to be in California. Long periods of time would pass when our only contact was by telephone. When we were together we had to squeeze private moments into hectic, and very public, schedules. I remember dinners and parties with New York literary figures and activists—a black-tie reception for the Bedford

Stuyvesant Restoration Project, for example—and rallies on behalf of political or social causes, such as a march to the Mexican border with Cesar Chavez to dramatize the unity between the poor of both countries. With us, it was never just a quiet dinner and a movie.

According to one of Gloria's biographers, I was the first of several black men with whom she had relationships. Reportedly, she found African-American men "more sensitive to the dangers and oppressions of sexism than their white male counterparts." Gloria felt that anyone who had been discriminated against because of an inborn, superficial quality like skin color would naturally empathize with women, who were held back because of their gender. Also, most black men have grown up with mothers and sisters who had to work and whose choices were limited by sex as well as race. I can't speak for others, but the basic goals of feminism—equality of opportunity, equal pay for equal work, and the like—are easy for me to comprehend and support. It seems not only wrong but a tragic waste of talent to keep women out of positions of power and influence.

On a personal level, Gloria's views were not an obstacle; they were an attraction. Maybe because I was raised by a strong, wise, courageous mother, I admired the same qualities in Gloria. Her independent spirit appealed to me as much as her concern for the disadvantaged. It's often forgotten that, long before she became an icon of feminism, Gloria put herself on the front lines of every social battle of the 1960s. (Evidently, my admiration for her was mutual. A magazine once asked Gloria to name the ten men she most admired; I was deeply moved to find myself on the same list as Bobby Kennedy.)

From time to time I'd have to laugh about the things that were said about Gloria by people who did not know her. There was nothing abrasive about her, for instance; she was warm, mild-mannered, and thoughtful. There was nothing phony or self-important about her either; she was as real as rain and often self-effacing. And she certainly didn't hate men. If Gloria hated anything it was injustice—that, and being singled out for her looks instead of what she stood for. But at the risk of offending her I must say that Gloria was as beautiful as she was intelligent, and she still is.

Although we loved, respected, and trusted each other, our lives were too chaotic even to consider an exclusive relationship. At the time, Gloria's star was on the rise. She wrote a regular column in *New York* magazine and articles for other influential publications, and she was constantly trying to raise money and awareness for the women's liberation movement, which was just taking shape (*Ms.* magazine wouldn't start up until 1972). She was constantly in demand by the media and various activist groups. But the connection between us was powerful. "This was not the kind of romance in which you're looking for the other person to complete you," Gloria once said. "Brief though it was, it was more like a mature love than most of the romances we think of."

My feelings for Gloria were strong enough for me to entertain thoughts of marriage. The thoughts didn't hold up to scrutiny, however. For one thing, I felt that being married to a black man might impede Gloria's mission. She was already under pressure; why should she have to deal with the added burden of an interracial marriage? I'm sure Gloria would say that was nonsense, and maybe it was, but at the time I felt that I might be a deterrent to her work. On a selfish level, I wasn't sure I wanted to live with the kind of constant scrutiny that Gloria seemed destined to attract. I longed for a quieter, more private existence.

Geography was another impediment. It would have been difficult for me to move to New York, and Gloria did not want to live in Los Angeles. More important, I wanted a traditional family life, complete with children. I wasn't sure Gloria shared that vision. In later years, in fact, she apparently decided never to marry or have kids.

Oddly enough, we never discussed any of this. Perhaps I was too private and Gloria too shy for either of us to bring up such issues. Maybe the answers were so obvious we didn't have to. In any event, the relationship just sort of faded. Years—in fact, decades—later, I learned that Gloria had fallen in love with someone else and had always felt badly about not telling me the truth. There was no reason for her to feel guilty. I had come to realize that marriage was not in our future and had begun to see more clearly that the woman I *should* marry was already in my life.

In retrospect, it seems that Betsy Thorsen and I were destined for each other. In a sense, we met before I knew it. As girls, Betsy and her older sister, Barbara, were track and field fans. Because they lived in nearby Arcadia, they knew all about Rafer Johnson, the UCLA star. In 1956, when Barbara was a high school senior, she talked her parents into sending her to Melbourne to see the Olympics. On the flight over, she happened to sit next to someone else who was traveling alone: my mother.

Back home, Barbara told her younger sister all about the Olympics, including the story of Rafer Johnson, who won a silver medal despite his injuries and whose mother was now her friend. The following year Barbara enrolled in the College of the Pacific in Stockton. Since Kingsburg was on her way, she would often visit my mother when driving between Los Angeles and school. On at least one of those occasions, Betsy was with her older sister and met the woman who would one day become her mother-in-law. She met me for the first time after a speech I gave at an *L.A. Times* track and field banquet. A couple introduced themselves as Paul and Maggie Thorsen, the parents of my mother's young friend Barbara. With them was their fourteen-year-old daughter, Betsy. To be honest, I don't remember that meeting. I suppose I saw it as just a pleasant handshake with a young fan.

When Barbara transferred to UCLA, I was a senior and student body president. Betsy continued to hear about me from her sister. The next year, the entire Thorsen family went to Rome for the 1960 Olympics. When it started pouring on the first day of the decathlon, the rest of Betsy's family left the stadium, but Betsy insisted on staying. "They were mad that I was late to a dinner they were having," she recalls, "but it was too exciting to leave. I couldn't wait until the next day to see the rest of it. When Rafer won, I was so thrilled I knew I would never forget it."

A year or two later I was invited to speak at a church in Pasadena. As I recall, it was a Rose Bowl breakfast sponsored by a Christian organization. Maggie Thorsen saw a mention of it in the newspaper and suggested that the family go hear me speak. As before, they came up to chat afterward. By now Betsy was a high school senior. Here's how she remembers it: "Rafer gave me a business card from People to People and wrote his home phone number on it. He was living on West Boulevard by then. I still have the card."

The next time we met was in 1966. Betsy had just graduated from UCLA and had started her first job, teaching school in Orange County. Feeling lonely in her first apartment, she took out her address book and started calling people, beginning with the A's and moving through the alphabet. When she got to J, she called me. We talked for a while, then she moved on to the K's.

I'd better let Betsy tell the next part: "One day I was in Westwood, and I thought I would call Rafer and see how he was doing. He invited me to dinner and gave me directions to his house. I remember him walking out to greet me. He was wearing a black golf shirt, a black alpaca sweater, and black pants. I said to myself, 'Oh, my God.' Something changed at that moment. I felt something I never had before. I was looking at him in an entirely different way. I went in and sat down. His mother, sister, and nephew were there. I was so nervous that I threw up three times."

Since I'd last seen her, Betsy had become a young woman—a young *attractive* woman. She was 23, I was 32. "We finished dinner and Rafer walked me out to my car," Betsy recalls. "I could sense that the attraction was mutual. I felt he was hesitating. I said, 'Why don't you come down to my apartment and have dinner sometime?' Not too long after that, he did. I cooked something, we went for a ride through the hills in Laguna. It was romantic. I remember him saying, 'From what I see, you would be very easy to fall in love with.' I don't remember what I said in response."

We started seeing each other on and off. The "off" periods were my doing. As I described earlier, the years 1967 through 1970 were stormy and chaotic. I was on the go constantly, and away from Los Angeles for long periods of time. I was unsure about a lot of things, including my career and the kind of woman that would be right for me. I wish things had been different, so Betsy could have had an easier time of it. She was more certain of her feelings than I was. I'm sure my inability to commit to a future together was difficult for her, especially since she would sometimes open a newspaper or magazine and read about me with Pat Morrow, the actress, or Gloria Steinem.

"People would tell me to forget about him," Betsy recalls. "I would make myself go out with other men, but I would usually be thinking about Rafer. Even when he was not being thoughtful, I could see the real person underneath. I loved him, and I just knew it would be okay." She had every reason to give up on me. I'll always be grateful that she did not.

Sometime late in 1970 or early in 1971, we began to see each other more steadily. I began to think in terms of marriage. Betsy seemed to be everything I could want in a lifelong partner. She had an unmistakable core of goodness. She was the kindest, most thoughtful and considerate person I'd ever known. She was also incredibly smart. I knew I could depend on her judgment. A hard worker, extremely efficient and well-organized, she was the kind of person you could turn to if you needed anything done. She shared the values that were closest to my heart, and had the same vision of family and community. Like me, she adored kids and wanted to have some of her own. She was involved with her church; in fact, we went to services together even while we were dating. I was also impressed by how she handled being with me in public. Often people would fawn over me and ignore her. She never got irritated, and never seemed terribly impressed. It just seemed to amuse her, and I liked that.

As sweet as she was, Betsy was also tough—very tough and very strong. If you were in a posse, you'd want Betsy riding next to you. This was very important to me. Anyone in an interracial marriage in those days had to be prepared to put up with all kinds of things. Even beloved figures like Harry Belafonte had drawn a lot of heat—from both races—for marrying across the racial divide. I knew that Betsy would not stand for intolerance or insensitive behavior. She had strong principles and when those principles were violated, she was more like a towering warrior than a petite schoolteacher. Her will was as strong as her values. When Betsy made up her mind about something, it was going to happen. She always persevered—as she did with me before I came to my senses. I knew I could count on her loyalty and tenacity the rest of my life.

Those are just the qualities I can articulate. I felt comfortable with Betsy. I could always be myself with her. Above all, we loved each other, plain and simple; that inexplicable something that binds two souls was, in the final analysis, the most compelling reason to get married.

And so, one night, I called her up and proposed. "We've been seeing each other for a long time," I began. Betsy's first thought was, Here we go, he's breaking up with me. Instead, I said, "I think we should get married." She said, "Yes."

Afterward, she tells me, she thought, I finally have what I've wanted all these years, but . . . do I *really* want this? It was the usual cold feet. My feet must have chilled a little as well. According to Betsy, after we hung up the phone that night she didn't hear from me for two weeks—until she called me. Honestly, I don't remember it that way, but I trust her memory better than my own. I may have been traveling, but that's no excuse for not calling. I worked for a telephone company, after all! I have no explanation. I can't even explain why I proposed on the phone instead of in person. I can only say, I'm glad she said yes.

When we first announced our engagement, I think my mother was a bit resistant—not because Betsy was white but because someone, *anyone,* was taking her son. As for Betsy's family, if there was any trace of *Guess Who's Coming to Dinner* in the Thorsens' home, I was not aware of it. They were as welcoming as any in-laws could be. "I don't think there were ever any racial worries," my mother-in-law told a reporter. "My kids are pretty independent thinkers." The only flack came from one of Betsy's uncles, an unrepentant bigot who refused to attend the wedding. He wasn't missed. Naturally, Betsy and I had discussed the racial factor, mainly in terms of the problems our children might face. Once we were in sync on that issue, we proceeded as if our skin colors matched as well as our hearts and minds.

We decided to get married in December. Later I tried to change the date to the following June. Betsy said, "No way!" We got married on December 18, 1971, at St. Andrews Presbyterian Church in Newport Beach. I imported my old friend and pastor, Lou Evans, to officiate. It was a beautiful ceremony, made all the more glorious by poinsettias and other touches of Christmas. The ushers included fraternity brothers, friends from Kingsburg, and C. K. Yang. My nephew Brian was the ringbearer. My brother Jim was best man. The only sad note was that my brother Ed was in Germany and could not attend.

The reception, an elegant affair with about 300 guests, was held in the Thorsens' home in Newport Beach. When it ended, the orchestra followed Betsy and me to the pier. Under a barrage of rice we boarded her parents' boat and sailed off into the starry night. It was a dramatic way to end a magnificent day, but it was really just a romantic flourish. The boat motored around the bend, where we disembarked to begin our honeymoon on land.

Pictures and accounts of the wedding appeared all over the country, including *Newsweek* and the front page of the *New York Post.* Soon, though, my public profile began to fade and I settled into a new, more normal existence. We rented an apartment in Santa Monica. Betsy continued to teach eighth and ninth grade in the Orange County town of Fountain Valley. I continued working at Continental. In 1973, when our daughter Jenny was born, we bought a house in Sherman Oaks. Two years later, our son Josh was born.

I had done big, exciting things in my life. I had enough plaques and trophies to fill a garage, and enough clippings to fill a small library. I'd been an Olympic champion, a Hollywood personality, a friend to a senator and presidential candidate. I had dated beautiful women, traveled the world, and been glorified in cover stories and network documentaries. I'd experienced things very few men had and many men craved. Now I had what most men cherish and live for: a good, steady job, a loving wife, two great children, a home in the suburbs, an honored place in my church and community. Ordinary pleasures, simple treasures. What they gave me was far more meaningful than anything I'd known before.

I had started this phase of my life lost and battered, on shaky legs. I had thrown myself like a javelin into a new life, hoping I was aiming in the right direction. Now I had landed. I was planted securely in the ground and I was content.

10

GOING THE DISTANCE

Let us lay aside every weight, and the sin which doth so easily beset us, and let us run with patience the race that is set before us.

—Epistle to the Hebrews, 12:1

IN 1960 *Time* magazine asked me about the grueling nature of my sport. "The whole decathlon is ridiculous," I said, "but the 1500 meters is insanity." When asked why I keep on doing it, I responded, "Because every time I walk out there I think maybe I'll do a little better than the time before."

The longest, most demanding event of all, the 1500-meter race comes at night, often late, after two full days of competition, when you're physically exhausted and emotionally drained. When, as in Rome, victory or defeat hinges on running nearly a mile, it's easy to rise to the occasion. In most cases, though, your performance will have little bearing on the final outcome, or on how you'll be remembered. But *you* will remember, and that's what counts. You give it your best because what stays with you longest is the last thing you did before you left the track.

It's not just speed and stamina that determine the outcome of the 1500 meters, but also strategy. Because you never know what the race is going to ask of you, it is essential to be aware of what's going on at every moment and be prepared to respond.

I've tried to approach the rest of my life the way I approached the 1500 meters. In maturity, when the glory days are over, the challenges are different. The race ahead takes foresight, endurance, and commitment. Mental toughness and emotional stamina play a bigger role than the sheer physical prowess that can carry a young athlete to victory. In the game of life, winning and losing are less cut-and-dried than in sports. You strive to do well, not for fame and medals but because you have a responsibility to others and because, when all is said and done, you want to know that you have always been the best that you can be.

Jack Maguire, the president of Continental Telephone, was kind enough, and smart enough, to give me a lot of autonomy. Throughout my fifteen-year tenure—as vice-president of personnel and, later, of community affairs—I was allowed to keep up my outside interests as long as I got my job done. While building a hiring program for women and for people of color, and mediating personnel complaints and equal-opportunity disputes, I lent time and energy to causes I considered important. On occasion, I even made some extra money. Jack not only respected my involvements but saw them as good public relations. Every time I was introduced to an audience or written up in a newspaper, I was referred to as a Con Tel executive. One of my greatest honors, for example, also helped the company's local image: Bakersfield's school for children with mental disabilities was renamed the Rafer Johnson Elementary School for Exceptional Children.

An unexpected reward for traveling so much in the 1970s was getting to know Jesse Owens. We met when I was in St. Louis on Con Tel business. When I heard that Jesse was in town to give a speech, I arranged to see him. I was impressed by how trim and fit he looked, and even more by something he said. A child in the audience said that he wanted to grow up to be just like Jesse Owens. Jesse asked how old he was. The boy said he was nine. "Then be the best nine-year-old you can be," said Jesse. "And when you're ten, be the best ten-year-old you can be. And when you're eleven . . ." I could see that the message would have a big impact on the boy, and perhaps on other kids in the audience.

Our paths crossed a number of times after that. Jesse was always friendly, dignified, and humble. One of my proudest moments was when we were both inducted into the first class of the Track and Field Hall of Fame.

Continental's flexibility allowed me to squeeze in some film and television work as well. I had a small role in a television movie called *The Loneliest Runner,* about a teenage athlete with the embarrassing problem of bed-wetting. It was written, produced, and directed by Michael Landon. In the James Bond movie, *License to Kill,* with Timothy Dalton, I play a Drug Enforcement Agency officer who helps Bond chase a villain. The shoot, on location in the Florida Keys, was wild and exciting, but brief. If you want to see me in this film, or hear me speak my one line, "No Sanchez," don't go for popcorn before the opening credits.

When I was asked to play the chief of staff of an idealistic U.S. senator on an episode of *Quincy,* I almost turned it down. Most of my scenes were to be shot in the Ambassador Hotel. I did not want to be reminded of the worst night of my life. Then I changed my mind and took the job, partly to see if I could handle it. I made a point of getting to the set early. I gazed at the now empty Embassy Room, where Senator Kennedy had made his last speech. I peered into the pantry area where he was assassinated. Ugly memories and painful emotions flooded through me, but I was glad that I did it. By the time the director called me to the set, I was ready to work.

It was on a film shoot that I learned an important lesson about the woman I had married. We were in Greece for a documentary about the ancient Olympics, to be aired during the 1972 Games. It featured a script by Erich Segal of *Love Story* fame (he was a classics professor at Yale and a former marathon runner, as well as a novelist). I appeared on camera with Bill Toomey, who had been the decathlon gold medalist in 1968.

After the shoot, Betsy and I went sightseeing. We had been married only a few months at the time. On the island of Crete we had dinner at a restaurant that let you choose your own fish from a large tank. When we were served, we saw immediately that the fish on the plate was two or three times bigger than the one we'd selected. We ate what we could and fed the rest to the cats that roamed around the restaurant. Our bill was huge. We realized that this was no mistake, but a scheme to rip off tourists. I shrugged it off, paid the check, and left.

Betsy fumed all the way back to the hotel. She wanted to return to the restaurant and tell the owner what she thought of his cheap trick. I tried to talk her out of it. I didn't want to make a fuss. She stood her ground. "If that's the way it is," she said, "give me my plane ticket, I'm going home." That got my attention. She said I was trivializing her feelings and that she was going back to the restaurant with or without me. I went with her. We told the humiliated owner what we thought, and that was that.

Only from that moment on I knew that when Betsy feels strongly about something I have to honor her feelings, get out of her way, and let her do what she has to do, especially if there is a principle at stake. A few years later, at a restaurant in Los Angeles, we heard someone at the next table use the phrase "nigger toes." He was referring to a form of nut on the dessert tray. I figured the guy was just using a slang term and didn't mean any harm. Betsy had the same look she had had in Greece. This time I knew she had to have her say. Together we gave the man a vocabulary lesson.

As the wife of a black man and the mother of interracial children, that strength of character has stood Betsy well. Because we've lived in a sophisticated city where I am often recognized, we have not had to put up with a lot of bigotry over the years. But when people have gaped at us the wrong way, or whispered, Betsy would stare them down or ask if they had something to say. One night, when I was doing some work on our front lawn, someone drove by and yelled, "Nigger!" Next thing I knew, Betsy was sitting on the fence with a gun in her lap in case they returned. She has made sure our children would also stand up for principle. When she heard that a playmate had tossed a racial slur at our daughter, she read the offender the riot act and told our kids that if anyone ever says such a thing to their faces they should teach them a lesson they won't forget.

Most of my non-Continental activities in the 1970s and early 1980s were on behalf of organizations I considered worthwhile. As a spokesperson for Reebok's athletic competitions for high school students, I made appearances throughout California, speaking at schools and advising athletes and coaches. That was the beginning of an affiliation with the company that continues to this day. For more than a decade I've been an unpaid board member for the Reebok Human Rights Awards, which honors people under thirty who "against great odds have significantly raised awareness of human rights and exercised freedom of expression." The money and worldwide attention help the recipients continue their important work.

I also became national head coach for the Hershey Track and Field Youth Program. The company sponsors competitions for youngsters aged nine to fourteen in conjunction with local departments of parks and recreation. Every August five hundred finalists, both boys and girls, are invited to a weekend in Hershey, Pennsylvania, where the company maintains headquarters, recreational facilities, and a theme park. Each state must be represented by at least five participants, who are then grouped into regional teams.

Much more than a track meet, the event is an enriching educational experience that has changed the lives of thousands of kids. In the dormitories each year are many youngsters who have never before been on a plane or slept away from home. They meet peers from all over the country, take a tour of the chocolate factory, visit the theme park, and purchase candy at a big discount to take home with them. One reason I'm proud to be associated with Hershey's is that it has never used the track and field program as a promotional vehicle. The company has a genuine interest in giving something back to the community.

Most of my outside commitments have been in the nonprofit sector. For example, I joined the board of directors of the Close-Up Foundation, which brings high school students to the nation's capital to learn how government works. (I've watched the program grow to include 25,000 youngsters of all ethnic and economic groups who participate each year.) At one time or another, I have served charities like the March of Dimes, the Muscular Dystrophy Association, and the American Red Cross; sports-related organizations such as the National Amateur Sports Development Foundation, the National Recreation and Park Association, the United States Athletic Foundation, and the Athletic Advisory Panel of the U.S. State Department; and community groups such as the San Fernando Valley Fair Housing Counsel and the Voter Registration Program. Speaking of voting, I campaigned for George McGovern in the 1972 presidential race. He was the closest thing to Bobby Kennedy that we had at the time, and his running mate, Sargent Shriver, was Bobby's brother-in-law, my good friend, and a major force behind Special Olympics.

I became devoted to Special Olympics quickly, and it has kept me busy ever since 1969 when I helped establish the California chapter with a competition for 900 athletes at the L.A. Coliseum. Over the years I've done my best to help administer the program, raise funds, and mobilize individual and corporate volunteers. (I'm currently national head coach and chairman of the board of governors for Southern California.) It's been enormously satisfying to watch the organization grow from humble beginnings to a year-round program of high-quality training and regular competitions in twenty sports. Over 25,000 athletes participate in California alone.

I've always considered the time and energy I've given to Special Olympics a gift from me to the athletes and to the Kennedy family. In truth, I've gotten more out of it than I've given. As I always tell volunteers, it's impossible to come away from the Special Olympics Games without feeling better about yourself. Each year I preside over the opening ceremonies at UCLA, in the track stadium named for my late coach, Ducky Drake. I never fail to be inspired when I lead the ringing chorus of voices in the athlete's oath: "Let me win, but if I cannot win, let me be brave in the attempt."

During the two-day competition, I'm constantly amazed at the courage and sportsmanship exhibited. You have not seen sports in its purity until you have seen a special athlete take an opponent's hand and help her across the finish line; or a boy on crutches fight with every ounce of strength in his body to complete a race that his opponents have finished long before; or a blind girl use her coach for eyes to compete in the softball toss; or a high jumper clear the bar and celebrate as if he'd set a world record. One of my favorite tasks is giving out the award for Most Inspirational Athlete, which is given in the name of my in-laws, Paul and Maggie Thorsen. When California Special Olympics was down to its last nickel, the Thorsens donated a piece of property they owned. The sale of that land saved the program. Paul has since passed away, but Maggie comes each year to present the award. She's not the only relative of mine who participates: I rope every member of my extended family into manning Rafer's Boutique, which sells hats, T-shirts, and mugs to raise money for the program.

I'm often asked why I give so much time to causes for which I'm not remunerated. I've even been rebuked because I've come close to burnout at times, and I would be better off financially if I'd spent more time earning money. To a degree, those criticisms are valid. Sometimes I wish I had learned to say no when I needed to. Overall, I can only say that in my experience the biblical expression is true: It *is* more blessed to give than to receive. My purpose in mentioning this is to encourage others, especially youngsters, to contribute to their communities. I know from experience that nothing feels better.

By freeing me from the restraints of a time clock, Continental made it easier for me to devote time to something I valued above all else: being a father. It's been hard to find the right words to describe certain key moments in my life, but when it comes to seeing my children enter the world I won't even try. I just knew from the start that being with them would be the most fun I would ever have, and that watching them grow would be the most profound experience I would ever have. Nothing was going to cheat me out of it, not wealth nor glory.

I vowed to be a part of my kids' lives, not apart from them. I wanted to be a constant presence, not just a provider and disciplinarian. I wanted to diaper them, help them get dressed and brush their teeth, read to them before they went to bed, make sure they did their homework. From the day each child was born I did whatever I could to be with them.

Even with my flexible schedule, it wasn't always easy. At one point I realized that I could spend more time with my family if I took charge of my own itinerary. Instead of having the company arrange my trips, I booked flights myself to make sure I could leave my house as late as possible and return as early as possible. No more hanging around someone's office for three hours between a meeting and my flight. No more late dinner meetings if the same business could be conducted earlier or on the way to the airport so I could get back in time to kiss my kids goodnight. No more hotel rooms if a red-eye could get me home for breakfast.

Juggling my travel schedule was one thing; coordinating my office hours was another. I have already mentioned one reason why I chose not to move to Bakersfield. There were others as well. Betsy and I did not want to be that far from our friends and extended families. Also, she had a teaching job she liked. Later, when she quit to be a full-time mom, we had yet another reason to stay in Los Angeles: we felt that a big, diverse city would be a better place to bring up interracial children and find the kind of schools wc wanted them to attend. And so we chose to move to the house in Sherman Oaks, where we still live, a one-hour-and-forty-five-minute drive from my office.

Fortunately I was able to meet my responsibilities to both employer and family. I had excellent secretaries and an exceptional assistant in George Valos, the man who had introduced me to Continental in the first place. And my office was so big I could convert it into a bedroom, complete with stereo and TV, when I needed to stay overnight. Some weeks I'd stay for two or three days; other weeks I'd drive back and forth each day. I did not mind the drive. It was a chance to listen to music and to think. There was no traffic, just open road, a good part of which weaved through mountainous terrain that seemed to offer a different vista every day: green and lush and speckled with wildflowers in the spring; gold and brown in the dry season; bathed in low fog or awash in rain; flooded by bright, fluorescent sunlight or painted with blue and purple shadows.

Once, when asked about my upbringing, my mother said, "We felt that we should implant in the children the desire to live a full life, rather than tell them how to do it. I have always believed that parents should be as close to their children as possible. This is the only way to really know how they think and feel." I tried to follow that example with Jenny and Josh. The most important thing was not to lead them but to let myself be led so that their natural qualities would guide their development. I always felt like a passenger on their journey, and the ride has been sheer joy.

Betsy and I saw eye to eye on how to bring up the kids. We did not force anything on them, not sports, nor schoolwork, nor religion. Early in our children's lives we took them to church every Sunday. It was, in many ways, the centerpiece of our family life. The kids went to Sunday School and participated in church youth programs. Once we gave them a foundation, we let them make their own decisions about spirituality.

The only issue Betsy and I disagreed on was spanking. I was for it, she was vehemently opposed. "I got whipped a lot," I argued, "and look how I turned out." She was not impressed. There are better ways to deal with misbehavior, she said. I was not entirely convinced, but I deferred to her judgment, and I'm glad I did. The kids were never touched in anger, and they could not have turned out better.

As an expert in education, Betsy found the best schools and gave the kids high-quality help with their studies. Somehow, they acquired her sense of organization and use of time. They both worked hard at their schoolwork; Josh was especially diligent. He would study over breakfast, in the car on the way to school, while waiting for sports practice to begin—whenever he could squeeze in a moment. I pitched in with homework from time to time, but mainly I found other ways to show them how important their education was to me. I got directly involved with their schools. If it was Parents' Day, I'd be there. If something on the grounds needed to be done, I'd show up in my work clothes to lay pavement, build a wading pool, or install a new bathroom. I did these things to support the school and to hug my kids during recess, but mainly to show them I cared. It connected us in ways that just driving them to school and picking them up would not have. Whatever Betsy and I did, it must have worked; Jenny and Josh were excellent students from grade school through college.

When the kids took up sports, I was concerned that they might feel pressured to live up to their father's reputation. I was so conscious of keeping my past in the background that I talked about it only when asked and kept my trophies either in storage or at my office. Fortunately they got involved in sports I was not associated with and this did not invite comparisons. For that reason, I thought it would be okay to coach Josh's soccer team. I learned about the game by assisting the team's head coach, and when he moved on I took over. I tried to transmit everything I'd learned about being an athlete, to bring out the best in each child. I made sure each boy played more than half of every game (the minimum mandated by the league), regardless of his talent level. Eventually I pulled back from coaching, but Betsy and I went to every game, meet, or match we could possibly get to, and we still do.

Throughout this book I've tried to describe my life without sounding boastful. Now I'm going to depart from that policy and shout about what I consider my proudest accomplishment: **I have been a very good father!**

Of course, as with everything else, I needed help. I could not have been a good dad if Betsy had not been an outstanding mom. I can't imagine a wiser or more devoted parent. She made me the best father I can be.

Compared to earlier years, I enjoyed relative anonymity during the seventies. Then, unexpectedly and gloriously, I was thrust back into the spotlight.

Earlier, when Los Angeles was awarded the 1984 Olympic Games, the Olympic movement had been in trouble. The 1972 Games in Munich had been marred by the tragic slaying of Israeli athletes by terrorists; the 1976 Games in Montreal had been a fiscal disaster that cost Canadian taxpayers a billion dollars. As a result, Los Angeles was able to negotiate an unprecedented deal with the International Olympic Committee (IOC): The city would not be held liable for the cost of the Games; the city would not build new stadiums or an Olympic Village, but use existing facilities instead; funds would not come from the government but would be raised from the private sector.

I was asked by Mayor Tom Bradley to join the board of directors of the Los Angeles Olympic Organizing Committee (LAOOC) and was later named to the executive committee. It was an honor I accepted eagerly. I had participated in the Olympics as a competitor, a journalist, and a spectator. Now I would be behind the scenes in the planning and organizing stage of something that meant the world to me.

One of the first things the executive committee had to do was choose a president. This person would answer to the board but would essentially be in charge of the entire operation. It came down to two candidates: Edwin W. Steidle, the chairman of the board of May Company, and Peter V. Ueberroth, a sports-loving entrepreneur who had built the second-largest travel agency in the country. At the key meeting, we went around the room and verbally cast our ballots. I was the last in line. The election was tied. I cast the deciding vote for Ueberroth. He proved to be an effective leader and a treasured friend.

The cynicism in Los Angeles was Olympian. Many Angelinos seemed more interested in how much rent they could charge for their houses during the Games than how to enjoy the spectacle or help make it a success. They feared everything from monumental traffic jams to terrorist attacks. When President Carter announced the boycott of the 1980 Moscow Games, to protest the Soviet invasion of Afghanistan, those feelings grew even more pronounced. To win over the public and the media, Peter Ueberroth formed a speaker's bureau and a spirit team, dispatching people such as me to garner support. In addition to my duties on the executive committee, I spoke to civic groups, corporations, schools and colleges, mainly in Los Angeles but elsewhere in the country as well. I tried to assure people that the Games would be a great success, and to let them know that the Olympics is not just a sports spectacle but a powerful force for good.

All the talk about how the Olympics increases brotherhood and understanding was sounding corny to jaded American ears. But I knew from personal experience the value of international competition. Athletes and spectators come to view other parts of the world not as outlines on a map or a collection of stereotypes but as the homes of human beings like themselves. I like to think that the Olympic motto, "Citius, Altius, Fortius" (Swifter, Higher, Stronger) applies to more than athletic prowess. It also stands for stronger bonds between diverse people, higher aspirations for humanity, and swifter progress toward world peace.

I also knew how determined the LAOOC was. We were going to make this the best Olympiad the world had seen, and, we hoped, turn a profit at the same time. At the very least, Los Angeles was going to put on a show like only the entertainment capital of the world could.

To mastermind the opening ceremonies, Peter turned to David L. Wolper, the renowned producer of theater, movies, and television programs ranging from *Roots* to a documentary about me. David set out to create a "twenty-goosebump" show that would be emotional without being corny.

Historically, the centerpiece of the opening ceremonies is the lighting of the Olympic torch that burns for the duration of the Games. In 1984 a new twist was added to the journey of the flame from Greece to the host city. This time, when it arrived in the United States, the torch would zigzag through all fifty states in a relay involving thousands of citizens and covering more than 9,000 miles. Relay legs were sold to sponsors at $3,000 per leg, with the proceeds going to finance sports programs for youth.

The torch run began on a rainy morning in New York. I had the honor of participating in the ceremony at United Nations Plaza. I ignited a caldron. From that flame Peter lit the first torch and handed it to the initial runners—Gina Hemphill, granddaughter of Jesse Owens, and Bill Thorpe, Jr., grandson of Jim Thorpe. It was thrilling to see them run through the glistening puddles, each with a hand on the torch. My next rendezvous with the flame was in my childhood home, Dallas, Texas, where Bob Hayes, the Olympic sprinter and football star, handed me the torch for one leg of the relay. At that time I had no idea I was destined to hold the torch again.

Traditionally, the identity of the person who is to light the torch at the opening ceremonies is kept secret until the last minute. In 1984 the choice was Peter Ueberroth's to make. Speculation ran rampant, not only within the LAOOC family but the media as well. Who would be given the honor? Would it be Bruce Jenner, who had set a new world record while winning the Olympic decathlon at Montreal? Bruce lived in Los Angeles and had been a popular figure ever since he took his memorable victory lap with the American flag. Would it be Mark Spitz, another Californian and the winner of an amazing nine gold medals in Olympic swimming competition? Would it be Wilma Rudolph, whose spectacular performance in Rome opened the doors to greater participation in sports by women? Or would it be Nadia Comaneci, the gymnast who, at age fourteen, had captivated the world with perfect tens in Montreal? More speculation surrounded Nadia than any other possible choice because the Soviet Union had retaliated for the U.S. boycott of the 1980 Olympics in Moscow with a boycott of its own. All the Soviet satellites were staying home, with the notable exception of Yugoslavia and Romania, Nadia's homeland, and Nadia was coming to Los Angeles at Peter's invitation.

About ten days before the ceremonies, I arrived at a senior citizens' home in Studio City to give a speech. I was given a message from Peter Ueberroth. He said he had to talk to me in person. By the time I finished my speech, a car was waiting to take me to his office. I was greeted by Peter and David Wolper. Peter said he'd like me to be the final torchbearer. I was so stunned all I could get out of my mouth was, "Thank you."

I did not know why Peter chose me. He joked that it was payback for my casting the deciding vote that gave him his job. In his own book, *Made in America,* he said it was because I represented "what the Olympics are all about" and because I "brought all of those ideals to our organizational efforts." It was his way, perhaps, of thanking me for being there whenever I was needed during the five years of preparation. I simply wanted to give something back to the Olympics; now the Olympics were once again giving me something, only this was an honor I had never dreamed of.

Once I got over the shock of Peter's announcement, David got down to business and told me what was involved. I would have to run a lap and a quarter around the Coliseum track, climb from the floor of the stadium to the top, then ascend an additional set of steps built on a 50-degree incline, turn around, face the crowd, and light the flame through a system of gas jets leading to a caldron atop the Coliseum's row of columns. "We had a college football player try it and he fell flat on his face," David said, "but I know you can do it."

I did not share his confidence. I had been working out regularly at the gym and playing tennis and golf, but I was forty-nine years old and twenty-four years removed from my last competition. I was going to give it my best shot, though. The week before the Olympics, I was on vacation with my family on Balboa Island (something we have done every summer for more than twenty years now). Inconspicuously, so as not to call attention to myself, I stepped up my workout pace. What worried me most were the steps, so every day I went to the condominium complex in Newport where Betsy's parents lived and ran up and down the indoor staircase.

It wasn't enough. David was an impresario, not a coach. He wanted me to light the flame just as the orchestra and chorus reached a crescendo. That meant I had to circle the track at a brisk pace and run up the ninety-nine steps. I might have been able to handle a slow jog, but not the speed he wanted. During a rehearsal, my leg cramped up on the stairs. I had to stop and sit down. As I massaged my leg, David came running over. "We'll think of something," he said. At the next rehearsal, Peter said they had come up with a new plan: Gina Hemphill would carry the torch into the stadium, run the lap, and hand the torch off to me.

All of this remained a secret as closely guarded as a military operation. At rehearsals, David had different people run up the stairs to safeguard the identity of the real torchbearer. Not even the other practice runners knew the truth.

• • •

I was too happy to keep the secret for long. Shortly after I learned about it myself, I told Betsy, my brothers and sisters, and a few close friends whose discretion I could count on. One other person I told was my neighbor, Michael Roth. He gave me the Star of David that was given to him at his bar mitzvah and asked me to wear it at the ceremonies. As with my fraternity brothers' mezuzah in Melbourne, I wore the Jewish symbol around my neck, along with a cross. I still have that star; I promised Michael I'd return it in time for his own son's bar mitzvah, but so far he hasn't had children.

The last two people on earth I could tell were the two I most wanted to tell. Jenny and Josh were eleven and nine at the time; if they found out, everyone in the neighborhood would know within the hour. I told them on the way to the ceremonies. To say they were thrilled is an understatement. "If anyone asks you who is going to light the flame," I said, "tell them, 'I don't know, ask my daddy.' " They made a song out of it. They sang "I don't know, ask my daddy" all the way to the Coliseum.

After we parked, I told the kids that the next time they saw me I'd be carrying the torch. To maintain secrecy and make sure I was in the right place at the right time, David hid me in a trailer in a fenced-off area adjacent to the Coliseum. I changed into a pair of white shorts and a white, sleeveless T-shirt with the Olympic logo on the chest, then settled down to watch the ceremonies on television. At times I wished I were watching in person with Betsy and the kids. David had promised it would be "majestic and inspirational, evocative and emotional." It was Hollywood magic at its best.

Trumpets and timpanis blared the opening theme. Skywriting planes formed the Olympic rings and scrawled "Welcome" across the heavens. Girls passed out flowers with "Welcome" written in several languages on ribbons attached to the stems. Powered by a jet pack, a man flew into the stadium and landed on the infield. "Welcome" was written on his back. Over a thousand marchers performed a drill with five-foot balloons while the huge video screen showed Angelinos waving to their guests and an animated film of the word "Welcome" spelled out in 23 languages. The drill team formed the Olympic symbol, then marched into the letters of "Welcome."

A marching band, an orchestra, a choir of a thousand voices, and hundreds of dancers depicted the nation's history through the music of American composers. Eighty-five grand pianos rolled through the Coliseum arches and played George Gershwin's "Rhapsody in Blue." The entertainment ended with the drill team forming a map of the United States. Then came a moment I wish I'd seen in person. Colored plastic cards had been placed on every seat in the Coliseum. On cue, 92,655 spectators held up their cards, forming a gorgeous mosaic of the flags of all 140 nations present.

During the traditional parade of athletes, someone came to the trailer to escort me into the Coliseum. We entered a tunnel built for dignitaries to safely enter the field. To keep loose I paced the floor, hardly using the chair that had been provided for me. I could barely see the legs of the athletes as they walked past the tunnel, but I could hear the announcements, the music, and the applause. Chills ran up my spine twice: when the Romanian delegation was welcomed with an ovation for having defied the Soviet boycott; and when the American team entered the stadium. The colossal response was more than a tribute to the home team, it was also recognition of the sacrifice that so many athletes had made four years earlier, when the U.S. boycott of Moscow robbed them of their Olympic dreams.

The parade of nearly 8,000 athletes took about an hour and a half. I later learned—and saw on tape—that it was the most festive opening parade anyone had seen. The gaiety resembled a closing ceremony, when the athletes let loose and party, rather than the stiffer, more formal atmosphere typical of openings. I also learned that a drama had unfolded while I waited. Someone discovered that the lock on the door leading to the caldron that would hold the Olympic flame had been broken. A bomb squad was sent in to investigate. It was feared that terrorists might have planted a device set to explode when I ignited the flame. It turned out that ABC had needed to do some wiring for the broadcast and couldn't find the key, so they broke the lock. David was smart enough not to tell me this, or else I would have been the first person in Olympic history to light the flame and duck for cover.

When I heard that all the athletes had been assembled, I walked up close to the tunnel exit and looked out onto the field. The U.S. team was right in front of me, decked out in red, white, and blue uniforms. I saw Edwin Moses, the great hurdler, with tears in his eyes. I ducked back into the tunnel so my emotions wouldn't get the best of me. I paced back and forth and shook my arms and legs to release some of the adrenaline.

Peter Ueberroth welcomed everyone to Los Angeles, paying tribute to the millions of Americans who turned out to cheer the torch on its journey across the country. Juan Antonio Samaranch, president of the IOC, ended his speech with "God bless America." President Reagan officially opened the Games. Then music played and the announcer said that the Olympic flag was being carried into place. I envisioned the Olympian flagbearers in their white uniforms: old friends Pat McCormick, Sammy Lee, Wyomia Tyus, Al Oerter, and Parry O'Brien; and two who were personal inspirations—Billy Mills, the Native American runner who had shined in Tokyo, and Mack Robinson, Jackie's brother. I thought of one flagbearer and smiled. Bruce Jenner was part of the backup plan for the torch ceremony. He was wearing running clothes under his official suit. If I were to falter going up the stairs, Bruce was to tear off his uniform like Superman and fly to the rescue. I was going to make sure he kept his clothes on.

A familiar feeling swept over me—nerve endings tingling and muscles aching to be used. I had been nervous before every speech I ever gave, on the set of every movie I acted in, and in every television studio while waiting for the red light on the camera to go on. This was a feeling I'd had only when competing. And now I was, in a sense, an Olympian again, preparing to will my body to do something exceptional. Was I concerned about making it to the top of the stairs? Yes. Was I thinking about whether I might trip or fall? Yes. Did I have any doubt that I would come through? No. I was going to be the best torchbearer that I could be.

Four thousand homing pigeons were released into the air. When the applause died down, there was a brief silence. Then I heard a drumroll and the announcer's voice: "Lit directly by the rays of the sun on the steps of the temple Hedra, the Olympic torch brings flame from Greece. Los Angeles is proud to accept again this ancient and sacred symbol." A Philip Glass composition, "The Olympian," opened like a fanfare and built dramatically, with organ and voices forming a recurring theme, almost like a chant. A roar went up as the crowd spotted Gina Hemphill entering the arena with the torch held high. I saw her run past my tunnel, looking stately but grinning like the Cheshire Cat. As she circled the arena, the athletes in the infield got so carried away they broke ranks and wandered onto the track to snap photos and touch her. The path got so congested that Gina had to slow to a walk until security guards cleared her path. The delay caused the prerecorded music to run out. Fortunately, David Wolper had thought of everything; a backup tape picked up the theme seamlessly.

A man with earphones at the entrance to the tunnel said,

"Get ready." A moment later, he said, "Now!" I walked onto the field and, for the first time, saw the immense, spellbound crowd. Everyone's eyes were on Gina. I crossed a patch of grass and took my place on the track. As Gina approached, I heard over the public address system, "The flame will be lit by one of America's greatest athletes, Olympic Gold Medalist Rafer Johnson." Gina and I shared a brief smile. She extended the torch. I grasped it and something surged inside me, as if giant cymbals had clashed. The crowd's roar was deafening as I started my run, and it only got louder. So did the music, as it built to a crescendo.

A month earlier I had fractured a finger playing baseball, and it hurt to carry the four-pound torch. But my other fingers did the job. I ran about a hundred yards on the straightaway, keeping my gaze straight ahead of me. I did not make eye contact with the athletes who crept onto the track to get a closer look, but I could feel them reaching out to me. It was as if each of their hands was on the torch, along with the thousands of other hands that had relayed the flame from Greece to my grip.

As I jogged up the steps, the grand arch of the Coliseum peristyle looked golden in the light of the setting sun. On either side of me, splendidly bedecked in white, the thousand members of the Olympic choir applauded. Atop the permanent steps, the metal stairway built for this moment rose like an ancient monolith on hydraulic lifts. It glistened like solid silver as it filled the archway. But it was as rickety as an old ladder and, with its 50-degree angle, just as steep. As I climbed it I touched each of the twenty-five steps to make sure I didn't miss one. All I could think was, "Don't stumble, keep your eye on the dots."

The dots had been my idea. To light the flame I had to be right in the middle of the top step. Since there was no rail, and the background offered no frame of reference, I could not gauge how straight I was as I climbed. In rehearsal I had ended up angled to one side. Having to adjust my position would not only look tacky, it would be dangerous; there was nothing behind the narrow top step to keep me from plunging a hundred feet to the concrete floor. So, to make sure I ascended in a straight line, I had had a black dot painted in the center of each step and two dots on the last one.

I made it. Sucking in air and holding the torch aloft, I turned to face the assemblage. What I saw then was so staggering I lost my breath. Thankfully, I had persuaded David Wolper to install a thirty-six-inch pole on the top step, just in case I needed something to hold onto. Otherwise I might have toppled off the back of the steps and disappeared. That's how stunning the view was: It was like a living painting, with colors more radiant, more dazzling than a sunset at the Grand Canyon—and the Grand Canyon does not have music with an incessant, driving rhythm and a hundred thousand people cheering like crazy. For a moment, time stood still and the noise melted into a kind of silence.

I raised the torch in the direction of the presidential box. I was saluting Peter Ueberroth as well as President Reagan. Then I turned toward the athletes and held up the torch as a tribute to them. The gestures had not been rehearsed, they just seemed to be the right thing to do. After a brief salute to the other side, I returned to the center and lifted the torch to the gas jet attached to the bottom of the arch. I heard a whoosh. The flame took hold, rose up to outline the five intertwined circles of the Olympic symbol, then followed a pipeline to the top of the peristyle. A moment later, the caldron burst into flame. The torch had reached its destination.

In a sense, so had I. Standing at the pinnacle of the Coliseum, having been afforded this singular honor, with my face being beamed to a billion homes around the world as ABC's Jim McKay called me "a great American"—well, it was a long way from the cotton fields of Hillsboro, Texas. It was all I could do to keep from weeping.

• • •

The hydraulic stairs lowered with me on them as the athletes recited the competitors' oath. I changed into street clothes and rejoined my family. I was emotionally drained, but there was still enough feeling left in me to enjoy the pride on Betsy's face and the joyful hugs of Jenny and Josh. That night, Jenny wrote the following in her diary: "Today at the 1984 Olympics my father Rafer Johnson lit the torch. I was so proud of him when he did it that I cried. Seeing him go up those stairs made me proud to be Rafer & Betsy Johnson's daughter. Wow! When my dad told me about it I thought that it was great. But I didn't realize how great it was until I saw him do it."

I did not get to see much more of the opening ceremonies, because bedlam surrounded me. I could hear Beethoven's "Ode to Joy" and the pop song "Reach Out and Touch," but I could not see everyone in the Coliseum holding hands and swaying, and I could not see the athletes dancing in the infield as if they did not have to compete the next day. I didn't see much of anything, because I was surrounded by people who wanted my autograph or to shake my hand or pat my back or ask me a question. I was mobbed all the way to the parking area too. I had not seen anything like it since the Robert Kennedy presidential campaign, only now *I* was the object of attention. It was as disturbing as it was thrilling.

It continued that way throughout the Olympics. I could not attend an event without being besieged. I felt like a Beatle. For years afterward I was constantly stopped by people who recognized me from the opening ceremonies. Never before had I fully appreciated the power of television. Earlier in my life I had been recognized often—but not like this. Not only had I been seen by millions more people, but they had seen me for an extended period of time, in close-up, at an incredibly emotional moment. The *L.A. Times'* critic, Howard Rosenberg, called the torch ceremony "one of TV's greatest moments, when the small screen seemed to expand ten-fold and become 3-D." I was etched into the viewers' brain cells.

The L.A. Games revitalized the Olympic movement. For one thing, it created a legacy of corporate sponsorship for amateur sports that has made a huge difference to American athletes. USA/Visa, for example, has been providing support for promising decathlon competitors, enabling them to devote time to training and to have access to quality coaching year-round. Periodically, the company brings decathletes to a training facility where, among other things, they benefit from the experience of five American gold medalists in their sport—Bob Mathias, Milt Campbell, Bill Toomey, Bruce Jenner, and me.

Thanks to Peter Ueberroth, whose success with the Olympics led to a stint as commissioner of baseball, the Games piled up a $200 million surplus. With those funds the Amateur Athletic Foundation was created. Housed in a handsome facility in Los Angeles and run by the capable Anita DeFrantz, a former Olympic rower, the AAF provides programs and training grants for young athletes. I've been proud to sit on the board of directors ever since AAF was established, and even more proud to have been given its Lifetime Achievement Award in a dual presentation with C. K. Yang. (At that event I said that without C.K.'s help I would not have beaten him in 1960; he said that without my help he would not have come as close to beating me.)

For me personally, the 1984 Games had a surprising and enduring impact. I was suddenly in such demand for speeches that I had to turn down many lucrative offers. Several corporations contracted with me to serve as spokesperson for community service programs. Adding to my proud and ongoing commitment to Hershey Foods, I made arrangements with American Express, which had a job-placement program for Olympians, and with the Southland Corporation (owner of the

Seven-Eleven Stores), which gave awards to men and women who made significant contributions to sports at all levels. At one point I was speaking to over 10,000 people a year, the bulk of whom, it seemed, wanted to know more about the torch-lighting than anything I'd done as an athlete.

This new source of employment could not have come at a better time. Earlier, Continental Telephone had moved its corporate offices to Atlanta. I had arranged to continue working out of Bakersfield, which remained the regional headquarters. But by 1986 the company felt the arrangement was no longer tenable. I would have to move to Atlanta or leave. I did not want to do either, and I don't know what I would have done if not for the new opportunities that cropped up for me after the Games. This made it possible to comfortably end my tenure at Con Tel.

Now I had even more scheduling flexibility than before, and I used it to help Jenny and Josh glide through their teenage years, and to step up my volunteer efforts. Invitations to join boards and committees kept piling up. I've just started my second term as chairman of the Mayor's Committee on Disability, for example, and my special relationship with Special Olympics is in its fourth fulfilling decade.

The years since the 1984 Games have been surprising and satisfying. I'll mention some of the most important highlights.

• When Kingsburg decided to build a new junior high school, someone proposed that it be named after me. Of the five-member school board, only one was in favor. Two wished to name the school for Thomas Jefferson and two wanted to call it Kingsburg Junior High. My old friend Karl Finley sampled public opinion and found a lot of support for naming the school after me. The board didn't budge. Some citizens were apparently concerned that something scandalous might be revealed about me and embarrass the town. Finally the townspeople were asked to decide the issue at the ballot box. With Karl and his wife Julie leading the charge, my supporters won 81 percent of the votes.

Rafer Johnson Junior High School was dedicated in 1993. At the ceremony I said to the assembled townspeople, "There's no way I can possibly repay you for your years of kindness." I meant it from the bottom of my heart. I promised to return often to work with the children attending the school, and I have. I've spoken at every graduation and I've presided over every Fun Run, an annual event that raises funds for school activities. The school's teams are called the Olympians, and a replica of the Olympic torch is the school symbol. When asked which school they attend, students say they go to "Rafer." Near the entrance is a marble slab with a bronze plaque bearing a likeness of me carrying the Olympic torch. The inscription reads, "This school is dedicated in the name of Rafer Johnson by the citizens of this community. It is his wish that all young people will be inspired to be the best that they can be. . . ."

• At the 1992 Olympics in Barcelona and the 1996 Atlanta Games, I got to renew old friendships and reflect on the changes in sports over the years. From adjustable starting blocks to artificial surfaces, the conditions for modern runners are far more favorable than they were in the days when we dug holes in the dirt to plant our feet and ran on crushed cinder block. Modern athletes have gained tremendously from strides in sports medicine, nutrition, and training (it's laughable to think back to when weight lifting was forbidden). The technology of shoe design alone has revolutionized sports. The sneakers we wore were like combat boots compared to today's lightweight shoes, and the variety available now is staggering. Until 1960 I wore two pair of athletic shoes, one for running and one for field events. Now there are shoes specifically designed for each event and custom-made for each athlete.

One of the most important changes has been the advancement of female athletes. In my day, the public suffered under the assumption that women could not compete in the same sports as men, or had to be protected if they did. I remember women's basketball, for instance, when each team had an offensive and a defensive unit so the players did not have to run full court. Most of the male athletes I knew had great respect for their female counterparts; we were not surprised to see the strides that women have made since Wilma Rudolph dazzled the world in Rome.

The biggest change, of course, has been money. I enjoy seeing athletes getting paid well. I love seeing track and field stars have enough support to pursue their careers longer and more efficiently. What I *don't* like is today's focus on individuals instead of team play. I don't like seeing athletes posture for the camera or the crowd, and I find the taunting of opponents repulsive. I love to see gracious athletes who know how fortunate they are and respect their teammates, opponents, and fans. A little gratitude and humility would go a very long way to ensuring the future of every sport.

• The Atlanta Games in 1996 were especially wonderful, partly because I got to kick off the torch relay when the Olympic flame was delivered from Greece. In a reverse of 1984, I ignited the torch from a caldron outside the Los Angeles Coliseum, ran the first leg, and handed off to Gina Hemphill. The competition itself was memorable for the performances of two magnificent athletes, Carl Lewis and Michael Johnson, and because Dan O'Brien finally won the gold medal he'd been expected to win in the 1992 decathlon. But the highlight for me was watching my old friend Muhammad Ali receive the honor I'd had the last time the Games were in the United States.

Watching him hold the torch in his trembling hand and light the flame was an experience I'll always treasure.

Almost as good was a precious private moment I shared with Ali. The story actually begins in 1960, when he—then known as Cassius Clay—and I, both fresh off our gold medal victories in Rome, traveled to some colleges in the South to speak about the Olympics. We were opposites in many ways, but I loved his brash self-confidence and he respected my quiet manner, and we had a lot of fun. On one campus we both were attracted to a gorgeous student named Carmelita. I exchanged letters with her for a while, but I never saw her again. Sometime later, Ali and I were at a banquet in Los Angeles. "By the way," he gloated, "I went back to see Carmelita, and she's my girlfriend now."

Flash forward to 1996. Ali is now a living legend, but sadly, he can hardly speak and Parkinson's syndrome has slowed his once-graceful body. At a Dream Team basketball game, I took my seat in the last row of the lower section and heard a familiar sound, like the noise of locusts in my ear. I thought of Ali; he had a way of rubbing his fingers together to make that sound. I turned and saw him smiling down at me from a VIP box just above my seat. We chatted as best we could. After the game, I turned to say goodbye. I took him by the hand, pulled him closer, and whispered one word: "Carmelita." He burst into sustained laughter. As I walked away, someone in his entourage ran after me. "What did you say?" he asked. "He hasn't laughed like that in years. Can you do it again?" "No," I replied, "it can only be said once."

• My entire family has been a great source of love and warmth. My sisters Erma and Dolores, my brothers Ed and Jim, and all my nieces and nephews (including one named after me) have grown dearer to me with every year that passes. In 1994 my pride overflowed when we gathered in Canton, Ohio, to see

Jimmy enshrined in the NFL Hall of Fame. I was given the honor of presenting him for induction. It was the culmination of all the years I dreamed my brother's dream with him. As a skinny teenager, all he wanted to do was play the game he loved. He played it with a vengeance. "Jimmy is a quiet man," I said, "but he played with determination and commitment. Most of all, Jim was and is a gentle man and a true gentleman." Now his greatness was carved in stone forever, in the bust of his likeness that was installed in the Hall. I could not have been prouder, not even when, in his speech, he called me his hero.

Over the years I've seen the marriages of many friends fall apart and far too many children suffer the breakup of their homes. I'm overjoyed that Betsy and I have not only endured, but thrived together. Through the usual challenges of marriage, plus the unique strains of an interracial union, our bond has grown stronger and stronger, and the family we created remains the most sacred part of my life.

In a book called *Fathers and Sons,* I was asked about being a dad. "It is as if fatherhood made me a complete person," I said. "I don't think there has been anything that made me feel the way I felt when I saw my children a few moments after they were born. The Olympic Silver Medal in 1956, the Olympic Gold Medal in 1960, and the opening of the Olympic Games in 1984 all were great and wonderful moments, but none matched looking into the newborn faces of Joshua and Jennifer. To see them grow and learn has been a glorious experience. Josh and Jenny have made me proud to be a father."

I'm proud of them for a lot of reasons. Jenny captained the UCLA volleyball team and is now a professional on the beach-volleyball circuit. I go to every match, and my nerves jangle every time the ball is hit in her direction. Josh lettered in four sports in high school. As a freshman at UCLA he took up the javelin almost by chance (despite the fact that he grew up with my javelin from the Rome Olympics in his room) and developed rapidly. Now entering his senior year, he is ranked in the top five in the nation. I'm proud of those achievements, but even more proud that both kids followed their hearts and never let anything they heard or read about their father get in their way. I was especially concerned about Josh in that regard. At one of his first meets, he was on the runway when the announcer introduced him as "the son of Olympic Gold Medalist Rafer Johnson." All I could do was keep a low profile and advise him never to let such things affect him. He never has.

Neither Jenny nor Josh has ever skirted a challenge or looked for a shortcut or easy way out. They worked hard to be excellent students in tough academic environments. Jenny majored in communications, Josh in sociology and Afro-American studies. He's a fine writer too; in his senior year at UCLA he wrote an editorial for the *Los Angeles Times* about what it's like to be the child of an interracial marriage and be treated according to society's stereotypes of black people. Happily, there was no mention of who his father was.

I'm proud too that the kids were strong enough to listen to Betsy and me when it mattered. They were not the type of teenagers who demean their parents in order to flaunt their independence. I'm proud that we made it through the complexities of the parent–child relationship with our love, respect, and trust intact. And I'm most proud that they turned into good, decent adults, dependable, friendly, and open, the kind of people who would help someone in need at the drop of a hat.

When she was a little girl I would tell people, "When Jenny is old enough to date, I'm going to drive. Her date can sit in the back seat." I made up tests to give any boy who got interested in her. For instance, he would have to run through the sprinklers on my lawn without getting wet. I got a lot of laughs with those remarks, but I wasn't sure I was joking. Naturally, Jenny set me straight when she was about fifteen.

Eventually, I had to get used to the fact that my little girl was a young woman. When she went away to college and I watched her car disappear over the hill, it was one of the most depressing moments of my life. She was moving to a dorm fifteen minutes from home! I guess letting go was the toughest thing to learn about parenting. In the spring of 1997, Jenny married her college sweetheart, Kevin Jordan, a wide receiver who was signed as a free agent by the Arizona Cardinals. It was one of the happiest and saddest days of my life.

I've won a number of awards in the last few years, including an honorary doctorate from Central Michigan University and the prestigious Theodore Roosevelt Award from the National Collegiate Athletic Association. The one I'm proudest of is the 1992 Father of the Year award from the West Coast Father's Day Council.

With the joys have come heartaches, most notably the passing of my father and mother. In his last years, my father lived in a series of apartments in Los Angeles. I watched him deteriorate. Perhaps it was the cumulative effect of all his drinking, or the early stages of Alzheimer's or some other form of dementia, but he often made no sense. At times he would refuse to eat. I think that sorrow over his unrealized potential ate away at him. He finally found peace at age seventy-five.

My mother passed away in 1990 in the house on West Boulevard. She had suffered from diabetes and had a small stroke about two years earlier. The stroke limited her mobility on the left side of her body, but she functioned well and lost none of her wit or humor. When the end came it was from a massive stroke and heart attack brought on by the diabetes. Thankfully, she did not suffer long. I miss her.

I only wish my parents had lived long enough to see their grandchildren come of age and their son Jim enter the Hall of Fame.

My heart aches too when I look around and see how little progress we have made toward social justice and equality. As a society, we're like a grown man who keeps smoking cigarettes even though he knows he's destroying his body. We keep on hating and blaming while neglecting those in need, even though we know it's going to kill us. Sometimes I look at the news and think, "Haven't we learned? Will we *ever* learn?"

As a Los Angeles resident, I was shaken and stunned by two events of recent years. One was the riot that followed the verdict in the Rodney King case. It brought me back to the 1965 upheaval in Watts. I remembered the terror I felt then, when I excused myself from a National Guard weekend to protect my mother and sisters from the encroaching mobs. I never thought I'd see anything like that again. And yet I understood, deep down, the anger and frustration that sparked the destruction in 1992.

For the most part I've been lucky enough to have been judged by the content of my character, not the color of my skin. I've been accepted and respected by the dominant society to a remarkable degree. Nevertheless, I've been stopped for no reason by harsh, insensitive police officers in my own neighborhood. I've encountered bigotry in my own church. I've been looked at with paranoia and fear because I'm a big black man. So has my son. In his *Los Angeles Times* article, my biracial son wrote, "In local stores, I would catch the eyes of suspicious storekeepers peering over the aisles at me just waiting for me to slide something into my pocket or stuff something under my shirt. . . . I would be asked if I wanted to check my bag at the front counter as other customers weren't questioned at all."

Such indignities enrage me, and I know that the average person of color, living in the inner city without a famous name, experiences far worse every day. The fact that they rioted in the light of yet another injustice was deplorable, but understandable.

The other local event that disturbed me was the O. J. Simpson trial. Partly because I had met O.J. on a few occasions and we had mutual friends, I followed the proceedings closely. I found the verdict in the criminal case, and the racial polarization it revealed, extremely disheartening.

When I first saw O.J. in handcuffs, I was infuriated. What a travesty, I thought. How dare they subject this friendly, affable man to such humiliation. As the trial proceeded and the facts came to light, I reluctantly changed my mind. We may never know the full truth, but if I were on that jury I would have voted guilty on the basis of the evidence.

I heard the verdict while eating. I was so stunned I dropped my spoon. The jurors must have used an entirely different thought process than I had. Later, when I reflected on it, I better understood what had happened but I did not find it comforting. During the trial I had made a point of speaking to people of color as I traveled around. It seemed that their opinions about the case depended on their perception of law enforcement. For those who had experienced brutality at first hand, or knew someone who had, it was not hard to imagine the police framing a black hero, even if there was no evidence to support that view.

These two incidents were messages of despair that must be heard. Things are certainly better than they were thirty years ago. But I'm tired of that cop-out. It only makes where we are now seem more painful. It's easy for people who are doing well to say, "We've come a long way, baby"; but what every comfortable, secure person—white, black, Asian, Latino, male, female—needs to ask is, what more can *I* do? How can *I* make the system work for everyone the way it has for me? Thanks to the victories of the 1960s, America will never be the same. But the problems are more complicated now, and the solutions more evasive. Most institutional barriers to equality have been eliminated, but hearts and minds are harder to change than laws.

History, and the voices of those who have traveled paths we have not, should have changed our minds and hearts by now. But we don't listen well enough or learn fast enough. Perhaps too many of us are too concerned with ourselves and not enough with our fellow citizens. It mystifies me that we can't see how interconnected we are, or appreciate that the welfare of the least of us affects the rest of us. Perhaps thinking of what's best for the community, instead of me and mine, takes a leap of faith that we are not willing to make.

I sometimes imagine Martin Luther King, Jr., and Bobby Kennedy looking down at us. I know they'd be dismayed, and I know they'd be angry, but I also know they would tell us to roll up our sleeves and do something constructive. They would tell us to stop being so divisive and not lose sight of the common ground. They would tell us to stop wasting time on ideological arguments and get practical; that families, charities, businesses, schools, churches, civic groups, and government all have a role to play in making things better. They would surely encourage self-reliance among the poor and disadvantaged, but they would not give up on social programs just because some haven't worked as well as planned and because "liberal" has been turned into a dirty word.

I, for one, would like to see more individuals pitching in where needed, and more businesses getting involved in their communities. Corporate America is regarded as greedy and callous. But Hershey, Reebok, Visa, and other companies I've worked with—and others, like Great Western Bank, Toyota, and Von's Supermarkets, who have supplied Special Olympics with funds and volunteers—know that social responsibility is not just morally right, it's also good business. Successful companies have the financial, human, and technical resources to help make things better. They should be doing more.

Despite my disappointments, I hold to my core belief: Americans can create an integrated, harmoniously diverse society, in which people treat one another with decency and take care of the least fortunate. I believe strongly that action on a local level, no matter how seemingly small, can have a big impact on society as a whole. To cite one example, Betsy and I have joined forces with educators we know to create a new school. We plan to focus on critical-thinking skills and give students a voice in policy and curriculum decisions. An important goal of the proposed Mosaic School will be to reflect the diversity of the real world. We want to give youngsters experience at an early age in dealing with people of all colors and cultural backgrounds.

Writing this book has been, in part, an attempt to encourage bridge-building. I've tried to show what hard work and focus can accomplish when people of goodwill look beyond their own self-interest and embrace their fellow citizens with compassion. I've had a good life, thanks to people with a generous spirit. I'd like to see every child given the kind of breaks I received. Perhaps my story will bring hope to young people and inspire their elders to build communities like the one I knew in Kingsburg.

"Life is a race," said Saint Paul. "You run it as well as you can for as long as you can." In a distance race there are always surprises. You try to have an overall strategy, but you have to be prepared to alter your plan as things around you change. Back in 1973, a reporter asked about my future. "I can't tell you where I'll be five, twenty-five, thirty years from now," I said. "But I know you've got to be flexible, interested in things, not standing still. You can't stagnate, mentally or physically.'' I would say the same thing now.

People have suggested all kinds of things for my future: run for office, start a business, head a foundation, go back into the media. I'm not sure what I'll do. All I know is, I want to run long and well and keep contributing.

I also told that reporter in 1973, ''I appreciate people who do things as well as they can—the guy who puts gas in my car, the plumber, the electrician. In a way, they're saying . . . that they owe themselves one thing, that they couldn't have done their job any better. If I can say that at the end of my life, I'll be happy.''

Recently, I was asked what I'd like my epitaph to be. What came to mind was a simple phrase: ''This guy tried to get it done.'' I'll be happy to be remembered as someone who was of service to his family and community, and tried to be the best that he could be.

INDEX

INDEX

INDEX

INDEX

INDEX

INDEX

INDEX